Mental Health in Intellectual Disabilities

A complete introduction to assessment, intervention, care and support

Fifth edition

Edited by Colin Hemmings

Pavilio

Mental Health and Intellectual Disabilities
(5th edition)

Published by:
Pavilion Publishing and Media Ltd
Rayford House
School Road
Hove
East Sussex
BN3 5HX
Tel: 01273 434 943
Fax: 01273 227 308
Email: info@pavpub.com

Published 2018

A catalogue record for this book is available from the British Library.

ISBN: 978-1-911028-96-3

Pavilion is the leading training and development provider and publisher in the health, social care and allied fields, providing a range of innovative training solutions underpinned by sound research and professional values. We aim to put our customers first, through excellent customer service and value.

Editor: Colin Hemmings
Production editor: Mike Benge, Pavilion Publishing and Media Ltd.
Cover design: Phil Morash, Pavilion Publishing and Media Ltd.
Page layout and typesetting: Emma Dawe, Pavilion Publishing and Media Ltd.
Printing: Print2Demand Ltd

Contents

Contributors

Dr Joanna Anderson has worked with people with learning disabilities for 12 years. Her work as an assistant psychologist started within schools for children with learning disabilities and autism spectrum conditions. She later became interested in working with adults with learning disabilities and the systems in which they often found themselves, whether these were family systems or residential services. Joanna completed her clinical psychology Doctorate at Southampton University in 2012. Since qualifying she has worked in Kent and Medway Partnership Trust, in the Mental Health of Learning Disability service. As a part of this role she has been involved in running a psychotherapy group for people with learning disabilities, providing individual therapy, and running multi-disciplinary clinics for complex clients in collaboration with other professionals from different mental health teams. She also teaches on the clinical psychology Doctorate at Salomons University for their learning disability module.

Jane Barnes was a social worker for over 30 years, specialising in mental health and learning disabilities. She is an approved mental health professional, best interests assessor and accredited practice teacher and assessor. For 12 years she was senior practitioner at the Mental Impairment Evaluation and Treatment Service, a national specialist inpatient unit for adults with learning disabilities and complex presentations run by the South London and Maudsley NHS Foundation Trust. She also spent four years with the Mental Health Act Commission covering forensic services including Broadmoor Hospital. Jane finished her full time career as a service manager with the London Borough of Southwark and now concentrates on teaching. She teaches on AMHP courses, provides AMHP refresher training for local authorities and trusts, and designs and delivers training days for provider agencies as well as contributing to the Institute of Psychiatry's teaching programme. She has presented to national conferences and contributed to several publications.

Dr Anna Bodicoat worked in an assistant psychologist post in a service for people with intellectual disabilities in York, and completed her clinical psychology doctorate at Hull University in 2013. Since qualifying, she has worked in Kent and Medway Partnership Trust, in the mental health of learning disability service. Her doctoral research was regarding intensive interaction, an approach used for people with profound and multiple learning disabilities and/or autism, and she has a review paper published on this subject. Anna has an interest in working with families and the complex systems around people with intellectual disabilities. She is curious about how families deal with times of transition and change, and how they use resources to get through periods of difficulty. She has been undertaking further training in systemic family interventions through KMPT, and hopes to develop this practice further.

Professor Nick Bouras, MD, PhD, FRCPsych, is Professor Emeritus of Psychiatry at the Institute of Psychiatry, King's College London and honorary consultant psychiatrist at South London and the Maudsley Foundation NHS Trust. Professor Bouras actively participated in the development of community based multi-professional mental health services, which have been supporting numerous residential facilities in local communities for people with intellectual disabilities and complex mental health needs. His research has been focused on health service related topics including assessment and clinical effectiveness of specialist mental health services, evaluation of multi-professional training methods, and social and biological determinants of behaviour in psychiatric patients. Professor Bouras held executive positions in several national and international organisations. He has published extensively on community psychiatry and the mental health of people with intellectual disabilities. Several of his books have been translated in to different languages. His last book, *Reflections on the Challenges of Psychiatry in the UK and Beyond* was recently published by Pavilion Publishing and Media.

Professor Eddie Chaplin is a professor in the Department of Mental Health and Learning Disabilities at London South Bank University. Eddie has extensive clinical experience in local and national mental health services for people with neurodevelopmental disabilities, including autism, intellectual disabilities and ADHD. He has also developed a number of Masters courses relating to offending and the mental health of people with intellectual disability. Eddie has an extensive publication portfolio and is principal editor for the *Advances in Autism* journal.

Dr Omaima Daoud completed her specialty registrar (ST4-6) training on the St George's (SW London) Scheme in Psychiatry of ID in 2017. This included gaining additional sub-specialist expertise in CAMHS ID. She is currently working as a consultant in CAMHS ID psychiatry with North East London Foundation NHS Trust. After initially graduating from the Faculty of Medicine at Zagazig, Egypt, she decided to pursue a career as a psychiatrist. This included completing an MSc in psychiatry and neurology, and a Doctorate in psychiatry. She went on to become a lecturer/consultant in psychiatry at Zagazig University, Egypt, a post which she continues to hold. After moving to the UK, Dr Daoud completed a postgraduate diploma in child and adolescent psychiatry, and an MSc in mental health studies (ID) at King's College, London. Her work covering autistic spectrum disorder (ASD) was the first internationally published research looking specifically at ASD in the Middle East. During her ST4-6 training she was actively involved in undergraduate and postgraduate teaching and examining, including at St George's University of London. She has also published papers on child abuse.

Dr Terence Davidson is a consultant clinical psychologist in a mental health of learning disability NHS team and a visiting lecturer at Canterbury Christ Church University and the Tizard Centre at the University of Kent. He has worked in services for people with learning disabilities and autism in the NHS since 2005. Terence has extensive experience in the application of positive behaviour support approaches to improving the lives of people with learning disabilities, incorporating behaviour analytic and systemic psychological models. Terence has published research and guidance regarding the assessment of learning disability and continues to investigate the role of clinical psychology in this area.

Dr Philip Dodd, MB, Msc, MRCPsych, MA, MD, is associate clinical professor at University of Dublin, Trinity College, and consultant psychiatrist at St. Michael's House in Dublin, Ireland. He has specialist training in general adult psychiatry and the psychiatry of intellectual disability. In 2016 he was appointed national clinical lead for mental health of intellectual disability with the Irish national health service, and in 2017 he was appointed national clinical lead for mental health, leading out on national mental health clinical programmes such as early intervention psychosis and eating disorders. His research interests include disability studies, complicated grief and mental health service development.

Dr Mo Eyeoyibo is a consultant psychiatrist in intellectual disability and interim assistant medical director for the Community and Recovery Care Group at Kent and Medway NHS and Social Care Trust. He was the lead consultant for Mental Health of Learning Disability Service for many years, until recently. His interest areas include healthcare governance, pathway development and research. Dr Eyeoyibo is the chair of the Intellectual Disability Faculty Specialty Regional Representative at the RCPsych, and co-chaired the publication of the *College Report 203: Role of Intellectual Disability Psychiatrist in Epilepsy Management*. He has been principal investigator for some intellectual disability research.

Dr Andrew Flynn is a consultant psychiatrist specialising in mental health of intellectual disabilities. He looks after patients with complex emotional and behavioural problems in the community and also in a specialist inpatient service. He has a particular interest in the field of personality disorder and has published academic research and review articles in this field as well as on psychotherapy, psychopharmacology and mental health service provision for people with intellectual disabilities. He has previously been a trainer on the Interpersonal Psychotherapy Program at the Anna Freud Centre and is a visiting lecturer at the University of Greenwich where he teaches on psychopathology and mental state examination.

Steve Hardy is practice development nurse in the Adult Learning Disability Service of Oxleas NHS Foundation Trust and a member of the *Can You Understand It?* team. He is also associate editor of the *Advances in Autism* journal and a member of LDNurse.com. He is widely published in the field of the mental health needs of people with learning disabilities and mental capacity. He has a passion for developing and sharing resources and works in co-production with people with learning disabilities to give them a platform to be heard.

Dr Colin Hemmings, BSc MBBS MSc MA MD(Res) MRCPsych, is the editor of this new edition of *Mental Health in Intellectual Disabilities*. He is a consultant psychiatrist in intellectual disabilities working in Kent and Medway Partnership (KMPT) NHS Trust. Colin trained at St Bartholomew's Hospital, and before moving to KMPT in 2015 he worked for over 20 years in London including at University College, The Middlesex, St Thomas', Guy's and Maudsley Hospitals. His academic interests include psychosis in people with ID, mental health of ID services and the relationships between mental illness and challenging behaviours in people with ID. He has contributed many journal articles and book chapters and also previously co-edited a textbook in the field of MHID.

Dr Sidney Tin Htut is a specialty doctor with Kent & Medway NHS and SCP Trust, CRSL. He started his career in the UK in 1990 as a research scientist in the Department of Applied Parasitology, Cambridge University, and worked as a research fellow in respiratory medicine, Clinical Sciences Division, Sheffield University, from 1996 to 2000. He made a career change in 2005 to be trained in adult general psychiatry, and in learning disability since 2010. His academic interests include ADHD, ASD and the mental health of people with intellectual disabilities.

Dr Andy Inett is a consultant forensic psychologist working in forensic services in Kent where he leads a team of psychologists in both the low secure inpatient services and community forensic outreach services. Andy has almost 20 years of experience of working in secure mental health services, particularly with service users with intellectual disabilities (ID) and other mental health needs. He is experienced in completing detailed, structured individual risk assessments with violent offenders, sexual offenders and fire setters, in addition to risk formulation and management planning, and the development and implementation of group and individual forensic psychology interventions. Andy holds an honorary lectureship in the Forensic Psychology Postgraduate programme at the Institute of Psychiatry (IOP), King's College London. He also lectures at the University of Kent and on clinical psychology training programmes. He has been an accredited risk assessment trainer for the IOP, training other clinicians in the use of structured professional judgement based risk assessment tools, such as the HCR-20. Andy has also trained to assess personality disorders, psychopathy, autism and cognitive functioning. He has research interests and publications in the use of structured risk assessments with offenders with intellectual disabilities, adapted group-based interventions for ID offenders, use of restorative justice in forensic MH/ID services, supporting staff following exposure to violence, and fire setting.

Dr Deepa Jain works as a specialty doctor with Kent & Medway NHS and SCP trust. Deepa obtained her science honours and medical degrees from Bhopal in India and she trained in paediatrics and psychiatry in Ireland. Deepa took a lead in developing a specialist paediatric ADHD clinic in Dublin and was actively involved in a research project on bipolar affective disorder. She has been working in the UK since 2010 in psychiatry of learning disabilities. Her areas of interests include bipolar disorder and physical health in mental health of people with learning disabilities.

James Kerrigan trained as a registered nurse in learning disability (RNLD Dip N) at Queens University, Belfast, in 1992, before taking a post at Longstone Hospital, a long-stay NHS hospital for people with intellectual disability in Armagh City. He qualified as a registered nurse in mental health (RMN Dip N) at Kings College, London, in 2001. He has worked across a range of clinical settings including neuropsychiatry, psychiatric intensive care, acute mental health, A&E psychiatric liaison and community mental health services for people with ID. James has been a commissioner of specialist health services for people with ID for over 13 years. He completed an MSc in Commissioning Health and Social Care at the University of Brighton in 2013 and published research on factors that influence the implementation of policy in ID services in 2017. He currently works as commissioner for integrated learning disability services in Kent and is the NHS and local authority project lead for the Transforming Care programme.

Dr Sarah Maber currently works for Surrey and Borders Partnership NHS Foundation Trust as a consultant psychiatrist for people with intellectual disability based at Bourne House (West CTPLD). She completed her core psychiatry training in North West London (Charing Cross Scheme) working in both in-patient and community settings in general adult psychiatry, older adult psychiatry and forensic psychiatry. Sarah undertook her higher psychiatry training specialising in learning disability psychiatry in South West London (St George's Training Scheme), mainly working with community learning disability teams in the London boroughs of Wandsworth, Kingston and Richmond. She has a BSc in the History of Medicine and an MSc in Psychiatric Research from University College London (UCL). She has special interests in dementia, challenging behaviour and animal-assisted therapy, having published on the latter topic in the journal *Research in Developmental Disabilities*.

Dr Jane McCarthy is working as a consultant psychiatrist at Puawai, Midland Regional Forensic Service, Waikato District Health Board, New Zealand, and is a visiting senior lecturer in the Department of Forensic & Neurodevelopmental Sciences at King's College London. Dr McCarthy's key research interests include the outcomes of psychiatric disorders in people with intellectual disabilities across the lifespan, including those with autism spectrum disorders. In the last five years she has significantly contributed to research in this area having obtained funding for a number of research initiatives including the assessment and early interventions for offenders with learning disabilities and autism, and neurodevelopmental disorders in prison'. From 2009 to 2010 Dr McCarthy acted as clinical advisor for adults with autism at the Department of Health in England, supporting the development and delivery of the national strategy for adults with autism titled *Fulfilling and Rewarding Lives: The national strategy for adults with autism in England.*

Dr Shirin Mishra (MRCPsych, MbChb (Hons)) is a CT3 trainee currently working at SW London & St George's Mental Health NHS Trust. Her passions include writing, teaching and promoting physical health in mental health. At university, Dr Mishra won the Mrs Bentley Prize for her writing and in CT3 year she also won 'best article', which was published in RCPSYCH Winter Edition London Newsletter '17. Enabling her to further her interests, Dr Mishra was appointed co-lead organiser of the London Specialty School of Psychiatry Annual Trainee Conference. A holistic theme to the day encompassing both physical and mental health was chosen and named 'Psychiatry Plus'. She was involved in all stages of this process including the chairing of the day. Dr Mishra also won first prize at the South London Trainee Conference '16 for her poster titled '5 Minutes in Physical Health'. With regards to medical education, Dr Mishra has engaged with St Georges Medical School to deliver seminars and lectures on mental state examination and schizophrenia, substance misuse and addiction. She also volunteers as an OSCE examiner for St Georges' medical students and has been involved in both formal and informal bedside teaching.

Dr Asim Naeem is a consultant psychiatrist in intellectual disability at South West London & St George's Mental Health NHS Trust. He works for the Sutton Community Mental Health ID Team and is also the training programme director for the St George's ST4-6 Scheme in Psychiatry of ID across South West London. He completed both his core and higher training on the St George's Psychiatry Training Schemes. His higher specialist training included a year spent in old age psychiatry, where he developed additional sub-specialist expertise in dementia. His clinical specialist interest areas include neuropsychiatry, dementia in people with ID, old age and LD, psychopharmacology and autistic spectrum disorders. Dr Naeem is actively involved in medical education/training, and is a MRCPsych

CASC and University of London MB BS Examiner. He has several UK peer-reviewed publications in psychiatry journals and text books. He has also presented at regional and national psychiatry conferences.

Dr Alice Nicholls began her career as a support worker for people with intellectual disabilities in Norfolk. She graduated with a first class honours degree in psychology from Anglia Ruskin University in 2007 and went on to complete her Doctorate in clinical psychology at the University of Leicester in 2012. Since qualifying, Dr Nicholls has developed her knowledge of, and skills in, functional assessment and positive behaviour support. She is the lead clinician within a specialist NHS service in East Kent for the assessment and treatment of people presenting with difficult to understand, complex and long-standing challenging behaviour.

Dr Ilias Partsenidis is a consultant psychiatrist in intellectual disabilities working at South London and Maudsley NHS Foundation Trust (SLAM). After qualifying from Guy's, King's and St Thomas' (GKT) School of Medicine, King's College London, he trained in psychiatry in Exeter, Surrey and then at SLAM and Oxleas NHS Foundation Trust. He has published research into substance misuse and involvement with the criminal justice system in adults with intellectual disabilities and mental health problems. He is a trainer recognised by the GMC and supervises core and higher psychiatry trainees. He has a special interest in autism spectrum disorder.

Dr Shama Parveen is a specialty registrar (ST6) on the St George's (SW London) Scheme in Psychiatry of ID. Her clinical specialist interest areas include dementia in people with ID, autistic spectrum disorders, ADHD, and epilepsy in people with ID. She completed her core psychiatric training in the West Midlands. She is actively involved in undergraduate and postgraduate medical education at St George's University of London. Dr Parveen currently leads on co-ordinating the local ID academic programme, and induction OSCEs (assessing for on-call competencies) for new core psychiatric trainees on the St George's scheme. She has presented research/audit posters at national and international conferences, and has an international journal publication on the side effects of Stevens-Johnson syndrome associated with lamotrigine.

Dr Rupal Patel is a consultant psychiatrist within Neurodevelopmental Services at Your Healthcare, CIC. She completed her psychiatry training in South West London and developed a passion and interest for working with adults with intellectual disabilities during this time. Her research interests focus on the management of challenging behaviour in people with intellectual disabilities and dementia in people with intellectual disabilities. She has a real enthusiasm for teaching and training and is involved in both undergraduate and postgraduate training and appraisal.

Dr Max Pickard is a consultant psychiatrist in the mental health of people learning disabilities. He trained at University College London medical school, and had specialist psychiatric training at the South London and Maudsley NHS trust. He has over ten years' experience working in this field as a consultant in community mental health teams for people with learning disabilities. Max has published on service innovations, training and medico-legal issues in this field. He continues to teach on autistic spectrum disorder and attention deficit disorder at under and postgraduate level, as well as being trust medical humanities lead working to integrate different fields into medical practice. He set up the Kent Medical Humanities network, which now runs an annual successful conference in this area. His specialist clinical interests and expertise are in psychodynamic aspects of mental health in learning disabilities and neuropsychiatric elements of mental health in learning disabilities, including joint working with neurology services.

Dr Anne-Marije Prins, MRCPsych, obtained her medical degree from Leiden University in the Netherlands. She came to the UK in 2008 and trained in psychiatry at the South London and Maudsley NHS Foundation trust. Her special interests include the assessment and treatment of perinatal psychiatric disorders in people with intellectual disabilities and developing specialised multidisciplinary care pathways in this field. She has recently moved back to the Netherlands to continue her work in psychiatry of intellectual disabilities, and she aims to develop an acknowledged subspecialty within the Dutch psychiatry training.

Dr Hugh Ramsay is a consultant psychiatrist in psychiatry of intellectual disability with St Michael's House, Dublin, and an honorary clinical lecturer with the Royal College of Surgeons in Ireland. He completed his specialist training in general adult psychiatry and intellectual disability psychiatry in 2016 before taking up his current post with St Michael's House, where he is currently leading the newly developing mental health of intellectual disability team. His clinical interests are in developing community mental health services for people with intellectual disabilities and in the assessment and management of psychosis and of mental disorders occurring in the context of autism. Alongside his clinical training, Dr Ramsay completed an MSc in epidemiology with the University of London in 2013, and a PhD in psychiatric epidemiology with the University of Oulu, Finland, which he completed in 2017. Dr Ramsay has published on a range of mental health topics, including genetic, metabolic and environmental risk factors for cognition and psychosis risk states, mental health law, autism, and mental health service developments for people with intellectual disabilities.

Martin Robb trained as a registered nurse in learning disability (RNLD Dip N) at the University of Ulster in 1994 before taking a post at Muckamore Abbey Hospital, a long-stay NHS institution for people with intellectual disability in Antrim, Northern Ireland. He qualified as a registered nurse in mental health (RMN Dip N) at Kings College, London, in 2001. He has worked across a range of clinical settings including psychiatric intensive care, acute mental health, early intervention in psychosis and community mental health teams. Martin has been a service manager for the Mental Health of Learning Disabilities Team (MHLD) for Kent & Medway NHS and Social Care Partnership Trust since 2014, where his work includes operational and strategic development for the Transforming Care programme, as well ongoing development of mental health services for people with intellectual disabilities.

Emma Rye is a consultant clinical psychologist and clinical lead for psychology in the Mental Health of Learning Disability service in Kent and Medway Partnership NHS Trust. She has worked with adults with learning disabilities ever since qualifying from the Salomons training scheme in Kent in 1994. At that time there was very limited access to any talking therapies for adults with learning disabilities. Emma has always been a passionate advocate for equality of access to psychological therapy for this client group. She has a particular interest in psychodynamic work with adults with learning disabilities and completed the year-long intermediate course at the Tavistock Clinic in 1996. Systemic approaches to working with people with learning disabilities, their families and carers are also important in informing her clinical work. Emma has recently had her portfolio approved by the regional panel to take on the responsible clinician role and is interested in the ethical debate surrounding clinical psychologists taking this on. Emma is also a visiting lecturer on the Canterbury Christ Church (Salomons) Clinical Psychology Doctorate Programme, teaching topics including the delivery of services in the NHS, ethics, philosophy and power.

Dr Aruna Sahni is a specialist registrar in ID at South West London and St George's Mental Health NHS Trust. She entered medicine later in life after a previous career in alternative medicine. She found her interest in psychiatry while working as a foundation doctor, and then her niche in ID as a core trainee in Tower Hamlets, East London. Aruna continues to be interested in evidence-based, non-pharmacological approaches to her work. This includes psychological treatments, particularly systemic work. Her special interest work last year was in a specialist family therapy group for families affected by disabilities, an avenue she would like to explore further in the future. Her current specialist interest work is in neuropsychiatry, particularly non-epileptic seizures. In the last year she helped organise the ID higher trainee conference, and has facilitated clinical problem-based learning sessions with St George's Medical School students.

Dr Abdul Sabir, MD, MRCPsych, is a specialist registrar, Psychiatry of Intellectual Disabilities, at South West London and St George's NHS Trust. Abdul started his training in psychiatry at Xavier University School of Medicine in the US as a foreign medical graduate before moving to the UK in 2009. He had his core training with the West London, Central and North West London NHS Foundation Trusts. He now works for people with intellectual disabilities and pervasive developmental disorders with ongoing mental health needs and has a special interest in the field of autistic spectrum disorders in interface with neuropsychiatry. Abdul has actively participated in various research projects, peer reviewed journals and taught the psychiatry of intellectual disability mainly to final year medical students from St George's and Imperial College, London.

Dr Nwamaka Uchendu is consultant psychiatrist at South London and Maudsley NHS Foundation Trust. Nwamaka completed her training in psychiatry in the East London and on the South London and Maudsley training schemes. She now works as a consultant psychiatrist in the Lewisham Mental Health Learning Disabilities Service in Lewisham, South East London.

Dr Robert Winterhalder is a consultant psychiatrist, Bromley Learning Disability Epilepsy Service, and Mental Health in Learning Disability Team in Oxleas NHS Trust. He graduated from Rome Medical School, La Sapienza, and completed his postgraduate training in psychiatry in South East London and the South of England. He is the clinical lead in his Trust for two specialist teams within a broader community learning disability team for learning disabilities (CTLD), which assess and manage epilepsy and functional and organic psychiatric disorders in people with significant intellectual disability. He has mostly published in the areas of epileptology, psychiatric disorders and pharmacological treatment in people with intellectual disability. He also helped develop and deliver the Diploma and MSC in mental health in learning disabilities, based at Guy's Hospital, in the 1990s. The aim of both his academic and service development work is to promote high standards of clinical practice, particularly among medical doctors and nurses, in the field of adult neurodevelopmental medicine. He has also campaigned against the concept of the overuse of the biopsychosocial model as currently applied by psychiatrists in the UK.

Foreword

I am very pleased to have been invited to write the foreword to this fifth edition of *Mental Health in Intellectual Disabilities*, having been co-editor of the previous four editions. The first edition in this series was published back in 1995 as a companion to a training resource called *Mental Health in Learning Disabilities*, which was itself part of the training activities of the specialist mental health in learning disabilities service based at Guy's Hospital and the Estia Centre in London. This training pack was an innovative idea – a comprehensive programme consisting of over 70 hours of learning, split into several themed modules that provided detailed lecture notes, slides, handouts, learning exercises and video case vignettes. The first edition of this book offered thorough supporting information for the training, guiding both the trainer and the learner step-by-step through each module.

That training pack and the accompanying first edition in this series were developed according to a training needs analysis with local service providers and produced in consultation with local groups of people with intellectual disabilities (ID), as well as with professionals who specialised in the mental health needs of people with ID. At that time, more than 20 years ago, the programmes to de-institutionalise and resettle people with ID in the community were well underway and there was an urgent need to support families, carers, frontline support staff and health and social care professionals. This included helping them to promote the positive mental health of those they cared for, to identify mental health problems, and to provide appropriate services. This training programme therefore filled a vital need.

A second edition of the training resource and this handbook was published in 1997, and a third followed in 2005, which attracted an international interest that resulted in adaptations being published in Australia in 2003 and in the US in 2006. A fourth edition of the handbook, as a standalone reader this time, was published in 2011.

Since that last publication we have witnessed enormous changes in the field of mental health services for people with ID, not least in the increased awareness of the many issues people face. Community services are now well established and the involvement of service users in all aspects of health and social care is considered of paramount importance. People with mental health problems and ID are supported to access mainstream services, psychological therapies have gained increasing recognition, and services are experiencing a growing rate of referrals of service users with offending behaviour. There is also research emerging that shows the effectiveness of psychosocial interventions for people with mental health problems and ID.

This fifth edition of the reader is a completely new iteration of what has become a 'classic' training resource for anyone working in this field. It explores advances in assessment and diagnosis, therapeutic interventions, the current legislative framework and policy governing the area, the ever-growing issues of dementia and old age, psychosis, mood and anxiety disorders, personality disorder and deliberate self-harm, the use of medication, advances in psychological interventions, the application of the Mental Health Act and the importance of capacity and consent. New chapters have also been added covering attention deficit hyperactivity disorder (ADHD), genetic syndromes, the relationship between mental health and challenging behaviour (which remains among the most important of clinical and therapeutic issues), as well as life events and issues around abuse. The book has a new editor in Colin Hemmings, who is joined by a host of new contributors with a wide range of disciplinary backgrounds, including psychiatrists, psychologists, social workers, family therapists, nurses and trainers – all experts in delivering mental health services to people with ID and all sharing a keen interest in staff training.

The 5th edition of *Mental Health in Intellectual Disabilities* is suitable for all staff who support people with ID in a variety of settings, in the community or in-patient services, and for those working in either mainstream or specialist services. It will be invaluable to training departments, as well as professionals and carers involved in health services and social care, such as nurses, psychologists, therapists, social workers and psychiatrists. It is clear, simple, practise-based and evidence-based, and presented in a format that is accessible and very easy to read, with technical and medical jargon being kept to a necessary minimum. This latest edition, published with exceptional care by Pavilion Publishing, will be of value to everyone concerned with the mental health of people with ID.

Nick Bouras
Professor Emeritus
King's College London
Institute of Psychiatry, Psychology and Neuroscience

Chapter 1:
The mental health of people with intellectual disabilities

By Mo Eyeoyibo

Introduction

The terminology used to describe individuals with intellectual disabilities has changed over the years. Terms such as 'idiocy', 'mentally subnormal', 'mental handicap' and 'mental retardation' have become obsolete and are now regarded as socially inappropriate and derogatory. These were terms prominent in legislation, including the UK's Mental Health Act and various UK government policies. The terms 'learning disability' or 'learning disabilities' (LD) are generally more acceptable socially and academic. However, there is a need to harmonise descriptions internationally and 'intellectual disabilities' (ID) is becoming the more preferred term worldwide.

There have been many policies to dictate how services are provided for people with ID to promote inclusion, rights and choices. These strategies have allowed significant gains to be made in the decommissioning of old, long-stay hospitals, promoting independence in smaller, community settings and less institutionalised environments. There is an emphasis on individualised care promoted through person-centred care planning, health action plans and robust safeguarding procedures.

With the closure of most institutional care settings in the UK, which started in the 1970s, health and social care workers have over the years developed specialised skills to support individuals with ID and coexisting mental health problems. But there is still a need to continue to develop this specialism through investment in workforce planning, training and research, and the development of appropriate policies specifically related to the discipline. Mental health in ID, as a specialist area of practice, is concerned with the development of clinical pathways, working with others to provide the right support and enabling an environment for recovery for individuals with ID and mental health problems.

The concepts of dual diagnosis and diagnostic overshadowing

When mental health problems coexist with ID, a condition described as dual diagnosis (Werner & Stawski, 2011), there is increased burden on the individual, their care givers, friends and families. There is also a need for additional services from multiple professionals. There have been various studies supporting the view that individuals with ID are more likely to develop mental health problems than people without ID (Smiley, 2005), however there is still a significant delay in the diagnosis and treatment of mental health problems in this population group. Many reasons are postulated, and one of the most important is the concept of *diagnostic overshadowing*. This is the term used to describe the tendency for clinicians to overlook symptoms of mental and physical health problems in individuals with ID and (mis)attribute them to being part of the person's ID. The effect of diagnostic overshadowing can be misdiagnosis and therefore delays in providing treatment, and both of these consequences can ultimately lead to other serious risks, including carers being unable to manage and placement breakdown.

In a study examining the impact of diagnostic overshadowing in individuals with mental illnesses who present in A&E departments, Shefer *et al* (2014) highlighted the risk of misdiagnosis and delayed treatment and described direct causes and background factors for these. This study recognised the direct causes of misdiagnosis as being the nature of the presentation and the behaviour of the individual reported by staff leading to complex presentations. The background factors noted were the environmental effects on the presentation of the individual or the impact on the motivation of the clinician. For example, a noisy environment will impact on the temperament of an individual with ID and a chaotic clinical environment will not allow clinicians the ability and motivation to dedicate the time and effort required for a thorough assessment.

Most psychiatric diagnoses rely on verbal reports from the patient. This can be difficult in individuals with ID as verbal communication becomes increasingly limited with increasing degrees of disability (RCPsych, 2001). Communication difficulties are also a major reason for challenging behaviour, and both contribute to misdiagnosis in ID.

For these reasons, it is important to have clinicians specially trained in the assessment and treatment of individuals with ID and mental health problems, as well as having systems and processes that support an environment that allows the necessary time for a thorough assessment and treatment.

Definition of ID and how it is diagnosed

The standard definition is provided by the government White Paper *Valuing People* (2001), which says that ID includes the presence of:

- a significantly reduced ability to understand new or complex information, to learn new skills (impaired intelligence), with

- a reduced ability to cope independently (impaired social functioning) and

- which started before adulthood, with a lasting effect on development.

This may be supported with an intelligence quotient (IQ) of 69 or below. The assessment of intellectual functioning usually involves the administration of the most common IQ test, WAIS-IV, which encompasses tests that provide a verbal comprehension score, a perceptual reasoning score, a working memory score and processing speed score. These combine to give a full-scale IQ score. An individual's performance on this measure is compared against the performance of similar-aged individuals. A score between 90 and 109 on each of the domains would represent an average score for the age group. Scores below 70 would be within the ID range.

Eligibility criteria for specialist ID services

This is sometimes described as access criteria and it is usually defined by commissioning organisations to allow providers to focus on services for which they receive funding. There is a general consensus that people with ID should receive care from the same services as the general population, and that the specialist healthcare services should be available when it is needed (Department of Health, 2009). Rigid application of IQ scores can exclude individuals with significant impairments in adaptive functioning because the IQ score is outside the ID range. In essence, provision should be needs-led and not just given on the basis of degree of ID.

Case study: Steven

Steven is a 34-year-old male who lives in a supported living placement where he gets 16 hours carer support with his bills and appointments. He worked for eight years at a local supermarket returning trolleys to the shopping area. He suddenly stopped going to work six months after the death of his mother, who he used to see once a month. His GP referred him to the local adult mental health team. He said that he missed his mother and that he was no longer interested in his job.

He also mentioned he was not sleeping and that he lacked energy during the day. The carers reported he had lost weight and that it took longer to encourage him to do his food shopping. The assessment concluded that his symptoms caused him significant distress and he agreed to take antidepressants. He was referred for psychological support and the initial assessment concluded that his comprehension was limited and that he would be better supported by an ID specialist. Steven completed his sessions with the Mental Health of Intellectual Disability (MHID) team and, during the course of therapy, he considered returning to work.

Mental Health of ID (MHID) Services

Chaplin (2009) described two service models for people with ID. First, the Community Team for People with Learning Disability (CTLD), which may or may not include a mental health element and is likely to have an integrated approach. Second, the Specialist Mental Health Service, which has the advantage of interfaces with adult mental health services but is less well integrated with other allied health care professions (e.g. occupational therapists and speech therapists) such as were to be found in the CTLDs.

As an example, in Kent and Medway Partnership NHS Trust, the mental health needs of individuals with ID are provided by the Mental Health of Learning Disability (MHLD) service, which is comprised of specialist nurses, clinical psychologists and positive behaviour support (PBS) therapists and psychiatrists, all of whom are experienced in the mental health of people with ID. Other allied healthcare professionals (speech and language therapists, occupational therapists and community ID nurses) are employed by the CTLD teams. The social care support provided by the care managers is managed from Kent County Council. Providing support for an individual with ID and mental health problems from three organisations can be challenging, especially if they are not co-located, operationally different (including information systems), and have different governance arrangements. The 'Alliance Contract' is an attempt to bring all three partner providers together to manage one budget and agree on a set of outcomes that allows easy access, quick responses and positive experiences by service users. This type of relationship between the MHLD (MHID) teams and the CTLDs, as described in Kent, can be seen elsewhere in the UK, although other service configurations are also seen.

Inpatient services

There has been a reduction of over 90% in the use of inpatient beds since 1987-1988 (RCPsych, 2013), and a further reduction is anticipated with the transforming care agenda following the Winterbourne View scandal. The role of inpatient services for people with ID has been under scrutiny since Winterbourne, with a call for clarity in its functions. The Royal College of Psychiatrists examined all inpatient beds and suggested the categories of beds should include: forensic (including high, medium, low and rehabilitation beds), acute admission beds within specialised ID units or within generic mental health services, complex continuing rehabilitation beds, and other beds including those for specialist neuropsychiatric conditions.

In reducing bed usage, building the right community support is required to prevent inappropriate admissions and to facilitate discharge (NHS England, 2015). This means having a clear service model and pathway, partnership working between all agencies including community ID teams, mental health services, social services, private providers and clinical commissioning groups. Driving quality through rigorous regulation with inspections will contribute to a culture that supports the best provision for individuals with ID.

In Kent and Medway Partnership Trust, the commissioners and the providers (NHS, social care and other private providers) developed the Complex Care Response (CCR) to support individuals with ID in crisis and at risk of losing their placement or being admitted because of mental illness or behaviour that challenges. The process can be instigated by any service provider, who will be regarded as responsible for the process until a multidisciplinary meeting has taken place to identify the responsible organisation for the CCR and determine whether it is primarily a social, psychological or medical need. This process allows all support organisations to provide resources to try to prevent an admission or to support the person with ID remaining at home. This process does not replace the Care Program Approach (CPA) or Person-Centred Planning (PCP), as both are required to co-ordinate the health and social care needs of the individual with ID. Anecdotal evidence so far suggests positive outcomes for the Complex Care Response process and better support for mainstream use of inpatient beds.

Interfaces and partnership working

Mental health services for people with ID provide services for those who would have had to be provided for by older persons' mental health services, early intervention services and personality disorder services. Sometimes this may take the form of supporting individuals who are able to access such services and, depending on the degree of ID, practitioners within mental health of ID services may have to provide such services.

Two specialist interface areas to consider in service development are transitions from child and adolescent services and the older persons' services for people with dementia. Transfer from child to adult services is often a time of high anxiety for both parents and their children, and there is often a need to manage expectations. Providing adequate information about the service, especially information about managing crises, can make a big difference. The partnerships between older persons' mental health services, social services and mental health in ID services will ensure individuals with ID and dementia receive a comprehensive assessment of their needs for a care plan and care package that addresses issues relating to dementia.

Key learning points

- People with ID should be supported to express their rights and choices and to live a fulfilling life.

- The coexistence of ID and mental health problems brings additional burdens to the individuals, carers and family members.

- Services must be setup to take complex presentations into account and allow time for an adequate understanding of their needs.

- Access to services must not be rigid and should be needs-led and not entirely dependent on IQ scores alone.

- There is a need for an integrated approach to service delivery so as to improve the experiences of people with ID.

- The emphasis of commissioners and providers should be on preventing inappropriate admissions (Department of Health et al, 2015), and when this is required, there must be clear outcomes from the admission.

References

Chaplin E (2009) Mental Health Services for people with intellectual disability: Challenges to care delivery. *British Journal of Learning Disability*. DOI: 10.1111/j.1468-3156.2008.00540.

Department of Health (2001) *Valuing People: A new strategy for learning disability for the 21st century*. London: DoH.

Department of Health (2009) *Valuing People Now: A new three-year strategy for people with learning disabilities*. London: DoH

NHS England (2015) *Building the Right Support* [online]. Available at: www.england.nhs.uk/learning-disabilities/natplan/ (accessed March 2018).

Royal College of Psychiatrists (2001) *DC-LD (Diagnostic Criteria for psychiatric disorders for use with intellectual disabilities / mental retardation)*. London: Gaskell Press.

Royal College of Psychiatrists (2013) *People with Learning Disability and Mental Health, Behavioural or Forensic Problems: The role of in-patient services* [online]. Available at: www.rcpsych.ac.uk/pdf/FR%20ID%2003%20for%20website.pdf (accessed March 2018).

Shefer G, Henderson C, Howard L, Murray J & Thornicroft G (2014) Diagnostic overshadowing and other challenges involved in the diagnostic process of patients with mental illness who present in emergency departments with physical symptoms – A Qualitative Study. *PLoS ONE* **9** (11).

Smiley E (2005) Epidemiology of mental health problems in adults with learning disability: an update. *Advances in Psychiatric Treatment* **11** (3).

Department of Health *et al* (2015) *Transforming Care for People with learning Disabilities – Next Steps* [online]. Available at: www.england.nhs.uk/wp-content/uploads/2015/01/transform-care-nxt-stps.pdf (accessed March 2018).

Werner S & Stawski M (2012) Knowledge, attitudes and training of professionals on dual diagnosis of intellectual disability and psychiatric disorder. *Journal of Intellectual Disability Research* **56** (3) 291-304.

Chapter 2: Policy, legislation and guidance

By James Kerrigan and Martin Robb

Introduction

This chapter will focus on policy, legislation and guidance as it relates to people with intellectual disabilities (ID) in the UK.

Policy is a document that outlines or defines what a government or an organisation such as the NHS is going to do and the steps that will be taken to achieve a set of objectives. National policy documents are known as White Papers and may indicate new legislation that the government intends to make.

Legislation in health and social care is the Acts of Parliament or laws that require or authorise public sector agencies to undertake certain actions or to provide certain functions. Legislation often requires local areas to develop specific policy and procedures that describe how the legislation will be adhered to in practice.

Guidance is published advice on how policy or legislation might/should be applied. It often includes examples of best practice. Guidance itself is not mandatory but *Statutory Guidance* is linked to legislation such as the Autism Act (2009), and therefore public sector agencies must adhere to it.

Most, if not all, policy, guidance and legislation on ID since the 1970s can be linked to the philosophy of normalisation, that is, that people with ID should be seen as and treated as equal citizens with the same rights as other members of society, including accessing the same public services and amenities.

Key policies

Valuing People

Valuing People: A new strategy for learning disability for the 21st Century (Department of Health, 2001) was the first national strategy to specifically address all aspects of the lives of people with ID in the community. It set out how the government intended to provide new opportunities for children and adults with ID and their families to live full and independent lives as part of their local communities. The four principles of *Valuing People* were rights, independence, choice and inclusion.

It identified 'problems and challenges' and 'what more needs to be done' with regard to the following areas:

■ Disabled children and young people – including educational services and transitioning to adult services.

■ More choice and control for people with ID – including person-centred planning, advocacy and direct payments.

■ Supporting carers – including information for carers and for the Carers and Disabled Children Act (2000).

■ Improving health for people with ID – through better access to mainstream services, reducing health inequalities and specialist services.

■ Housing, fulfilling lives and employment – including closing remaining long-stay NHS hospitals, and improving leisure, transport and benefits.

■ Quality services – including regulation, workforce planning and training and services for people with complex needs.

It defined the structures and actions required locally and nationally. One of the key structures was 'Learning Disability Partnership Boards', which were required to be set up in each local authority area to be responsible for the delivery of the government proposals that related to services for adults with ID.

Transforming Care

Transforming Care is a national programme of work that began in 2012 to expand and develop the range of community services and support available, and to close specialist in-patient hospitals for people with ID or autism. Transforming Care was previously known as the 'Winterbourne Programme' and followed the BBC Panorama investigation into the abuse of people with ID at Winterbourne View Hospital.

Building the Right Support (NHS England, 2015a) is the policy document that underpins the overall Transforming Care programme. Its key statements are:

■ A commitment to fundamentally change how people with ID or autism who have additional mental health or challenging behaviour needs are supported to live a normal life as members of their community.

■ A target range of no more than 10-15 assessment and treatment beds and 20-25 secure hospital beds being used at any point in time per one million population.

■ The closure of 50% of in-patient beds for people with ID or autism resulting in a reduction in total in-patients nationally from 2,600 to 1,300 by March 2019.

■ The transfer of funding from in-patient care to community services.

■ When in-patient care is required it will be high quality and will be close to the person's home area in order to enable them to maintain links with their relatives.

■ A reduction in lengths of stay in in-patient care when it is required.

■ Commissioners will be organised into 49 areas called Transforming Care Partnerships and will be responsible for delivering change within their respective area.

■ Provider organisations will be engaged to develop innovative housing care and support solutions in the community.

■ A finance framework will underpin transformation and a national budget made available to support change based on matched funding from local areas.

From *Care and Treatment Reviews: Policy and Guidance* (NHS England, 2015b), care and treatment reviews (CTRs) were developed to support the achievement of the Transforming Care objectives. CTRs bring together the patient/person and their family with commissioners and clinical experts to ensure that the care and treatment, and the differing support needs of the patient/person and their families, are being met, and that barriers to progress are challenged and overcome. CTRs focus on the following key lines of inquiry so that feedback can be provided to the patient and their family:

■ Am I safe?

■ What is my current care like?

■ Is there a plan in place for my future?

■ Do I need to be in hospital for my care and treatment?

All in-patients who have ID or autism should be offered a CTR every six months, or three months for children. Any person in the community who is at risk of, or who has been referred for, in-patient treatment must be offered a CTR to explore the rationale for admission and to consider alternatives that might prevent the admission.

Care Programme Approach

The Care Programme Approach (Department of Health, 1990) was introduced in England to improve the care received by people with severe mental health conditions. It provides a framework within which to co-ordinate the delivery of health and social care interventions, and one of its aims was to help services to remain in contact with service users. Key features of the CPA include:

- a system for assessing health and social needs
- provision and regular review of a written care plan
- close monitoring and co-ordination by a named keyworker
- involvement of users and carers
- inter-professional and inter-agency collaboration.

The CPA stresses the importance of close working between health and social care services and other relevant individuals or organisations e.g. wider NHS services, residential care and supported living providers. The need to involve service users and their carers in the assessment and planning of their care and support is paramount. CPA is therefore recognised as a valuable framework when planning care for people with ID who have mental health problems because people with both ID and mental health problems often require support from a range of health and social care agencies and because it espouses a person-centred approach.

The principles underpinning the CPA are:

- working in **partnership** with people who have complex mental health and social care needs and those supporting them
- striving to **empower** people using services to have choices and make decisions to determine their well-being and recovery
- integrating and **co-ordinating** a person's journey through all parts of the health and social care system
- enabling each person to have a **personalised care plan** based on his/her needs, preferences and choices

- ensuring that the person receives the **least restrictive care** in the setting most appropriate for that person

- supporting the person to attain **well-being** and recovery

- ensuring that the **needs of carers/families** are addressed

- brokering **partnerships** with health and social care agencies and networks which can respond to and help to meet the needs of the person who is experiencing mental health problems.

Case study: John

John is a 43-year-old man with a diagnosis of mild ID and bi-polar affective disorder. He was admitted to a local acute mental health unit from a residential care home following a relapse of mental illness and was detained under Section 3 of the Mental Health Act. When he was in hospital he displayed challenging behaviour, which the ward found hard to manage, and he was transferred to an out of area assessment and treatment unit for people with ID. He continued to display challenging behaviour while in hospital and remained in hospital for 11 years and his care and treatment was delivered under the Care Programme Approach. His care co-ordinator maintained contact with him throughout his time in hospital.

Following a Care and Treatment Review, John was identified for discharge from hospital under the Transforming Care programme. John does not have any family, and commissioners worked with John's care co-ordinator, the in-patient team, the local authority and a supported living provider to plan John's discharge. The in-patient team were asked to co-ordinate a process of person-centred planning. This involved talking to John regularly to identify and document what his wishes and aspirations for the future were, and in particular whether he would like to live with others or in his own accommodation and in which area. The views of other people who knew John were also recorded. This information was captured in a person-centred plan, which John kept a copy of.

The person-centred plan and information in clinical assessments and risk assessments were combined into a detailed placement specification document, which included information on the type of skills and experience support staff would need to be able to support John. The care co-ordinator and the care manager from the local authority then approached some providers of supported living to determine which one could best meet the requirements of the placement specification, including the specific type of training that staff were provided with to help them understand mental health problems and how to manage challenging behaviour. A decision about who would be the best provider was reached following discussion between everyone involved, and after an assessment was carried out John was supported to visit his new placement in the community.

He said he would be very happy to live there. The commissioner then approved funding for the supported living placement and John was discharged following a short period of Section 17 leave from hospital. The care co-ordinator made arrangements for local mental health services to continue to support John's mental health needs after his discharge, including regular appointments with a consultant psychiatrist. John's day-to-day care and his mental state are now managed under the Care Programme Approach. John is supported by his care co-ordinator to chair his own CPA reviews every six months, which are attended by his supported living key worker, psychiatrist, psychologist and care manager.

Safeguarding

'Safeguarding' is a term used to describe how adults and children are protected from abuse or neglect. It is an important shared priority of many public services and a key responsibility of local authorities. All health and care agencies, large or small, should have a safeguarding policy to underpin how they identify and respond to abuse or neglect. Each organisation providing care and support has a responsibility to ensure that they provide an environment free from fear and abuse. Their responsibilities also include investigating any complaints and reporting concerns and allegations about abuse to social services. Each provider organisation is expected to have its own internal guidelines on safeguarding vulnerable adults (or adults at risk).

It is essential that organisations identify and prioritise groups of people who are at the highest risk of abuse and harm, such as:

- people who are distressed and harm themselves or others
- people who are placed 'out of county'
- people with a very significant ID/high support needs
- people who are survivors of past abuse.

While not directed specifically at practitioners and care staff who work with people with ID, *Safeguarding Adults – Everyone's Responsibility* (RCN, 2015), set out professional and organisational safeguarding responsibilities which apply broadly. It involves making effective use of training, staff appraisal and supervision, and clarifying an organisation's policies and procedures. Professionals and care staff should be aware of abuse and neglect and their roles and responsibilities in reporting it. This includes:

- knowing what abuse and neglect is and what the potential signs are

- reporting concerns, and knowing who to report them to

- ensuring there is understanding within the service about how to make referrals for health and social care support

- taking early, proactive action where there is evidence of poor practice or 'low level' abuse

- being aware of fixed staff shift patterns

- ensuring that staff know that if they report abuse wrongly, but in good faith, they will not get into trouble

- ensuring that managers spend time working alongside service users and direct care staff

- ensuring that poor attitudes and disrespectful behaviours are challenged without delay

- ensuring that staff have good communication skills, both in communicating effectively with people with ID and understanding the ways in which people with ID communicate, especially with regard to individuals who use non-verbal communication or have sensory impairments.

Some changes to safeguarding legislation were been included in the Care Act (2014).

Case study: David

David is 35 years old. He has a diagnosis of moderate ID and autistic spectrum disorder. Although he has no diagnosed mental health issues, he was recently discharged from an ID specialist hospital having been detained under the Mental Health Act.

David was moved to a specialist community placement, where he lives on his own in one of a small complex of flats, and he is supported on a 2:1 staffing basis due to challenging behaviours, which include aggression to others and significant property damage. David has comprehensive behavioural support guidelines that also includes physical intervention as a last resort for the staff to keep David and others safe. He is supported by the local MHLD team under the Care Programme Approach (CPA). David lacked capacity to be involved in decision making in any aspect of his care, and therefore all his support was provided under best interest decisions.

During a routine community visit by an MHLD specialist nurse it was discovered that night staff had been removing David's front door handle to prevent him from leaving his flat and displaying aggression to staff. This had become adopted practice by all night staff with the intention of managing the risk David posed. However as this was not a part of current care plans or risk assessments it was considered a deprivation of liberty. A safeguarding alert was raised by the practitioner through the agreed local process as a result of this concern.

The outcome of the safeguarding investigation determined that David was being illegally detained within his home and this was not part of his current care plan. There was also concern that David could not be adequately monitored from outside his flat while restricted within.

Subsequently, a Court of Protection order was applied for restrictive practices including the locked door, physical intervention and removal of the door handle in severe situations. David remains in his current placement and all agencies involved in his care continue to be co-ordinated through the CPA process.

Without the safeguarding framework, which allows for independent review of concerns, restrictive practices could have continued for David putting him at risk of harm and continuing to deprive him of his liberty.

Key legislation

The Autism Act (2009)

The Autism Act (2009) was the first disability-specific law in England. It sought to address two key areas:

- To place a responsibility on the government to produce a strategy for adults with autism.
- To place a responsibility on the government to produce strategy guidance for local authorities and local health bodies on implementing the adult autism strategy.

Think Autism: Fulfilling and rewarding lives (DoH, 2014) was the government's updated plan to ensure that adults with autism get the help they need, and it explains how they will achieve this. The strategy also tells local authorities and health services how they can help adults with autism. It does not cover children with autism. The Adult Autism Strategy led to the Autism Statutory Guidance (see p20).

The Care Act (2014)

The Care Act focuses on improving and consolidating social care and support for adults with a mental or physical impairment or illness in England. It covers a broad range of aspects of social care and sets out a number of new statutory duties for local authorities as well as rights for individuals and their carers.

In carrying out its duties under the Act, a local authority must give due consideration to the well-being of the individual and their family, which involves:

■ the individual's views, wishes, feelings and beliefs

■ the need to prevent/delay the development of needs for care and support

■ the need to make decisions that are not based on stereotyping individuals

■ the importance of individual's participating as fully as possible in relevant decisions (including providing them with necessary information and support)

■ the importance of achieving a 'balance between the individual's well-being and that of any friends or relatives who are involved in caring for the individual'

■ the need to protect people from abuse and neglect

■ the need to ensure that restrictions on individual rights/freedoms be kept to the minimum necessary.

One of the other key aspects of the Care Act is the integration of health and social care, for example at the point of transition from children's to adult services. Legislation, policy and guidance for children's services is very distinct from adult services and service provision is very different as a result. Children with ID and complex needs and their families therefore have often experienced their care and support 'dropping over a cliff edge' at the age of 18 years. In response to the Care Act, many areas are now seeing the development of 16-25 years' social care teams in an attempt to bridge this service gap, and these are likely to be mirrored in health services in the near future.

The Care Act also places a duty on local authorities to make enquiries if an adult with health and social care needs is experiencing, or is at risk of, abuse or neglect and is unable to protect him/herself. Each local authority area is also required to have a Safeguarding Board to oversee all local policy and procedures.

Key guidance

Services for people with learning disabilities and mental health or challenging behaviour needs – The Mansell Report

The Mansell Report was originally published in 1993 and a 'revised edition' was published more than a decade later (Department of Health, 2007). The report provided, *'guidance for councils and health bodies on the development of services for adults with ID whose behaviour or mental health problems present a challenge to services'*. The 19 key recommendations for commissioners provide, *'a means to plan strategically; to develop preventative strategies that avoid crises; and to make the most effective use of available funding'*.

The Mansell Report highlighted the following:

- The need to put the individual and their family at the centre of service planning through individual person-centred plans and to focus on avoiding the burden on family carers by providing support options such as respite and day opportunities that are funded through direct payments.

- The risks associated with placing individuals in out-of-area residential schools or hospitals.

- The need to develop local services including small individualised support packages rather than large residential settings.

- The need for people with challenging behaviour or mental health needs to be supported by a range of community-based services including specialist multi-disciplinary teams with expertise in challenging behaviour, including 24/7 emergency support.

- The role of local psychiatric in-patient services to offer short-term, highly focused assessment and treatment interventions.

- The need for advanced and specialised training in challenging behaviour to be a requirement for staff at all levels that support people who present with challenging behaviour.

Practically all of the recommendations of the original report were restated due to a lack of progress in implementing good practice for this population nationally. A continued failure by health and social care agencies to implement the report's recommendations was a factor that led to the abuse of people at Winterbourne View Hospital (Flynn, 2012).

Healthcare for All

This guidance document was published in response to the Mencap report *Death by Indifference*, which told the stories of six families whose relatives with ID died prematurely while in the care of the NHS. *Healthcare For All* (DoH, 2008) describes how people with ID find it much harder than other people to access assessment and treatment for health problems that have nothing directly to do with their disability. The report indicated the following learning points for health and social care practitioners and care staff supporting people with ID to access healthcare:

- The NHS must make *reasonable adjustments* to support the delivery of equal treatment, as required by the Equality Act (2010). Reasonable adjustments are not 'one size fits all', but rather they are based on a detailed knowledge of each individual and their health needs, their expressive and receptive communication needs, and their preferences and any anxieties about procedures or the environments in which they will be carried out.

- Often parents and care workers are ignored in healthcare professionals' assessments, even though they often have the most detailed knowledge about the people with ID they support.

- Health service staff often have very limited knowledge about ID. There is often a lack of understanding that equal treatment does not mean receiving the same treatment as someone who does not have ID, rather it means that everyone has an equal right to treatment that meets their specific needs. Practitioners and care staff have a role in educating the wider NHS about the general needs of people with ID either through awareness training or by describing the specific needs or reasonable adjustments needed.

- The NHS is not good at identifying people with ID who access health services, either as a cohort or as individuals. This makes it difficult to assess the quality of care that people with ID receive from the NHS and therefore to understand the changes that need to be made to improve the quality of care. Professionals and care staff should support the process of improving this situation by, for example, asking GP practices whether the individuals they support are identified on GP registers as having ID.

- There is a striking lack of awareness of the health needs of people with ID in primary care. This is a concern because primary care is the point of access to health promotion and prevention of ill health, as well as most specialist health care and treatment. All people with ID are entitled to have an annual health check, which should inform the development of a health action plan. Professionals and care staff should support people with ID to achieve this.

Case study: Michael

Michael is a 22-year-old man with a diagnosis of mild ID and autistic spectrum disorder (ASD). With no history of mental illness and with little known antecedents, he gradually stopped eating and experienced disturbed sleep. This caused severe anxiety which, over a short period of time, led to further decline in his mental health and he was detained under the Mental Health Act under Section 2 and was admitted to a mainstream mental health ward.

The ward staff contacted the community MHLD team as there was difficulty engaging with Michael. MHLD attended the ward and made several recommendations regarding communication and interaction with Michael, especially in regard to his ASD e.g. information given in basic written and visual format; the importance of daily routine and structure; as much as possible using the same staff members to work with Michael to ensure a consistent approach to his care. Michael's parents were also able to visit on a daily basis and provided the ward staff with information and advice that helped them to understand his needs better.

While on the ward, the care team, in collaboration with MHLD, were able to formulate an individualised treatment plan that was effective and Michael was able to be discharged after two weeks and was subsequently followed up by MHLD. Although these adjustments may be considered quite minor, they had a significant impact on Michael's treatment pathway as he was able to have his care delivered on a local mainstream mental health ward.

Autism Statutory Guidance

Statutory guidance to support the implementation of the Adult Autism Strategy (DoH, 2015) was updated to ensure the implementation of the revised adult autism strategy by stating the actions that local authorities and NHS bodies should take to meet the needs of adults with autism. Actions required are to:

- provide autism awareness training for all staff
- provide specialist autism training for key staff, such as GPs and community care assessors
- not refuse a community care assessment for adults with autism based solely on IQ
- appoint an autism lead in their area
- develop a clear pathway to diagnosis and assessment for adults with autism
- commission services based on adequate population data.

As the guidance is statutory, local councils and local health bodies have a legal duty to implement it.

The Green Light Toolkit

The Green Light Toolkit was first published in 2004 to support local efforts to improve mental health services for people with ID. Under the Equalities Act (2010), organisations have had to make changes in how they deliver their services to ensure that they are as accessible to disabled people as everybody else. Mental health services, whether provided by the NHS, the local council, or by the voluntary and independent sector, must presume that people with ID will want to use mainstream adult mental health services and therefore arrangements must be made in advance to accommodate them.

The toolkit was well used in some places but not all, and it was therefore updated in 2013 (NDTi, 2013). This guidance provides practical tools to help services review their quality and share and replicate good practice. Its development brought together commissioners of services for people with ID, providers, user and carers, to share issues and identify solutions. It provides a framework to support reviews of how mental health services support people with ID. It includes an Easy Read version to enable service user involvement and also provides a database of examples of reasonable adjustments made by services to support innovation and to share learning.

Conclusion

Policy legislation and guidance together play a critical role in improving the lives of people with ID. Policy can help to challenge assumptions and accepted norms ascribed to people with ID. For example, prior to Transforming Care it was accepted that a person with ID and a mental illness might spend up to 10 years or more in a hospital, while other members of society would typically only spend weeks or months. Historically, the majority of people with ID may have been admitted to specialist in-patient units for assessment and treatment often far from their local community. The concept of reasonable adjustments has allowed people with ID to benefit from a broad range of mainstream health services that were previously thought to be unable to meet their needs. The role of specialist services for people with ID is crucial in supporting mainstream health services. Legislation and policy protect the people caring for individuals with ID as well as the individuals themselves. It provides a framework to deliver care and support (e.g. CPA) and also provides a means to check the validity of certain aspects of clinical practice and care delivery that a person with ID may not be able or empowered to challenge themselves (e.g. Deprivation of Liberty Safeguards).

Learning points

■ Policy, legislation and guidance are linked, and together they provide direction for what and how health and social care services should be provided.

■ They are subject to continuous review and update.

■ Legislation is law and must be adhered to. Policy describes the overarching approach that should be used across the country. Guidance describes good practice but is not mandatory. Statutory guidance is linked to legislation and is mandatory for local authorities and the NHS.

■ Policy on ID over many years has supported the rights of individuals to live a normal life as part of society with a specific focus on the move away from institutional or hospital care.

■ Failure to implement policy and guidance in local areas can result in the neglect and abuse of people with ID.

References

Department of Health (1990) *Care Programme Approach*. Circular HC(90)23/LASSL(90)11. London: Department of Health.

Department of Health (2001) *Valuing People: A new strategy for the 21st Century*. London: Department of Health.

Department of Health (2007) *Services for People with Learning Disabilities and Mental Health or Challenging Behaviour Needs (Mansell Report – Revised Edition)*. London: Department of Health.

Department of Health (2008) *Healthcare for All: Report of the Independent Enquiry into Access to Healthcare for People with Learning Disabilities*. London: Department of Health.

Department of Health (2014) *Think Autism: Fulfilling and rewarding lives, the strategy for adults with autism in England: an update* [online]. Available at: www.gov.uk/government/publications/think-autism-an-update-to-the-government-adult-autism-strategy (accessed March 2018).

Department of Health (2015) *Statutory guidance for Local Authorities and NHS organisations to support implementation of the Adult Autism Strategy* (2015) available at: https://www.gov.uk/government/publications/adult-autism-strategy-statutory guidance (accessed March 2018).

Flynn M (2012) *Winterbourne View Hospital: A serious case review*. South Gloucestershire Safeguarding Adults Board/South Gloucestershire Council.

NHS England (2015a) *Building the Right Support: A national plan to develop community services and close in-patient services for people with a learning disability and / or autism who display behaviour that challenges, including those with a mental health condition* [online]. Available at: https://www.england.nhs.uk/wp-content/uploads/2015/10/ld-nat-imp-plan-oct15.pdf (accessed December 2017).

NHS England (2015b) *Care and Treatment Review: Policy and guidance*. London: NHSE.

National Development Team for Inclusion (2013) *Green Light Toolkit 2013: A guide to auditing and improving your mental health services so that it is effective in supporting people with autism and people with learning disabilities*. Bath: NDTi.

Royal College of Nursing (2015) *Safeguarding Adults – Everyone's Responsibility*. RCN Guidance for Nursing Staff. London: Royal College of Nursing.

Chapter 3: Assessment

By Max Pickard and Emma Rye

Introduction

This chapter looks at referrals for assessment and discusses the process and challenges of specialist mental health assessment. It also considers the importance and potential complications of involving carers and family in the assessment process. Finally, it briefly looks at some standardised assessment tools that might be used.

Primary care assessment of mental health needs

Most mental health problems in the general population are assessed and treated (usually effectively) by primary care health professionals. In the UK, this is normally by a GP in the first instance, but not necessarily, and there are a growing number of other primary health care practitioners, such as nurse specialists, clinical psychologists or councillors, who are involved with primary care level assessment and treatment.

This is, in principle, no different for people with ID who also develop mental health problems. However, the local community ID team (CIDT) will also be available as a primary health care option. How these teams operate varies according to locality, but they will normally have ID-trained nurses and may have other specialist mental health professionals. In any case, while the CIDT will not be set up purely as a mental health service, they will normally have some expertise in mental health and may also be the first point of call for assessment.

Primary care by its very nature is normally about straightforward health problems that do not require in-depth assessment, and offers relatively simple treatment. For instance, most GPs would rarely provide more than ten minutes' of assessment, although they are trained to make the most of those ten minutes. Sometimes, but not always, they can offer longer appointments when problems are more complex.

People with ID do present more challenges in terms of assessment of mental health, particularly as the level of ID increases. Primary care assessment is normally required in order to access secondary care services. There are sometimes 'grey areas' in this principle, such as emergency situations, but it remains an integral part of the NHS.

When to refer for specialist assessment

If primary or generic health care practitioners do not feel they can adequately assess and treat (and this is, of course, a subjective judgement), then a specialist assessment is indicated. This would normally mean there is at least a suspicion of mental health problems, and they are of a more serious nature, and/or there are additional complexities (such as associated risks).

A GP would normally be able to treat common straightforward mental health problems with medication, such as depression, anxiety or phobias. Psychological treatment may need specialist intervention. More serious mental health problems, such as schizophrenia or bipolar disorder, are normally at least assessed by specialist services (although are often discharged back to primary care once stable).

In people with ID, communication difficulties and a large number of additional complicating factors (such as epilepsy, autistic spectrum disorder (ASD), and other physical health issues) often 'lower the bar' for assessment by specialist services, and rightly so.

There are some screening tools available, such as the mini PAS-ADD (Prosser *et al*, 1998), which are fairly short-structured questionnaires that can be completed by non-specialist health care professionals. These screening tools are not in themselves diagnostic, but can be used to suggest when a referral for specialist assessment is needed.

It is important that any referrer and assessor take into account the principles of capacity and consent.

Who assesses?

Depending on the service model, mental health assessments may be conducted by differing mental health professionals. These may include clinical psychologists, psychiatrists or specialist nurses. For the most complex presentations, a joint assessment may be helpful that includes two or more of these professions. This is because the different professionals will bring different professional perspectives on the person's difficulties.

For some referrals it may be decided that a joint assessment by a mental health professional and a social worker (who might be called a 'care manager' in some services) would be most appropriate. This may be because it is thought that the person's social circumstances are having a significant effect on their mental health, and that offering social care may be the most appropriate way of reducing the person's distress.

Differing agendas and language in an assessment

It behoves everyone involved in an assessment to be aware of the different agendas and priorities that can occur. At a minimum, an assessment will involve the person with ID and an assessing health care professional. Normally, however, there will be at least one informant: perhaps a care staff member or family member, and often both.

Case study: Roy

Roy, a gentleman in his 50s with ID, has become extremely withdrawn. He is spending most of his time in his room. He has stopped eating, fearing his food is poisoned. He has high blood pressure and has started refusing to take his medication for this. He has physically attacked staff on a number of occasions recently. He is up and about all night, waking other residents. He is seen for assessment by the psychiatrist in the Mental Health of ID Team, supported by the manager of the residential service where he lives. His sister and the ID nurse from the Community ID Team also attended the assessment.

The various agendas might be:

Patient: is fearful he might be injected with poison by the doctor, and wants to leave as soon as possible.

Sister: thinks her brother needs more care, that the staff are not feeding him properly, and is worried that Roy might starve to death.

Manager of service: thinks that Roy needs sedative medication so he can sleep and will stop attacking staff. She is worried about the impact of Roy's behaviour on other residents.

Nurse: is worried about the risk to Roy's health if he does not start taking his blood pressure tablets again. He thinks that the priority is to get Roy engaged with his GP and make sure his physical health is attended to.

Psychiatrist: thinks that Roy is showing signs of paranoia. She is concerned that Roy's late onset delusions might be due to a brain tumour and is keen for further investigations to be arranged to rule out physical causes.

Of course, often a range of agendas are present in all the individuals involved. The oft-repeated phrase 'We just want what's best' is unenlightening as – hopefully – everyone wants what is best for Roy, but there may be disagreement about the priorities. It would be wrong to imagine in the above example that the psychiatrist is not concerned with the patient's blood pressure or inner distress, or to presume that Roy's sister is not concerned about the reasons for late onset psychotic symptoms. However, their priorities may well differ and managing these conflicting agendas (by discussing them openly and respecting them all) is a helpful way to proceed in any assessment.

Complicating factors in mental health assessment in people with ID

People with ID often have difficulties with communication. This obviously complicates the assessment process. The person may struggle to describe their thoughts and feelings. This difficulty is often even more pronounced for people who also have an ASD. It requires great skill on behalf of the assessing professional to help the person being assessed to put their psychological difficulties into words by asking questions that take account of the person's verbal ability. The mental health professional needs to adapt the words used for each individual person assessed in order to elicit the quality of information required to complete a good quality assessment.

The assessing mental health professional needs to be cautious about the potential impact of suggestibility. People with ID are more likely than the general population to just agree with whatever they are asked, especially if they do not fully understand the question (Finlay & Lyons, 2002). Asking questions using different wording can help to clarify if suggestibility is having an impact on the assessment. For example, if a professional were to ask, 'Do you feel happy most of the time?' and 'Do you feel unhappy often?', and answer to both questions was 'Yes', although the questions may not be entirely inconsistent, it is a sign that further exploration will be required.

Sources of information

It usually helpful to obtain information from a range of sources in order to complete a thorough assessment. The referred person may find it difficult to explain their issues for the reasons outlined above, or may have no verbal communication at all. Moreover, by obtaining multiple perspectives, a clearer picture of the issues will be developed. There is never one truth when it comes to mental health. Speaking to the staff who support the person will give a valuable insight into their concerns. However, it must be borne in mind that different staff working with the same person may have widely differing views. Sometimes a member of staff who barely knows the person will support them to the assessment. This will hamper the assessment process, and in some circumstances make it impossible to conduct the assessment in a meaningful way.

When possible and appropriate, it can be helpful to also speak to family members. They are usually the only people who can give a full developmental history. However, again, it is important to bear in mind that their perspective is indeed just that: one perspective.

In some cases, it may be appropriate to observe the person in their home or at the day centre in order to get a clearer picture of the difficulties in the context of their environment. It may also be important to obtain results of medical investigations in order to complete the picture. For example, blood tests and scans might be helpful when looking at underlying medical conditions.

Assessment tools

In order to gather more information, the assessing mental health professional may request the referred person and/or those around them complete some forms. These may be standardised assessments of anxiety or depression, such as the Glasgow Anxiety and Depression Scales (Cooper *et al,* 2003; Espie & Mindham, 2003), which have been designed for people with ID to complete. However, all such questionnaires require the person to have a certain level of linguistic ability. There are other questionnaires which are designed for family or staff to complete, either by themselves, or in discussion with the mental health profession e.g. ADI-R (Lord *et al*, 1994) to assess for possible ASD.

If it is decided that it would be helpful to understand more about a person's cognitive functioning, a clinical psychologist may ask the person to do some psychometric tests, such as the WAIS-IV (Weschler, 2008). This can help to develop a picture of the person's strengths and difficulties, which may give insight into the context of their psychological difficulties. There are also specific assessments for conditions such as dementia.

Staff may be asked to go off and record the setting factors for all challenging behaviour for a few weeks, which would then be analysed by the mental health professional (e.g. ABC charts). They may be asked to complete mood charts for a few weeks, to give day-by-day information about the person's mood alongside details of activities, and who was on shift each day etc.

Common questions in the assessment

Assessment in people with ID normally requires increased time, both because of communication difficulties and the complexity of problems. Questioning and lines of inquiry should be tailored to the patient and their problems. While adapting the assessment to the individual is vital, there are a number of key questions and topic that are asked.

Current problems

What problems does the person being assessed think they have? What are their concerns and worries? What do they want help with?

The problems that other parties (such as family or carers) perceive in the individual are also important, but any assessment should look at the individual's perception of problems as far as possible. There are times (such as in the case of formal incapacity in an issue) when the individual does not perceive there to be a problem but others do, and this must be addressed.

When looking at current problems, noting 'behaviour' is not sufficient. Mental life is not behaviour on its own, but what lies behind the behaviour. What emotions caused the behaviour?

Caution should be taken when certain words are used that are open to misinterpretation, such as 'agitation' or 'mood instability', both of which can mean a wide variety of behaviours or emotional states. A good assessment will drill down and ask precisely what these descriptions mean. Agitation, for example, could mean restlessness, aggressiveness, anxiety or anger (among other things). Mood instability could mean anything from being irritable now and again, to the mood variation in bipolar disorder (changing over weeks), to the changes in emotional state characteristic in frontal lobe problems. The problems inherent in accepting these terms without a clear description of what they mean precisely are obvious (and dangerous).

Whether it be behaviour, communication, mood, thoughts, or any other aspect of mental health, a longitudinal history must be obtained, and this can be quite detailed. How long has it been a problem for? Has anything changed in the person's life that might explain mental changes? Is it variable? Is it getting better, or worse?

Past mental health history

Has the person had any mental health problems in the past, and if so, were they treated? (They may still be being treated.) Of particular importance with treatment (whether that is psychological or pharmacological) is whether it helped or not.

Past and current medical problems

Physical health is intertwined with mental health (and some argue that no distinction should be made in the first place: health is health). Mental health assessment should include an understanding of physical problems and treatment. Some particular issues that should be considered are the interaction of medication on mental health, epilepsy (which can cause many associated mental health issues), and pain or discomfort (which can lead to mood problems, or challenging behaviour).

Background history

No mental health assessment is complete without understanding the personal life history of the individual. Of particular importance is early experience, including trauma. While this may be hard for the individual to discuss (and one should respect the individual's wishes in this regard), it is important in understanding mental health. The person may not be able to tell the assessor about their early life: either because they do not have verbal skills, or they are too defended to recall. In such cases information from the carers is extremely important. However, sometimes the carers do not know the person's history, or only to a limited degree. Vague unqualified terms like 'abuse' or 'difficult upbringing' are far from ideal – what was the nature of the trauma? How severe was it? How often did it occur? What effect did it have? In addition, an assessment should look at the nature of attachments and relationships, particularly during the childhood years. Did the person feel safe and secure? Where they bullied? Neglected?

Developmental milestones (such as age of walking and speech) and educational achievements (or provision) are helpful in estimating level of ID and particular areas of strength or difficulty. There might also be clues to ASD in the background history.

Background history should not purely be about childhood, however. There is a wealth of important information beyond the age of 18. Occupation, interests, friendships, living arrangements to name but a few. Lastly, sexual and romantic relationships should not be ignored.

Social factors

Any mental health assessment should include the world in which the individual lives. What type of care and support (if any) do they receive? With whom do they live? It can be helpful to understand how many other people with ID they live with (for instance in a care home), and how many staff are in their home (or specifically dedicated to the individual). It can also be useful to understand if there are night staff, and whether they are waking or sleep-in.

In addition, activities and interests during the day, education, friendships, relationships, and contact with (and nature of relationship with) family should be included. Aside from the possibility that some of these factors may be pertinent in mental health problems, they might also offer avenues for improving mental health in the future.

Risk issues

Any assessment should consider risk from the outset.

Case study: Scott

Scott was referred to the Mental Health of ID Team by his GP. He was 28 years old and lived in his own tenancy. He had two hours' support a day from an agency, commissioned by his care manager from the local CIDT. The referral stated that he had a long history of anxiety, but that this had become more severe recently. He was experiencing night terrors and panic attacks. He had stopped going to his supported employment, which he used to enjoy: three days a week working in a kitchen at a community café.

Scott was invited to an assessment with the clinical psychologist. He told her about his childhood, with seven younger brothers and sisters, all of whom had ended up in care. Scott became very tearful as he talked about being regularly beaten by his father. He had a difficult relationship with his mother, too, who was verbally abusive towards him, and was not able to protect him from his father's violent rages. Scott remembered that the whole family were verbally abused and bullied by local children. He had lost touch with all his family many years before, but had recently found out that his father had died. He went to the funeral, and had hoped to maintain contact with the family, however they all made it clear to him that they were not interested.

In this assessment it was possible to get enough information from Scott himself in order to develop a psychological formulation, which helped Scott make sense of his increased anxiety and panic in the context of a history of trauma. For years

Scott had tried – quite successfully – to repress the memories of his childhood. However, when he attended the funeral and was rejected again by his family, this brought the memories flooding back and his previous strategies to cope by keeping himself busy were no longer working.

Key learning points

- Everybody can be assessed, even if they have no verbal communication skills.

- People with ID often have communication difficulties, other developmental problems (such as autism), and other health problems (such as epilepsy) that can make assessment much more complicated and challenging.

- For these reasons, informants are often important sources of information. However, different individuals (carers, family, professionals) may have competing agendas.

- While behaviour is an important part of assessment, it is not the only component. A person's emotions, thoughts and their inner world are also vital (although they may be difficult to understand).

References

Cooper S, Cuthill F & Espie C (2003) Development and psychometric properties of the Glasgow depression scale for people with a learning disability. Individual and carer supplement versions. *British Journal of Psychiatry* **182** 347-353.

Espie C & Mindham J (2003) Glasgow anxiety scale for people with an intellectual disability (GAS-ID): development and psychometric properties of a new measure for use with people with mild intellectual disability. *Journal of Intellectual Disability Research* **47** 22-30.

Finlay WM & Lyons E (2002) Acquiescence in interviews with people who have mental retardation. *Mental retardation* **40** 14-29.

Lord C, Rutter M & Le Couteur A (1994) Autism diagnostic interview-revised: a revised version of a diagnostic interview for caregivers of individuals with possible pervasive developmental disorders. *Journal of Autism and Developmental Disorders* **24** 659-85.

Prosser H, Moss S, Costello H, Simpson N, Patel P & Rowe S (1998) Reliability and validity of the Mini PAS-ADD for assessing psychiatric disorders in adults with intellectual disability. *Journal of Intellectual Disability Research* **42** 264-272.

Weschler D (2008) *Wechsler adult intelligence scale-fourth edition (WAIS-IV)*. London: Pearson.

Chapter 4: Dementia and old age

By Asim Naeem, Aruna Sahni & Shirin Mishra

Summary

This chapter explores the challenges of age-related conditions in people with intellectual disabilities (ID), with a particular focus on dementia. It includes an overview of: the presentation of dementia in people with ID, including the difficulties of accurate diagnosis; conditions that can mimic dementia ('pseudo-dementia'); dementia-screening investigations; management of dementia; and a brief look at other age-related conditions. Three case studies focus on the complex area of correctly diagnosing and managing dementia in people with ID, incorporating nine additional learning points for readers.

Introduction

The increasing life expectancy of people with ID brings about important challenges in terms of age-related conditions. Compared to the general older adult population, people with ID have greater rates of mental and physical illness. They are more likely to have complex atypical presentations of illness (e.g. dementia) and comorbid medical conditions (e.g. hypothyroidism, epilepsy).

Adults with Down's syndrome have increased rates of early-onset Alzheimer's dementia, with the average age of onset being 50–55 years (Prasher & Krishnan, 1993). After this, the rates of dementia increase exponentially, such that 30-40% of people with Down's syndrome have a clinical diagnosis of dementia by 60 years of age (Coppus *et al*, 2006). The age of onset and risk of dementia does not appear to be associated with the level of ID.

It is now known that older people with ID (>60-65 years age) who do not have Down's syndrome also have higher rates of dementia (Strydom *et al*, 2007). Alzheimer's dementia is the commonest dementia type seen; up to three times more than in the general population. Lewy body dementia and frontotemporal dementia are seen more commonly than vascular dementia.

The presentation of dementia in people with ID

Early detection and accurate diagnosis of dementia is important to ensure that optimum management strategies can be put in place. These may include starting anti-dementia medication and making adaptations to the person's home. This can improve quality of life for people with ID, reduce carer burden, and reduce the risks of placement breakdown.

In people with Alzheimer's dementia, the classical microscopic brain changes seen are the presence of neuritic plaques and neurofibrillary tangles. Some people with Down's syndrome start developing these brain changes before 40 years of age, but not all develop 'clinical dementia' at that time. Box 1 shows why the diagnosis of 'clinical dementia' is complex in people with ID.

Box 1: Why is it difficult to diagnose 'clinical dementia' in people with ID?

■ There are significant individual variations ('heterogeneity') in the pre-existing ('baseline') cognitive, behavioural and functional skills of people with ID (Raji & Naeem, 2011).

■ Diagnosis is dependent on good collateral information from carers/family. In residential settings, the rapid staff turnovers can reduce this likelihood.

■ Presenting with 'atypical' symptoms e.g. changes to their behaviour and/or mood, rather than memory.

■ There are no universally accepted quick screening tests to use directly with people with ID. The Mini-Mental State Examination (MMSE), which is used in the general older population, is not validated for use in people with ID.

■ A number of reversible conditions (see Box 2 on p39) can 'mimic' the signs of dementia.

■ Some people with ID have 'baseline' abnormal brain neuroimaging (CT/MRI brain scan) findings.

Table 1 shows the different domains of dementia, and how they may present in people with ID. It is important to establish current abilities and compare these with the person's abilities at their best previous level of functioning.

Table 1: The clinical domains of dementia in people with ID

Cognition (memory)	■ Forgetfulness of recent events e.g. meals/social outings (episodic memory impairment). ■ Getting muddled in familiar surroundings. ■ Not recognising familiar people (semantic memory impairment). ■ Forgetting where they have put familiar items (spatial memory impairment). ■ Not being able to perform previous skills e.g. making a drink, using the phone (procedural memory impairment).
Abstract reasoning (judgement/planning/ organisation)	■ Difficulty following instructions. ■ Decline in daily living skills e.g. eating, dressing, brushing teeth (apraxia). ■ Difficulty with reading (alexia), writing (agraphia) or language (aphasia). ■ Inappropriate use of common items (agnosia) e.g. trying to write with a spoon. ■ Loss of day-night awareness.
Behavioural & psychological symptoms of dementia (BPSD)	■ Low or labile mood (e.g. unexplained tearfulness or irritability). ■ Restlessness. ■ Sleep cycle changes. ■ Increased dependence on others. ■ Personality changes e.g. aggression, obsessional slowness. ■ Repetitively saying 'sorry' when asked to complete tasks.
Perceptual abnormalities	■ Hallucinations (auditory, visual or tactile).
Neurological abnormalities	■ Altered gait/falls/fear of stairs or uneven surfaces. ■ General slowness in movements (bradykinesia). ■ Seizures (may occur as the first sign of dementia, in the absence of past epilepsy). ■ Incontinence.

In exploring for symptoms suggestive of dementia, it is important to try to 'screen out' any individual 'baseline' deficits in a person with ID. For example, if a person presents with difficulties following carer instructions, clarification would be needed as to whether this is a new symptom, a pre-existing symptom that has got worse or a pre-existing symptom that has not worsened. In the absence of other causes (e.g. physical illness or environmental changes), only new symptoms or pre-existing symptoms that have worsened are likely to indicate dementia.

The different types of dementia can also have specific variations in their presentation. Alzheimer's dementia symptoms usually occur gradually and get progressively worse. Vascular dementia symptoms have a more sudden onset and get worse in a 'step-wise' manner, with a greater fluctuating course. They are also more likely to occur if there are other vascular risk factors (e.g. hypertension, diabetes mellitus, history of stroke). Usually, insight is relatively preserved in vascular dementia, while it is absent in Alzheimer's dementia. In Lewy body dementia, movement difficulties and visual hallucinations are common. However, there can be significant individual variations in all of these presentations, including from day to day and hour to hour.

Case study: Helen

Helen is a 50-year-old lady with mild ID secondary to Down's syndrome who lives in a residential home. Staff there had noticed that she had been getting more forgetful over recent events (including her birthday). Her sleep pattern had changed, so she was getting up several times during the night. She started to put her daytime clothes on when staff entered her room to prompt her back to sleep. There had also been occasions of her refusing to move from the landing area to the kitchen for mealtimes. Her GP had excluded any underlying physical cause for her memory deterioration.

On review by the psychiatrist, it was clarified that these symptoms were new. The psychiatrist noted that Helen appeared to 'freeze' at the different floor patterns between the landing and kitchen area. Helen's altered 'depth perception' was probably causing this. Helen's day-night disorientation was worsened when night staff wearing formal day-clothing tried to encourage her back to sleep at night. The Dementia Screening Questionnaire for Individuals with ID (DSQIID) revealed a score of over 20, suggesting a high likelihood of early-onset dementia. This was also supported by additional psychology testing using standardised screening tools.

A CT brain scan showed changes consistent with Alzheimer's dementia, including overall shrinking of the brain (cerebral atrophy), particularly prominent in the temporal lobe areas (temporal atrophy). An ECG showed a regular heart rhythm of ~ 60 bpm.

Helen was started on the anti-dementia medication donepezil, which was slowly increased to its maximum dose. This helped to stabilise her symptoms. There are plans to switch the donepezil to memantine when the dementia reaches the moderate-severe range. Some personalised environmental adaptations were also suggested to the home, including advice on consistent flooring between the landing and kitchen areas, and for night staff to put on a dressing gown (over their formal dress wear) when entering Helen's room at night.

This case highlights the following learning points:

- The altered depth perception and day-night disorientation in Alzheimer's dementia can present in different ways in people with ID.
- Accurate detection of Alzheimer's dementia in people with ID allows the early introduction of anti-dementia medication.
- Personalised adaptations to a placement can allow a person with ID to successfully remain there after being diagnosed with dementia.

Case study: John

John is a 60-year-old man with mild ID of unknown cause, who lives in a supported living placement. His care worker noticed that John's short-term memory had progressively deteriorated over the last six months, including occasions of him forgetting appointments. John appeared disorientated at times and had difficulty using his TV remote. Over the last three months, John appeared to be 'imagining' items in his flat, including flowers and other people. He has also had a number of falls. After some tests no underlying physical cause could be found for either the memory decline or the falls, and he was referred to the psychiatrist.

On psychiatric assessment, although John was sometimes seeing 'imagined items' (e.g. thinking a pile of socks was 'snakes'), he did not appear distressed by this. On examination John had a marked tremor in both hands and feet, apparent both at rest and on intentional movement. His gait appeared unsteady. He walked slowly with a 'shuffling gait'. Formal psychology testing revealed some deterioration in John's short-term memory. A CT brain scan showed only age-related brain shrinking (cerebral atrophy).

A clinical diagnosis of Lewy body dementia was made on account of the: progressive but fluctuating memory decline; recurrent well-formed, but non-threatening visual hallucinations; spontaneous features of Parkinsonism (tremor, altered gait); and repeated falls. John was started on the anti-dementia medication rivastigmine, which helped to improve his memory and reduce the visual hallucinations he was experiencing. He was also referred to the physiotherapist to help reduce some of the mobility and tremor difficulties.

It was decided not to add any anticholinergic medications (normally used to treat Parkinsonian side-effects) or antipsychotics as they can make confusion worse in Lewy body dementia.

This case highlights the following learning points:

■ The presence of progressive but fluctuating memory decline, recurrent visual hallucinations, spontaneous symptoms of Parkinsonism and recurrent falls strongly indicate Lewy body dementia.

■ Acetylcholinesterase anti-dementia medications can be of use in the management of Lewy body dementia.

■ Anticholinergics and antipsychotics (except low dose quetiapine) cause worsening confusion in Lewy body dementia.

Pseudo-dementia (including causes of delirium)

A number of conditions can 'mimic' the symptoms of dementia (see Box 2). These are collectively known as causes of 'pseudo-dementia'. Acute physical health problems such as infections, can cause sudden episodes of confusion known as 'delirium'. Once identified and correctly treated, the confusion resolves. People with diagnosed dementia may also have rapid worsening in their memory and confusion, due to developing a comorbid acute physical health problem, again such as an infection. This is referred to as 'acute on chronic' confusion.

The recommended physical health investigations to exclude pseudo-dementia (including delirium) include:

■ FBC (full blood count)

■ Vitamin B12 and folate levels

■ U & Es (urea & electrolytes)

■ Blood glucose

■ Liver function tests

■ Lipid profile

■ Thyroid function test

■ Urinalysis

■ Visual and hearing check

Box 2: The causes of pseudo-dementia in people with ID?

Medical

Physical

- Hypothyroidism
- Diabetes Mellitus
- Infections (e.g. ear, urinary, chest)
- Constipation
- Anaemia
- Visual (e.g. cataracts)
- Hearing (e.g. ear wax, sensorineural problems)
- Worsening epilepsy
- Cognitive side-effects from medications e.g. anticonvulsants.

Psychiatric

- Depression
- Anxiety
- Worsening obsessions within the context of OCD or autism
- Sedative side-effects from psychotropic medications.

Psychological

- Loss events e.g. bereavement/key staff members or peer group moving/college or day centre closing down.
- Emotional traumas (including abuse).

Social

Changes in routine/staff/home/daily activities.

Case study: Ralph

Ralph is a 53-year-old man with moderate ID secondary to Down's syndrome who lives in a community residential home. He has long-standing hearing impairment, for which he wears hearing aids in both ears. Over the last three months Ralph had found it more difficult to follow simple instructions (e.g. put on your coat), and he had episodes of becoming more confused. Staff had noticed that Ralph needed greater prompting. His self-care had deteriorated, with him having episodes of daytime urinary incontinence. However, he had retained enjoyment in his regular activities, including going bowling. He does not have a history of epilepsy and he is not on any regular medications.

Psychology dementia testing showed a marked deterioration in Ralph's functioning compared to that of a year ago. The Dementia Scale for Down Syndrome (DSDS) showed an unusual profile, with Ralph having symptoms indicative of early, middle and late-stage dementia. In view of this, the psychologist referred Ralph for an assessment by the Mental Health ID Team psychiatrist.

On psychiatric review, Ralph was able to give a 'thumbs up' sign to indicate that he was happy and was able to answer that he was eating, drinking and sleeping well. However, the psychiatrist noticed that Ralph needed significant prompting to answer these questions. There was no evidence that Ralph was depressed or experiencing any psychotic symptoms, or having any seizures. In view of Ralph's history of hearing difficulties and his recent episodes of daytime urinary incontinence, the psychiatrist arranged for Ralph to have an up-to-date hearing test and a urine test. It was found that Ralph's hearing had deteriorated over the last year, and that he also had a urine infection. He was fitted with a new pair of hearing aids and treated with antibiotics for the urine infection.

After treatment, staff noticed that Ralph appeared more alert and needed less prompting. The episodes of urinary incontinence also stopped. Repeat psychology dementia testing showed an improvement in his scores, back to those of a year ago.

Ralph's initial deterioration was due to a combination of a deterioration in his long-standing hearing difficulties, and episodes of delirium secondary to recurrent urinary tract infections. He did not have the early signs of dementia.

This case highlights the following learning points:

- Although people with Down's syndrome are at greater risk of developing Alzheimer's dementia, it is important to exclude other causes of 'pseudo-dementia' first.
- Episodes of delirium due to undiagnosed recurrent physical health problems (e.g. urinary tract infections, constipation) can 'mimic' the deterioration seen in dementia.
- While the scoring from standardised dementia screening assessments can help identify deterioration, it is essential to treat the patient and not the scores!

Screening assessments for dementia in people with ID

There are a number of validated dementia screening tools for people with ID. Where necessary, these screening tests can also be done at serial intervals (e.g. yearly) to help monitor change in functioning.

Some involve a detailed interview with an informant who has known the person with ID for some time. Examples include:

- The Dementia Screening Questionnaire for Individuals with Intellectual Disabilities (DSQIID) (Deb *et al*, 2007).

- Dementia Scale for Down Syndrome (DSDS).

- Dementia Questionnaire for People with ID (DLD).

There are also some structured assessments of daily living skills that can be completed to assess for change.

Other screening tools allow direct testing of the person with ID, usually by a specialist psychologist. Examples include the Neuropsychological Assessment of Dementia in Adults with ID (NAID) and a modified part of the Cambridge Examination for Mental Disorders of the Elderly (CAMDEX- DS).

While neuroimaging (CT or MRI brain scans) can be useful, it is seldom diagnostic in its own right for people with Down's syndrome. It is not therefore considered an essential investigation in the diagnosis of dementia (British Psychological Society & Royal College of Psychology, 2015). The reason for this is that some people with Down's syndrome have pre-existing, smaller (atrophy) temporal lobes. The presence of greater shrinking in the hippocampus (known as 'disproportionate hippocampal atrophy') can sometimes be a helpful indicator of dementia, but usually requires a MRI brain scan to be identified. However, neuroimaging can be helpful to explore for features of vascular dementia or to exclude space-occupying lesions (e.g. tumours).

CT brain scans are usually better tolerated than MRI brain scans due to their shorter scanning times. If a person with ID lacks capacity to consent to this, best interest principles need to be applied. If sedation is needed, it can sometimes be preferable to give sedation the night before the scan (to reduce the baseline anxiety), with a further dose being given on the morning of the scan.

Anti-dementia medications

Anti-dementia medications ('cognitive enhancing drugs') help to slow down the progressive deterioration that occurs in Alzheimer's dementia. There are two types of medications that can be used – 'acetylcholinesterase inhibitors' (AChEIs) and memantine. AChEIs are used in the treatment of mild to moderate Alzheimer's dementia. Memantine is used to treat severe Alzheimer's dementia. AChEIs are also used in the treatment of Lewy body dementia.

AChEIs act by reducing the breakdown of a brain chemical (neurotransmitter) called 'acetylcholine' (ACh). In Alzheimer's dementia there is a decrease in ACh levels. The use of AChEIs can help reduce further drops in ACh, thereby helping to alleviate some of the decline seen in this type of dementia. Donepezil, galantamine and rivastigmine are examples of medications belonging to this class of drug.

Donepezil is often considered for use with people with ID who develop Alzheimer's dementia as it is generally well tolerated, the dosing is easier (once daily), and it has the greatest evidence-base (as it has been around the longest). However, it is important to ensure that a baseline pulse/ECG check is done before starting any AChEI, as they can cause slowing of the heart rate (bradycardia). People with Down's syndrome sometimes have pre-existing bradycardia, so this class of medication should be avoided if the 'baseline' heart rate is <50 bpm. In such cases, memantine (which does not cause bradycardia) can be considered as an alternative treatment at an earlier stage of dementia. Other potential side-effects of AChEIs include diarrhoea, leg cramps and seizures.

Memantine acts by blocking the effects of a neurotransmitter called glutamate in the brain. Abnormally high levels of glutamate are known to occur in moderate to severe Alzheimer's dementia, causing destruction of brain cells. Memantine has a role in providing protection against this. It is available in drops for cases where there are difficulties swallowing (dysphagia), which tends to occur in the later/ severe stages of dementia.

As the dementia progresses to the severe stage, any AChEI medication should be gradually switched to memantine. In some circumstances, people with severe dementia can be treated with a combination of an AChEI and memantine. However, such combination treatment is not currently approved by UK NICE (National Institute for Health and Clinical Excellence) guidance.

In vascular dementia, the mainstay of treatment is good control of the underlying vascular risk factors (e.g. hypertension, raised cholesterol, diabetes mellitus, smoking). In some cases, aspirin can be used where there is evidence of ischaemic (blood vessel wall thickening) changes in the brain. However, this needs to be balanced against its potential risks such as bleeding.

Non-pharmacological treatments of dementia

There are a number of non-medication interventions that focus on either improving or reducing the deterioration in two of the major domains of dementia – cognition and BPSD (see Table 1 on p35).

Cognitive strategies

Reality orientation involves reminding the person with dementia about themselves and their environment, and may include the use of signposts, notices and other visual aids (Douglas *et al*, 2004). Cognitive stimulation involves discussions (either individually or within groups) around past and present topics, as well as engagement in activities such as cooking or gardening. Cognitive rehabilitation encourages the person with ID and their carers to create their own realistic goals in everyday settings. While all of these person-centred approaches are labour intensive, they can result in significant benefits in an individual's cognition and functioning, and reduce long-term carer burden.

BPSD strategies

Aromatherapy using lavender oils or melissa balm are well-tolerated in people with ID, and can help to reduce the need for anxiety-relieving medications. Hand massage can also help reduce overall anxiety symptoms, while gentle touch on the forearm with verbal encouragement can facilitate eating (Hulme *et al*, 2010). Music therapy can reduce agitation, aggression, wandering and restlessness, especially when individualised around a person's favourite old songs (that are part of their long-term memory). Maintaining regular exercise can also help mood, sleep and maintain functional skills (Hulme *et al*, 2010).

Other mental/physical illnesses in older people with ID

Anxiety and depression are common mental illnesses in older people with ID, and can co-exist with or without dementia. Co-morbid depression is particularly common in vascular dementia. Occasionally, psychosis may present for the first time in old age and may be misinterpreted as 'challenging behaviour'.

The physical health of people with ID as they age is connected with any concomitant syndrome they may have. For example, older adults with Fragile X syndrome have increased rates of epilepsy, mitral valve prolapse, visual impairments and musculoskeletal disorders. As well as premature ageing in Down's syndrome, there is an increased tendency to have hypothyroidism, sensory impairments, epilepsy, cardiac and musculoskeletal impairments and infections.

Pain is common in older people with ID, and can be due to age-related osteoarthritis or from other conditions such as constipation and dental problems. The DisDAT (Disability Distress Assessment Tool) can be used to assess pain.

Key learning points

■ The prevalence of dementia is greater in all adults with ID (not just those with Down's syndrome) compared to the general population.

■ After the 50-55 years of age, the rates of Alzheimer's dementia increase exponentially in people with Down's syndrome.

■ People with Down's syndrome are more likely to present with the behavioural and psychological symptoms of dementia rather than traditional memory ('cognitive') symptoms.

■ There are a range of medical, psychological and social conditions that can 'mimic' the symptoms of dementia. It is important to exclude these in people with ID.

■ Anti-dementia medications should be considered in adults with ID who develop Alzheimer's dementia or Lewy body dementia.

■ There are a range of non-pharmacological treatment strategies that can be used to tackle the cognitive and behavioural/psychological symptoms of dementia.

■ Older people with ID may develop some age-related conditions (e.g. arthritis) earlier than the general population.

References

British Psychological Society and Royal College of Psychiatrists (2015) *Dementia and People with Intellectual Disabilities: Guidance on the assessment, diagnosis, interventions and support of people with intellectual disabilities who develop dementia.* Leicester: The British Psychological Society.

Coppus A, Evenhuis H, Verberne G-J, Visser F, van Gool P, Eikelenboom P & van Duijin C (2006) Dementia and mortality in persons with Down's syndrome. *Journal of Intellectual Disability Research* **50** (10) 768–777.

Deb S, Hare M, Prior L & Bhaumik S (2007) dementia screening questionnaire for individuals with intellectual disabilities. *British Journal of Psychiatry* **190** 440–444.

Douglas S, James I & Ballard C (2004) Non-pharmacological interventions in dementia. *Advances in Psychiatric Treatment* **10** 171-179.

Hulme C, Wright J, Crocker T, Oluboyede Y & House A (2010) Non-pharmacological approaches for dementia that informal carers might try or access: a systematic review. *International Journal of Geriatric Psychiatry*. **25** 756-763

Prasher V & Krishnan V (1993) Age of onset and duration of dementia in people with down syndrome: integration of 98 reported cases in the literature. *International Journal of Geriatric Psychiatry* **8** (11) 915–922.

Raji O & Naeem A (2011) Old Age and Learning Disability. In: M Abou-Saleh, C Katona & A Kumar (Eds) *Principles and Practice of Geriatric Psychiatry* (3rd Edition). London: Wiley-Blackwell Publishing.

Strydom A, Livingston G, King M & Hassiotis A (2007) Prevalence of dementia in intellectual disability using different diagnostic criteria. *British Journal of Psychiatry* **191** 150–157.

Chapter 5: Psychosis spectrum disorders

By Colin Hemmings

Summary

Schizophrenia and other psychotic illnesses are more common in people with ID than in the general population. They are, however, more difficult to detect and the symptoms are often more subtle or less typical than those in the general population. Due to the difficulty of assessment, psychosis can either be more easily missed or wrongly diagnosed in people with ID. Schizophrenia in people with ID may cause more severe problems for the person and be harder to treat than when it occurs in the general population. The treatment of schizophrenia and associated disorders in people with ID broadly follows that in people who do not have ID.

Introduction

This chapter will look at the symptoms, prevalence, presentation, assessment and treatment of psychotic illnesses in people with intellectual disabilities (ID). Two case studies will provide examples of psychotic illnesses in people with ID.

What is psychosis?

The term 'psychosis' describes a situation in which a person has lost touch with reality or lost insight. Psychosis can also be described as the experience of various symptoms, such as showing disorganised or bizarre speech and behaviours. Psychotic illnesses, including the schizophrenias, are among the most severe mental illnesses. The best known and most described psychotic symptoms are delusions and hallucinations. Delusions are false beliefs that are firmly held despite obvious proof or evidence to the contrary. The beliefs are not those ordinarily accepted by other members of the person's culture or subculture. Hallucinations occur when people see, hear, feel, taste or smell things which are not present in reality, and yet the person has a compelling sense that these experiences are happening.

People with ID are also thought to be more susceptible to developing short-lived episodes of psychosis, which can be brought on by stressful life events because they often have more limited coping abilities. They also have higher rates of sensory problems such as hearing and visual impairments. Sensory impairments may make people more susceptible to misinterpreting things they see and hear. Psychotic symptoms can occur in a wide range of mental and physical disorders and people with ID can experience all of these.

Some conditions in which psychotic symptoms can occur include:

■ Dementia.

■ Delirium e.g. due to an infection or alcohol withdrawal.

■ Drug and alcohol misuse.

■ Epilepsy.

■ General medical conditions e.g. thyroid hormone excess.

■ Schizophrenia, schizoaffective and persistent delusional disorders.

■ Mania.

■ Severe depression.

■ Acute Stress Reactions.

The best known and most studied psychotic disorders in people with ID, as well as in the wider population, are the schizophrenias and associated disorders. This chapter will focus on these.

How common is psychosis in people with ID?

People with ID have higher rates of psychotic illnesses compared to the general population for a variety of reasons. These are thought to include increased genetic predisposition and increased psycho-social stressors. It is widely accepted that about 3% of people with ID will have schizophrenia-type psychotic symptoms at any one time (Deb *et al*, 2001). This is around three times higher than the prevalence rate in the general population. However, even this may be an underestimate because psychotic illnesses, and schizophrenia in particular, are generally more difficult to detect and diagnose in people with ID.

How does psychosis affect a person with ID?

Psychotic illnesses may be short-lived or long-standing, and symptoms may fluctuate even without treatment. The onset of a psychotic episode may be less noticeable in people with ID because they are less likely to have very obvious or clear-cut symptoms. The symptoms of schizophrenia in people with ID can be a decline in functioning, a deterioration of skills or social withdrawal, rather than obvious hallucinations and delusions (James & Mukherjee, 1996). The reduction in functioning may be temporary, but a long-standing psychosis may lead to a prolonged or even permanent reduction in a person's functioning. Due to their reduced opportunity to take part in normal life experiences, the delusions of people with ID, when they occur, may not be complicated. Complex hallucinations, such as hearing voices that give a running commentary of a person's actions, are also less commonly reported.

The DC-LD guide (*Diagnostic Criteria for Psychiatric Disorders for Use with Adults with Intellectual disabilities/Mental Retardation*) (Royal College of Psychiatrists, 2001) noted that early signs of a psychotic illness could be new behaviours (especially those that are odd, bizarre or uncharacteristic), or an increase in frequency or severity of pre-existing challenging behaviours. Certainly some challenging behaviours can sometimes be improved with antipsychotic medication, so it is possible that, in a minority of cases, mental health problems like psychosis might be driving the behaviour. It has also long been recognised that catatonia is more common in schizophrenia when a person has ID. Catatonia can include disturbances of movement – for example a person may adopt a motionless posture for long periods. Alternatively, in a catatonic state the person may become constantly overactive and be in a state of continual excitement.

Difficulties in assessment

There are many possible problems in the assessment and diagnosis of schizophrenia and its associated psychoses in people with ID. Psychosis can be missed but also it can be wrongly diagnosed. First, the symptoms of schizophrenia depend on the person being able to articulate their experiences, thoughts and beliefs. It is impossible to diagnose schizophrenia with any certainty in people with limited verbal communication. In practice, this means people with ID with an IQ level of about 45 or less.

Second, the difficulty in differentiating psychotic symptoms and features related to a person's ID may lead to the problem of psychosis being under-diagnosed. Sometimes it may be suggested that the person's ID accounts for their odd or unusual behaviours, rather than whether or not they may in fact be psychotic symptoms. This error has been termed 'diagnostic overshadowing' (Reiss *et al*, 1982). John's case study below illustrates a case of psychosis in which treatment was delayed because of diagnostic overshadowing.

Case study: John

John is a young man in his 30s who lives with his parents. The family had to move to a very remote house because neighbours had complained about John's loud night-time screaming. John did not talk much, did very few spontaneous activities and showed a general lack of interest. He even needed to be prompted to dress himself and to walk with his parents. John appeared to have severe ID. However, evidence from when he was a teenager suggested that in the past he could do more for himself and had shown much more interest in activities and talking up until his late teenage years.

When being assessed John seemed to be distracted by possible noises or visions, as he turned around and mumbled occasionally. It seemed as if he might have developed a psychotic illness and needed to go to hospital to start treatment. However, the social worker who was asked to see him to support an admission under the Mental Health Act had no experience of working with people with ID. She argued that his problems were only due to his ID and would not agree to the psychiatric in-patient admission.

Some months later John was seen by a different social worker who had experience in ID and he was admitted to hospital and given antipsychotic medication. John's interest in his environment increased and he stopped screaming at night. His overall functioning improved so that he appeared now to have mild ID.

A tentative diagnosis of schizophrenia in ID may be made on the basis of observations rather than a person's account. For example, behaviour that suggests auditory hallucinations could be a person with ID shouting at people who are not present when this has not been their previous behaviour. Similarly, suspiciousness and social withdrawal that were not previously part of the person's personality and behaviour could also suggest schizophrenia. Non-verbal evidence for possible psychosis is of greater importance in the assessment of people with ID who have limited verbal abilities.

It can also be the case that behaviours that may be appropriate for someone with ID at a certain developmental stage may be wrongly thought of as psychotic behaviours. It can also be difficult to separate hallucinations from self-talk or conversations with imaginary friends. These can all be appropriate for a person's developmental stage if they have ID (Hurley, 1996). People with ID may often recall previous conversations and rehearse them or think out loud. They often do not recognise that this is considered socially odd. Incoherent speech may also be hard to judge in people with ID as it can be difficult to follow the thread of their conversation.

It is often difficult to determine whether a person with ID has true delusional beliefs. For example, they may have fantasies that they are famous, such as being a great singer, which may lead to the wrong conclusion that they have grandiose delusions. In schizophrenia, people often have delusions that they are being controlled (delusions of passivity). However, people with ID may have a real lack of autonomy, or at least a perceived lack of control over their lives, and may complain. This can sometimes be misunderstood as a delusion. People with ID are also often sensitive to how they are perceived by others, which can often be based on real life experiences of being mocked and rejected (Hurley, 1996). They may then be mistakenly thought to show persecutory delusions.

Some symptoms of long-standing schizophrenia have been described as 'negative' symptoms and include social withdrawal, reduced speech and reduced motivation. These apparent 'negative' symptoms can also be misattributed to a psychotic disorder when they may be due to other factors, such as institutionalisation, over-sedation, lack of environmental stimulation, and severe problems with processing information (James & Mukhergee, 1996).

A guide to whether an odd or unusual belief may be delusional is whether the experiences or beliefs are distressing. A person does not generally tend to fantasise or imagine hearing or seeing things which are frightening or upsetting, or believe things that cause them distress. However, this can only be a rough guide, because sometimes genuinely psychotic symptoms are not upsetting for the person. It has also been suggested that people with ID are more likely to be able to be temporarily persuaded that delusional beliefs are false because of their increased suggestibility. It may be more important to observe them for their readiness to return to these beliefs when not being persuaded against them (Hurley, 1996).

Box 1: Questions to consider during assessment of possible psychosis

- Is this experience or behaviour new or very different for the person?
- Is this experience or behaviour odd or unusual for the person?
- Does this experience or behaviour seem to trouble the person?
- What is the usual mood or temperament of the person with ID?
- Have there been any other changes in their usual routines?
- Is this person in good physical health?
- Have they been checked recently by a doctor?
- Are there any dangers in these experiences or behaviours, for themselves or for others?

When trying to assess whether a person is psychotic there are some guiding principles to consider. Psychotic symptoms tend to come in clusters and therefore one odd or unusual experience on its own may be of less significance for a diagnosis of psychosis than if the person has multiple symptoms. People with ID who have a family history of psychosis are also more likely to develop psychosis than those with no family history. Finally, the basis of health care is accurate diagnosis followed by appropriate treatment. There are circumstances when, even though the diagnosis of psychosis is not clear-cut, it may still be ethical and in the best interests of the person to have a trial of an antipsychotic medication. The response, or lack of response, to the medication can then be used to help determine (but not prove) whether the tentative diagnosis of psychosis was correct. Quite often clinicians are using information from various sources to try and build up an overall guide to the diagnosis and it may not be impossible to give an absolutely conclusive opinion either way.

Autism and psychosis

It can be difficult to differentiate schizophrenia from autism in people with ID. Psychotic episodes can occur in autism but it is not yet clear whether the risk of developing schizophrenia in people with autism is any more frequent than that of developing schizophrenia in the general population. Social withdrawal and lack of empathy can often occur in schizophrenia as well as autism. Unusual preoccupations held rigidly by people with autism may be particularly difficult to differentiate from delusions. Flattened and odd moods, poor non-verbal communication and low amounts of speech are commonly seen in autism as well as schizophrenia. People with autism can be concrete and often preoccupied with their special interests and their view of themselves, and the world can appear so odd to others as to appear delusional. A very detailed history about someone's early life and development is necessary to help establish the right diagnosis.

Epilepsy and psychosis

Epilepsy can also lead to problems with diagnosis, for example differentiating temporal lobe epilepsy from schizophrenia, as psychotic symptoms such as hallucinations can occur in some types of epileptic seizures. Epilepsy can also cause difficulties in treatment, since antipsychotic medications can make seizures more likely. The phenomenon of 'forced normalisation' in epilepsy can occur whereby a reduction in seizures following the introduction of antiepileptic medication can be associated with an exacerbation of psychosis.

Treatment

The principles of treatment of psychotic disorders in people with ID are essentially similar to those in the general population. Treatment with antipsychotic medications in ID appears broadly similar in efficacy, with no significant increase in side effects. Some antipsychotic medications can make thinking, memory and word-finding more difficult, and also make someone more at risk of having an epileptic seizure. There is a consensus that antipsychotic medication prescribing often needs to be instigated and increased more cautiously than in people without ID. People with ID are more likely to have general physical health problems and they tend to be more sensitive to medication. Distinguishing between movement disorders and medication side-effects is more difficult in people with ID as movement disorders are more common, even without antipsychotic medication.

Many doctors have reported that effective dosage levels of antipsychotic medications can sometimes be lower in people with ID (see case study below).

Case study: Inzamam

Inzamam is a young man in his 20s who lives in his own flat near to his mother and younger siblings. His father had left the family, which had been very traumatic for the whole family. Inzamam is suspicious of others and almost mute. He is withdrawn and unkempt. He lives in squalor with takeaway leftovers all over his flat and flies swarming around. Neighbours often complain about the flies and the smell. Inzamam refuses to see his mother but she leaves food for him on his doorstep. Some people believe Inzamam is withdrawn as he has been so hurt by his life experiences. While this seemed true, from reports of his earlier years Inzamam seems to have undergone a massive change in his demeanour.

Inzamam is admitted into a specialist unit for people with ID and mental health problems. He is given a test dose (very low) of an antipsychotic medication injection and within days there is a dramatic improvement as he starts to speak more, become less suspicious and much more cheerful. Inzamam had a psychotic illness which has gone undiagnosed and untreated for many years.

Although psychosocial strategies may be used in practice for psychosis in people with ID, there is as yet very little published evidence regarding the use of psychosocial (including family) interventions for people with ID. A case series of cognitive behavioural therapy for five patients with psychosis and mild ID has been reported (Haddock *et al*, 2004). Hopefully the use of specific psychosocial interventions for psychosis in ID will become more established.

The course of schizophrenia

Schizophrenia can occur at any age but it is most likely to begin in early adulthood. When it begins in childhood or adolescence it may itself be a cause of ID by severely disrupting learning and normal development. Most clinicians believe that the course of schizophrenia in people with ID will tend to be more severe than in the general population. Doody *et al* (1998) found that people with ID and additional schizophrenia had fewer admissions to psychiatric hospitals than people with schizophrenia alone. However, when they were admitted they needed to be in hospital for longer periods of time, and when discharged they needed more support in the community than people with schizophrenia alone.

Conclusion

- Schizophrenia and associated psychoses are more common in people with ID than in the general population.

- They are more difficult to detect and often the symptoms are subtler or less typical than those in the general population.

- Due to the difficulty of assessment, psychosis can either be more easily missed or wrongly diagnosed in people with ID.

- Schizophrenia in people with ID may cause more severe problems for the person and be harder to treat than when it occurs in the general population.

- The treatment of schizophrenia and associated disorders in people with ID broadly follows that in people who do not have ID.

References

Deb S, Thomas M & Bright C (2001) Mental disorder in adults with intellectual disability: prevalence of functional psychiatric illness among a community-based population aged between 16 and 64 years. *Journal of Intellectual Disability Research* **45** 495–505.

Doody GA, Johnstone EC, Sanderson TL, Cunningham Owens DG & Muir WJ (1998) 'Pfropfschizophrenie' revisited. Schizophrenia in people with mild intellectual disability. *British Journal of Psychiatry* **173** 145–153.

Haddock G, Lobban F, Hatton C & Carson R. (2004) Cognitive behaviour therapy for people with psychosis and mild intellectual disability: a case series. *Clinical Psychology and Psychotherapy* **11** 282–298.

Hurley AD (1996) The misdiagnosis of hallucinations and delusions in persons with mental retardation: a neurodevelopmental perspective. *Seminars in Clinical Neuropsychiatry* **1** 122–133.

James DH & Mukhergee T (1996) Schizophrenia and Intellectual disability. *British Journal of Intellectual disabilities* **24** 90–94.

Reiss S, Levitan GW & Zyszko J (1982) Emotional disturbance and mental retardation: diagnostic overshadowing. *American Journal of Mental Deficiency* **86** 567–574.

Royal College of Psychiatrists (2001) DC-LD *(Diagnostic Criteria for psychiatric disorders for use with intellectual disabilities / mental retardation)*. London: Gaskell Press.

Chapter 6: Mood disorders

By Rupal Patel, Sarah Maber & Abdul Sabir

Introduction

People with intellectual disabilities (ID) are affected by the same mental health problems as the general population. In this chapter, we will discuss common mood disorders and how they might present in people with ID.

What is depression?

Depression is a common mental health disorder that will affect one in five of the general population at some time in their lives (RCPsych, 2017a). It is a disorder of mood that is persistent, characterised by a continuous low mood (for over two weeks) and that is pervasive to such a degree that it significantly affects or disrupts a person's day-to-day life and their ability to function as normal.

Depression is more common in those that have had significant negative life events or stressors. We know that people with ID will unfortunately face many difficult events throughout their life due to, or because of, their disability. These may include problems with the education system, the social care system, family dynamics, bereavements, disability discrimination, a lack of access to services and communication difficulties.

It is important to recognise the symptoms of depression promptly and, by accessing services and getting treatment early, significantly shorten the duration of the illness and reduce distress for the person and the network around them, such as their family, friends and carers.

What are the common symptoms of depression?

There are typically three core or main symptoms of depression: low mood, low energy or fatigue, and anhedonia (lack of pleasure/enjoyment). Other common symptoms that are often seen include problems with sleep (especially early morning wakening), lack of appetite and weight loss, loss of interest in sex (low libido), slow movements (psychomotor retardation) and agitation. These collective symptoms are frequently referred to as 'biological' or 'somatic' symptoms because they refer to the body or bodily functions. People with ID who have more verbal skills may also be able to describe some psychological symptoms: feelings of hopelessness, helplessness, poor concentration, feelings of guilt, worthlessness and low self-confidence and self-esteem.

People with severe depression may occasionally experience psychotic symptoms such as delusions (a fixed, unshakeable and abnormal belief), for example of presumed guilt; that they are deserving of punishment; nihilism (they are dying, for example, or their body is decaying); or hallucinations such as hearing voices accusing them, bad smells or scenes of death. Feelings or thoughts of wanting to end their life or thoughts of self-harm may also be experienced in severe depression.

The severity of depression is usually rated as mild, moderate or severe, which is used to guide clinicians in decisions about the best treatment options. For example, mild depression usually responds better to talking therapies and lifestyle modifications rather than medication (Barbui *et al*, 2011), whereas in moderate to severe depression, antidepressants may have a more effective role alongside talking therapies (NICE, 2009). Severe cases of depression may require additional medications such as antipsychotics, or other treatments such as electro-convulsive therapy, although this is usually only given in emergency cases where a person has stopped eating and drinking.

Distinguishing depression from unhappiness and dysthymia

Unhappiness or sadness is a normal emotional response to negative life events. Where it differs from a clinical diagnosis of depression is that the duration is shorter-lived and less consistent, the symptoms may be less intense and the impact on daily activity and functioning are minimal or less marked. The symptoms also generally resolve/improve without any specific treatment or intervention after a short period of time.

Dysthymia is very similar to depression in its presentation but it tends to manifest as an on-going low mood in a chronic pattern over many years with low-intensity symptoms and minimal impact on daily life.

How does depression present in people with ID?

Depression in people with ID may present in the same way as in the general population, especially for those people with ID who have good verbal communication and where the severity of their ID is milder (Pawlarcyzk & Beckwith, 1987). However, as the severity of the ID becomes more severe, the symptoms displayed will not always be typical. It is important to note that clinical expertise plays an indispensable role in understanding the person's presentation and there should not be a heavy reliance on strict diagnostic criteria, especially as the degree of ID becomes more severe.

Case study: Katie

Katie is a 27-year-old woman with mild ID and autism. Her mother took her to see the GP as she was concerned about Katie's behaviour. Katie seemed tired, was going to bed very early and not wanting to go to her day centre, which she is normally very excited to do. At the day centre, staff mentioned that she seemed lethargic, not wanting to engage in activities she normally enjoyed, and she was becoming short-tempered and had thrown her belongings on the floor a few times. She had also stopped snacking and was not eating much of her regular meals.

Katie had difficulty describing her feelings and could not tell the GP whether she feels happy or sad. Katie's GP checked her blood tests to exclude any physical cause for her presentation (such as low iron, diabetes or an under-active thyroid), all of which were normal, and so referred her to the community ID team. Katie was diagnosed with a depressive episode and started on a small dose of an antidepressant (citalopram, 10mg, once daily). She was followed-up four weeks' later and her symptoms had much improved.

Learning points

- People with ID can present with the typical features of depression, similar to the general population.

- It is important to obtain a detailed history of the person's existing baseline as people with ID have varying functional abilities. This could be obtained from carers, support staff, family or friends.

- Often lower doses of medication are used in people with ID when treating mood disorders. This fits in with a 'start low, go slow' approach.

Factors to take into consideration during assessment

There can be several factors to take into account when assessing and diagnosing mood disorders in people with ID:

■ A diagnosis of depression in people with ID can be completely overlooked or not recognised (also known as diagnostic overshadowing – where the symptoms of depression are erroneously attributed to the ID rather than other causes, such as depression in this case).

■ People with ID that have difficulty with verbal communication, especially those with moderate to severe ID, may have problems expressing their symptoms.

■ People with ID who are also on the autistic spectrum may have difficulty recognising and describing their emotional states or moods.

■ Depression as a diagnosis should not be disregarded in people with ID if they present in a way that is atypical e.g. increased sleeping or eating more.

■ Symptoms of depression could be wrongly attributed to other causes or conditions e.g. physical or other mental health problems, or changes in environmental or social circumstances.

Case study: Jane

Jane is a 57-year-old woman with mild ID living in a residential home. She was referred to the community ID team for dementia screening as she started wandering, feeling confused with poor concentration and motivation. Her behaviour changed significantly: she was unwilling to see her twin sister and brother, with whom she used to meet regularly, and she started screaming and spitting at staff and hitting her stomach. Jane's self-care also declined – she was reluctant to take showers and left her room untidy.

The DLD (Dementia Questionnaire for people with Learning Disability) was performed and she did not fulfil the criteria for dementia. During the process of a thorough assessment, it was established that Jane's symptoms were noted shortly after witnessing an unsuccessful resuscitation incident of her close friend in her residential place. Her symptoms successfully responded to an antidepressant. She reached her baseline functioning, resumed her interest in daily activities, and her concentration and cognition normalised. She stopped wandering, her sleep improved, and she also managed to re-establish a good relationship with her family, staff and residents.

Learning points

■ In older people with ID who exhibit memory problems, it is important to consider alternative diagnoses to dementia. Exclusion of physical health problems should be prioritised, as well as excluding depression.

■ People with Down's syndrome are at greater risk of developing Alzheimer's dementia, and they often present at an earlier age compared to the general population.

- In Jane's case, depression was masquerading as dementia, known as 'pseudo dementia'.

- Depression can occur concurrently with dementia. If concerns remain over memory or a decline in functional skills despite depressive symptoms improving, further monitoring and investigations for dementia should continue.

- Depression in people with ID can commonly present in an atypical fashion – either through behaviour disturbance, self-harming behaviour and disruption in daily functioning.

Case study: Paula

Paula is a 26-year-old woman with moderate ID living in a residential home who was referred to community mental health services for treatment of depression as her symptoms had not responded well to different antidepressant medications prescribed in primary care. Paula presented in the clinic as ungroomed with poor eye contact. Her speech was logical but quiet and non-elaborative (with 'yes', 'no' and 'don't know' responses to most of the questions). She admitted to feeling low, tired and unmotivated. She was spending most of her days in bed and was not keen to participate in most activities. Staff at her home noticed she had put on weight and her levels of concentration were poor. Blood tests revealed she had an underactive thyroid. Shortly after initiating thyroxine treatment her symptoms of depression started to improve.

Case study: Benjamin

Benjamin is a 26-year-old man in a residential living placement with moderate ID, epilepsy and challenging behaviour under the care of the community ID team. His main carer reported that in the last two months Benjamin had been more volatile and aggressive in his behaviour and his seizure episodes had become more frequent. His carer stated that Benjamin had become less interested in his hobbies or socialising, and he had been sleeping and eating significantly more than before. On a few occasions when he was prompted to attend his college he was witnessed hitting himself and damaging property in an aggressive and angry manner. The carer was of the opinion that a change in his individual 1:1 carer package from 30 hours weekly to five hours, which had happened in the last three months, could have played a major role in his recent presentation. A review of his carer package took place and his supporting hours were increased. He also attended adapted CBT (cognitive behavioural therapy) sessions combined with a small dose of an antidepressant. His mental state, behaviour, functioning and even his seizure episodes became less frequent. His epilepsy medication was also reviewed and monitored by the neurologist but no changes were made.

Case study: Robert

Robert is a 20-year-old male with severe ID and autism who had been living in a residential home for the last two years. Robert's key worker along with other staff were concerned that his mental state had deteriorated and his behaviour had changed in the past two months. He had become more isolated and withdrawn, and had been tearful on a few occasions. He was reluctant to come into the lounge for his meals, declining to participate in his previously favourite activities (colouring and gardening). On two occasions he screamed at the staff when they wanted to assist him with his shower and personal hygiene. He had also been refusing to visit his mother at the weekends for the last two months, when in the past he had always been extremely keen and it was a normal part of his routine.

Robert's key worker raised a safeguarding alert when his mother's new partner visited Robert in his home and the staff witnessed he was intoxicated and bullying Robert, trying to get him to give him money. Further collateral information was obtained from Robert's mother's neighbour who had witnessed Robert being verbally abused by his mother's partner on a regular basis. As part of the safeguarding process, Robert's mother agreed not to allow her partner in the house when Robert visited, following which Robert resumed his home visits again. Robert attended some art therapy sessions, which helped him to express and process his emotions about these experiences in a safe way. He started to settle in his mental state and his behaviour improved significantly.

Learning points

■ People with ID may have risk factors that increase the likelihood of abuse due to problems with communication and social skills, physical dependence on others, a lack of awareness of appropriate sexual behaviour and how to protect themselves against abuse (Bruder & Kroese, 2005).

■ An abuse victim may often exhibit changes in their mental state and or baseline behaviour. They may become withdrawn, less engaged, less motivated, irritable, confrontational etc., which may be interpreted as depression.

■ It is vital that carers, family, friends and professionals consider abuse as a possible reason for any observed behavioural changes and that professionals and carers involved work closely and communicate effectively, allowing early detection and safeguarding processes to be implemented to reduce future risk.

Case study: Richard

Richard is a 43-years-old man with moderate ID and autism who lives in a residential home. He has a history of a recurrent depressive disorder and was referred to the community ID team for his challenging behaviour. His carers reported that he had begun actively avoiding meeting new people or going to new places. If there was a sudden or unexpected change in Richard's plans or activities, he responded by screaming, biting his hand and banging his head against a wall. Staff also noted that his behaviour was agitated, irritable and confrontational. Staff reported that Richard was spending more time in his bedroom, appeared reluctant to engage in usual activities and would need repeated prompting with regards to his self-care. They had also noticed changes in his sleeping pattern – he would only sleep for a few hours – and that he had also lost weight due to decreased interest in eating.

During assessment, Richard looked tired with a perplexed affect and appeared to have poor concentration. At times he was fidgeting, sweating and picking at his skin. He was noted to have a hand tremor which worsened when questions were directed towards him.

Learning points

- Anxiety symptoms commonly feature in depressive episodes and in people with autism.

- Co-morbid neurodevelopmental conditions, such as autism and attention deficit hyperactivity disorder (ADHD), are much more common in people with ID than the general population.

- People with ID and autism can present with flattened, restrictive or odd affects in addition to difficulties with eye contact and limited emotional expression or reciprocity, which could be misinterpreted as low mood or a depressive episode. For people with ID and autism, their restrictive pattern of interests may superficially appear as a lack of engagement or interest in general activities, which could be erroneously perceived as anhedonia (a common core symptom of depression). It is therefore essential to establish a functional baseline in this particular group when assessing if a mood disorder is present or not.

Case study: James

James is a 50-year-old man with moderate ID. He moved to a residential home eight months ago following the death of his mother from bowel cancer, whom he used to live with. He has not been engaging with staff, appears withdrawn and has been missing his meals. His carers report that James is frequently asking to see the GP, calling the emergency services and has now started to turn up at the local A&E department complaining of stomach pain and difficulties going to toilet. It was noted by medical staff and home staff that James seemed preoccupied about not being able to open his bowels. Repeated physical investigations were all unremarkable (blood tests, X-rays and colonoscopy). He was prescribed oral laxatives to help with mild constipation. However, despite James complying with the treatment he continued to present to medical professionals with the same symptoms. His GP then referred and sought an opinion from the community ID team. Following review by the team he was diagnosed with a moderate depressive episode and commenced on antidepressants and started talking therapy. Improved fluid and food intake and uptake of more activities led to a concurrent improvement in his symptoms of constipation.

Learning points

- Constipation can commonly occur in people with depression due to poor food/fluid intake and low levels of activity with consequential reduction in gut motility.

- Sometimes people with depression can have difficulties acknowledging emotional distress and instead their symptoms can manifest through physical symptoms, such as headaches, abdominal discomfort and general body aches.

- People can occasionally become preoccupied with physical symptoms, which lack an organic cause, and repeatedly seek help and are not reassured by negative investigations. This is described as *somatoform disorder*. It is important therefore to consider depression as a potential reason in this presentation.

Bipolar affective disorder

Bipolar affective disorder is a relatively common mood disorder; approximately one in every 100 adults will experience bipolar disorder at some point in their life (RCPsych, 2017b). Rates are even higher in people with people with ID (NICE, 2016). Symptoms tend to first be noticed during adolescence or young adulthood.

What is bipolar affective disorder?

Bipolar affective disorder used to be known as 'manic depression'. This is because the disorder is typified by alternating episodes of mania and depression over the course of the illness with each discrete mood episode lasting several weeks or more. Mania and depression represent the two extremes of the mood spectrum, being polar opposites – hence the current terminology of 'bipolar'. For a diagnosis of bipolar affective disorder, a person must have had one episode of depression and one episode of either hypomania or mania.

Mania

Mania represents a state of extreme elation and happiness that significantly disrupts and impairs a person's ability to function on a day-to-day basis. Typical symptoms include feeling extremely happy, excited and full of energy, overly active, having an exaggerated sense of importance and self-confidence, irritability, decreased need for sleep and food, interest in new ideas and projects that are likely to be unrealistic, and moving quickly from one thing to another. This may also be evident in the person's speech; they may change topic frequently, speak very fast and be difficult to interrupt. Other behaviours include impulsivity, including recklessly spending money and being disinhibited and over familiar. In some cases, people can experience psychotic symptoms, including holding odd beliefs and hearing voices (auditory hallucinations).

In hypomania, the symptoms described above present in a milder form and have a less disabling impact on the person's ability to function normally.

How is bipolar affective disorder different from 'mood swings' and cyclothymia?

Mood swings can be normal responses to significant environmental changes and life events. People may experience episodes of sadness or elation, neither of which are severe or prolonged enough to justify a diagnosis of mild depression or hypomania respectively.

Cyclothymia has a similar presentation and pattern to bipolar affective disorder with fluctuations in mood. However, the symptoms are less severe and do not persist for a prolonged period of time.

How does bipolar affective disorder present in people with ID?

Bipolar affective disorder in people with ID may present in a similar fashion as in the general population, especially for those on the milder end of the ID spectrum and those with good verbal skills. The signs and symptoms of bipolar affective disorder can become more difficult to recognise in people with moderate to severe ID and communication difficulties. As with the presentation of depression in people with ID, there should not be a prescriptive adherence to the diagnostic criteria (ICD-10 and DSM-V), but a thorough clinical assessment of the person's functioning including changes from their usual baseline and incorporating collateral history.

Case study: Shazia

Shazia is a 20-year-old woman with mild ID who lives with her family. She is known to the local community ID team where she has previously received treatment with fluoxetine (a selective serotonin re-uptake inhibitor (SSRI) antidepressant) for a depressive episode. Shazia responded well to this and is now off treatment. Shazia volunteers two days a week at a local charity shop and is at college three days a week.

However, her family contacted the community team with concerns over Shazia's behaviour. At assessment, the psychiatrist found that Shazia was excessively talkative; it was difficult to get answers from her as she frequently changed the topic of conversation. She appeared restless, irritable and constantly on the go. Shazia has been telling her friends and family that she is now a 'heptathlete' and will be training for the Olympics with Jessica Ennis Hill, an Olympic champion. Shazia has been sleeping less and telling her family she needs to train. When her family questioned Shazia's perception of being an Olympic athlete she became angry and didn't believe her family's view. Her family have also reported they are concerned over her safety as she has been hugging strangers and buying lots of new clothes in the incorrect sizes. Staff at the college were also concerned about Shazia's behaviour and have spoken with the family – as she has been disruptive, rude and chaotic in class, which is unusual for her. For the last two weeks Shazia has no-longer been interested in her volunteering work stating she needs to prioritise her Olympic training.

Learning points

- It is important here to obtain collateral information about a person's current presentation to understand how this is deviating from their normal baseline functioning.

- In light of a previous depressive episode, when a person presents with a current manic state they would fulfil the diagnostic criteria of bipolar affective disorder[1].

- A full risk assessment should be part of the clinical review; assessing risk to self, to others and from others. In the case study in particular there are concerns that Shazia appears vulnerable to risk from others due to overfamiliarity and disinhibited behaviour.

---

1   To help distinguish a manic episode rather than a hypomanic episode, there should be a clear functional impairment to indicate the former. For example, in Shazia's case study above, the symptoms affect most areas of her life: social, education, employment and personal/home. Similarly, the presence of firm, unshakeable beliefs (delusions) – in this case, a belief of being an Olympic athlete – also distinguishes this as a manic episode. If it was the case that normal daily activities were not affected and there was less functional impairment, as well as no psychotic symptoms, then this presentation may have been qualified as a hypomanic episode, and in combination with a previous history of depression would fulfil diagnostic criteria for bipolar affective disorder.

- Again, in Shazia's case, she has good verbal skills and the assessment of psychopathology can be discerned akin to the general population. A greater emphasis will need to be placed on behavioural changes in someone with a more severe ID or those with limited verbal communication e.g. irritability, confusing signing (if using Makaton) and aggressive or confrontational manners.

- Caution and careful monitoring should be applied when treating people with depression with antidepressants as there is a small risk that this can precipitate a manic episode in a medication-induced reaction.

Management of mood disorders

Pharmacological

There are a number of medications that can be used to treat mood disorders. These include antidepressants, mood stabilisers, anxiolytics and antipsychotics. These are usually prescribed by the GP or a psychiatrist. People with ID are more prone to side effects, and medication should therefore be initiated at low doses and carefully monitored. In severe forms of depression, electroconvulsive therapy may also be an option.

Psychological

Talking therapies (also known as psychological treatment) are proven to be effective in the management of mood disorders. One of the most common talking therapies is cognitive behavioural therapy (CBT), which helps to challenge and change negative thinking (or cognitive errors), and strengthens alternative, more positive thoughts. There are several other psychological therapies including interpersonal therapy (IPT) and psychodynamic psychotherapy. In its simplest form, one of the first psychological therapies offered could be counselling and is delivered in primary care.

People with ID can benefit from different modalities of psychotherapy, which may need to be adapted according to their needs and cognitive abilities, for example inclusion of pictures and Easy Read information.
Alternative therapies may have a useful role in complementing the traditional management of mood disorders with medication and psychotherapy. This includes art, music, drama, dance, animal-assisted therapy etc. These may be particularly useful for people with moderate to severe ID with limited verbal communication skills who may be unable to engage in more traditional talking therapies as they allow them to express themselves.

Lifestyle modifications

Simple lifestyle changes can help to reduce stress levels and, consequently, chances of relapse. The following may be helpful:

- Adopting a good sleep pattern.
- Eating a healthy diet and drinking well.
- Keeping active and engaging in regular exercise.
- Avoiding or reducing alcohol consumption.
- Not taking illicit substances.
- Making time to relax e.g. hobbies and having a good work-life balance.
- Maintaining supportive relationships.
- Keeping a mood diary.

Key learning points

- People with ID are more prone to develop mood disorders than the general population.
- Their mood disorder symptoms often have an unusual (less typical) presentation, and at times can be difficult to identify.
- Mood disorders in people with ID can be easily missed or misdiagnosed due to assessment difficulties.
- Gathering collateral information from carers and family can play a vital role in appropriate assessment and offering timely therapeutic interventions.
- Standard therapeutic interventions are available to manage mood disorders in people with ID, sometimes requiring reasonable adjustments.

References

Barbui C, Cipriani A, Patel V, Ayuso-Mateos JL & van Ommeren M (2011) Efficacy of antidepressants and benzodiazepines in minor depression: systematic review and meta-analysis. *The British Journal of Psychiatry* **198** (1) 11–16.

Bruder C & Kroese BS (2005) The efficacy of interventions designed to prevent and protect people with intellectual disabilities from sexual abuse: a review of the literature. *The Journal of Adult Protection* **7** (2) 13–27.

Kwon OY & Park SP (2014) Depression and anxiety in people with epilepsy. *Journal of Clinical Neurology (Seoul, Korea)* **10** (3) 175–188.

NICE (2009) *Depression in Adults: Recognition and management (CG90)* [online]. Available at www.nice.org.uk/guidance/cg90 (accessed December 2017).

NICE (2016) *Mental Health Problems in People with Learning Disabilities: Prevention, assessment and management (NG54)* [online]. Available at: www.nice.org.uk/guidance/ng54 (accessed December 2017).

Pawlarcyzk D & Beckwith BE (1987) Depressive symptoms displayed by persons with mental retardation. *Mental Retardation* **25** 323–30.

Royal College of Psychiatrists (2017a) *Depression: Key facts* [online]. Available at: www.rcpsych.ac.uk/healthadvice/problemsdisorders/depressionkeyfacts.aspx (accessed December 2017).

Royal College of Psychiatrists (2017b) *Bipolar Affective Disorder: Key facts* [online]. Available at: www.rcpsych.ac.uk/healthadvice/problemsdisorders/bipolardisorder.aspx (accessed December 2017).

Chapter 7:
Anxiety disorders

By Amy Uchendu

Introduction

Research has found that anxiety disorders, along with other mental illnesses, are higher in people with intellectual disabilities (ID) than in the general population. The prevalence of these disorders is even higher in people with Down's syndrome (Collacott *et al*, 1998). Diagnosis of mental illness in people with ID can be complicated by a combination of cognitive impairments and difficulty with communication. When specific intellectual disorder diagnostic criteria was used with adults with ID (RCPsych, 2001), the most common comorbid mental ill health found by Cooper *et al* (2007) was problem behaviours (18.7%), while anxiety disorders were found in about 3.1%. This chapter looks at the anxiety disorders in people with ID and how to seek help from professionals.

Anxiety disorders

DSM-IV describes anxiety as the apprehension we feel when we anticipate future danger or misfortune. Anxiety is a distressing emotion that can motivate, protect and help us cope with adversity when at its peak level. Many people will feel anxious at some point in their lives. With limited ability to solve daily challenges, people with ID are likely to feel anxious more often without having an anxiety disorder. Anxiety becomes a disorder when the intensity or duration of anxiety is disproportionate to the potential for harm or in the absence of recognisable threat to the person. Anxiety disorders may present differently than they do in the general population because people with ID have problems with their intellect and communication. This can make diagnosis using the usual criteria or diagnostic tools difficult, and hence anxiety can go undetected and untreated with serious consequences for the person. There is also a risk of the symptoms being attributed to the ID (diagnostic overshadowing). When it is present, it is important that anxiety is recognised and diagnosed quickly by the professionals and carers in regular contact with the person.

Anxiety disorders may manifest with a combination of the following mental, emotional and physical symptoms:

- Dry mouth.
- Panic or fear.
- Shortness of breath.
- Sleep problems.
- Sweaty or tingling palms or feet.
- Feeling restless.
- Heart palpitations.
- Feeling sick.
- Tense muscles.
- Dizziness.

Anxiety disorders include the following conditions:

- Generalised anxiety disorder (GAD).
- Panic disorders.
- Agoraphobia.
- Specific phobias.
- Obsessive compulsive disorder.
- Acute and post-traumatic stress disorder (PTSD)

Generalised anxiety disorder

A person with generalised anxiety disorder feels fear and tension that is excessive and unrealistic, for little or no reason. This happens frequently, and while in some cases it is possible to identify the cause, at other times no cause can be identified.

Case study: Lee

Lee is a 28-year-old man with moderate ID and autism. He recently moved from a rehabilitation hospital to live in a supported placement with 24-hour staff support. Lee was taken to his local accident and emergency department in a distressed and agitated state after he assaulted another resident at his placement. In hospital, he was calm and appropriate in behaviour. Lee could not explain the incident initially, however it was later discovered that he often worries about various things, including living in the community. He was afraid that if he was unwell it would take time before anyone came to help him; he worried he would not get along with the other residents and that things would go wrong at the day centre and he would not be able to cope. When the other resident approached him and asked for a cup of tea (he does this with most residents and staff), Lee hit him. It was reported that Lee felt tense, his stomach was unsettled, his palms were sweating and his heart was beating faster and loudly in his ear. His sleep was reported to be poor but he denied being depressed. His adopted grandmother, Katy, described Lee as feeling safer in institutions such as hospitals. He had lived in care for most of his life, where most decisions were made for him. After he was adopted by Katy's daughter it took him awhile to settle at home. Katy's daughter passed away 13 years ago. After her death, Lee lived briefly with Katy but had a major outburst that led to his admission to hospital and eventual stepdown to a rehabilitation unit and then to the community.

Lee was seen by a psychiatrist in A&E who diagnosed him with generalised anxiety disorder. He was referred to the local ID mental health team. He was prescribed medication and referred to a clinical psychologist for anxiety management.

Panic disorder

In panic disorder, a person experiences an intense anxiety or terror. These 'attacks' occur randomly and can be so intense that the person believes they will have a heart attack or that they will die. They may start to panic at the thought of having another panic attack.

Case study: Uchechi

Uchechi is a 24-year-old woman with mild ID who was brought to A&E after reporting an episode of extreme chest pain and difficulty breathing. She described walking the family dog with her mother in a park near their home. On their way home, she suddenly started sweating, her heart was beating fast and felt like it would explode in her chest, and she had difficulty breathing. She thought she was having a heart attack and that she would die. Her ECG was normal and the doctors thought she may have had a panic attack. She was referred to the local ID mental health team and when she was seen three weeks later, she told the psychologist that she had about six panic attacks since the initial one that led to her visit to A&E. She was avoiding going to the day centre, walking the dog, or going out with the family.

The psychologist taught Uchechi to use relaxation technique and to breath slowly and deeply when she has a panic attack. She continues to use these techniques and reports a significant reduction in the number and intensity of the panic attacks.

Acute and post-traumatic stress

Many people experience traumatic events at some times in their lives, such as accidents, sexual or physical assault, illness and the loss of a caregiver or loved one. Some will respond with temporary distress, others will have an acute stress reaction within one month of the trauma and others will go on to develop a severe form of anxiety disorder known as post-traumatic stress disorder (PTSD). People with ID who develop PTSD often present initially with violent or disruptive behaviour.

Case study: Linda

Linda is a 29-year-old woman with mild ID and epilepsy who lives with her mother. She attends adult education courses at a college some distance from her home. Sadly, she was sexually assaulted by the shopkeeper who runs an off-licence close to the college when she went into the shop to buy goods.

When she saw her psychiatrist in clinic about one month after the incident, she described dreams of the incident, and was experiencing confusion and feelings of guilt. Her sleep and appetite were good and she had been attending college and felt able to concentrate in class, however when she was seen again four months after the incident she described symptoms of intrusive recollections of the assault through nightmares. She felt numb after the initial feelings of guilt had subsided, she had difficulty sleeping and increased irritability, especially towards her mother. The frequency of her seizures had also increased.

She was seen by a neurologist and her medications were increased without noticeable change on her seizure disorder. A change in anti-epileptic medication was then advised, which was being effected at the time of her second psychiatric review. She was diagnosed with post-traumatic stress disorder (PTSD). After careful discussion about medication, it was agreed to commence therapy alone, initially, and to combine this with medication if required in the future. She successfully engaged with psychotherapy. She was also deemed vulnerable in the community and needed additional help to ensure her safety. She was referred to social services and a social worker completed her 'needs assessment' and arrangements were made for her to have an outreach worker to support her in the community.

Obsessive-compulsive disorder

Individuals with obsessive compulsive disorder (OCD) have unwanted and repeated thoughts, feelings, ideas and sensations (obsessions), and behaviours which may drive them to do something repeatedly (compulsions). The person often carries out these repeated actions to get rid of the obsessive thoughts. The challenge of diagnosis of OCD in people with ID is that often people with ID have baseline repeated behaviours, are unable to express symptoms of anxiety, or to describe the ego-dystonia. However, in their assessment of repetitive behaviours in patients with autism, McDougle *et al* (1995) concluded that OCD symptoms differ significantly from other repetitive thoughts and behaviours seen in this population.

Case study: Sandra

Sandra is a 30-year-old woman who was seen in the mental health ID clinic with her parents, who reported a gradual onset of repetitive hand washing, excessive cleaning, bathing and refusing to touch anything when out of the house. When stopped from washing her hands repeatedly, she would become very irritated and aggressive and would only calm down when she washed her hands again. She had no significant past or family history of psychiatric illness and had no history of substance abuse. On examination, her vital signs were normal and there was no abnormality on systemic examination. Her blood sugar levels, blood count, liver function tests, kidney function tests, thyroid function tests and urinalysis were all within normal range.

An assessment of her IQ by Wechsler Adult Intelligence Scale-Performance Scale (WAIS –IV) was found it to be 46, which put her within the moderate ID range. A mental state examination showed her to be very anxious during interview. She had obsessions of contamination and had compulsive cleaning and washing rituals but there was no other significant mental illness elicited. A Yale-Brown Obsessive-Compulsive Scale Symptom Checklist was administered, which found her to be within the severe OCD range.

In a psychoeducation discussion with her family members, an explanation was given about the nature of the illness and the requirement of treatment, and Sandra was started on an anti-depressant (a selective serotonin re-uptake inhibitor (SSRI)). On review two weeks later, her parents reported development of episodic irritability and aggressive behaviour which responded to a mood stabiliser. The psychologist started differential positive reinforcement, exposure and response prevention. At the three-month follow-up review, her parents reported significant reduction of her symptoms and improvement in her daily functioning.

Phobias

A phobia is described as an extreme or irrational fear of, or aversion to, something. This includes agoraphobia (marked fear of or avoidance of crowds, public places, travelling alone or travelling away from home), social phobia (fear of social situations that involve interaction with other people) and specific phobias (intense fear and avoidance of certain objects or situations such as flying, driving, heights, enclosed spaces, animals, injections or blood). The fear of choking, vomiting or contracting an illness has also been described. Research suggests a higher prevalence of fears and phobia in children with ID and/or autism compared to typically developing peers. This trend appears to continue into adulthood.

According to the fourth edition of the Diagnostic and Statistical Manual of Mental Disorders (DSM-IV; American Psychiatric Association, 2000), the fear reaction occurs in anticipation of, or immediately upon, encountering the feared stimulus, and may escalate into a panic attack. In adults, the individual must recognise that the fear is excessive or irrational. For a diagnosis, the phobia must cause significant impairment in everyday functioning or be associated with distress about having the fear, and cannot be better accounted for by another mental disorder. A fear of needles/injections may have negative medical consequences as it could result in refusal to have blood tests or dental health checks. The case described below is of a young man with ID and autism and a phobia of dogs.

Case study: Martin

Martin is an 18-year-old man with history of moderate ID and autism who, on transition from child to adult services, was reported to have a severe phobia of dogs. When he was seen at home, his family reported an intense anxiety, especially with unfamiliar dogs or dogs running loose. Encounters with dogs would result in Martin screaming, crying, hitting out at others, hitting his face and head and refusing to leave the house. Consequently, he misses out on usual activities including school and various evening clubs and leisure activities. He reported that he missed going to school and attending his usual social clubs. However, as the likelihood of meeting a dog each time he went out was high, to avoid this and the resulting unpleasant feelings, he would much rather stay at home. His annual health review, completed recently, showed no underlying physical health condition. On examination of his mental state, he appeared well kempt and relaxed, however he quickly became tense at the mention of dogs or going out into the community. His speech was dysarthric (a difficulty articulating words) and limited in quantity, and he required help from his family to describe his fear of being chased or bitten by dogs. There was no co-morbid mental illness elicited.

He was commenced on Sertraline, an antidepressant, and he was due to be seen by a psychologist for exposure therapy. At his review two weeks later, there had been some reduction in his anxiety level and he had been able to go grocery shopping with the family at the local superstore.

Association with drugs, alcohol and caffeine

Avoidance behaviours are shown in anxiety models to be the primary factor that maintains anxiety. These behaviours can be as overt as avoiding the feared object or situation, or escaping a fearful situation. Other behaviours can be subtle and involve the use of safety behaviours, distraction or maladaptive coping behaviours when in the feared situation. Safety behaviours are coping strategies intended to reduce one's anxiety and prevent the feared outcome from occurring (Salkovskis, 1991). Common safety behaviours include the use of alcohol, drugs and caffeine to decrease anxiety in the feared situation, or wearing heavy gloves or protective clothing in the basement or garden to prevent contact with spiders, for example. Avoidance behaviours may help to reduce fear in the short term, however they are thought to maintain the disorder in the long term because individuals may come to believe that the coping behaviour was responsible for preventing the feared outcome or that it enabled them to manage their fear in the situation (e.g. 'The dog didn't bite me because I didn't leave the house). However, this does little to change one's inaccurate beliefs about the dangerousness of the situation. When identified, avoidance and coping strategies can be targeted in exposure therapy and gradually eliminate reliance on safety strategies as the treatment progresses.

Assessments

These may include:

- Clinical interviews.
- The use of specialist rating instruments where relevant, such as the Yale Brown Obsessive Compulsive Scale used in OCD.
- Behavioural assessments.
- Physical examination.
- Investigations.

Treatment

These may include one of or combination of the following:

- Psychotherapies – exposure therapy, cognitive behavioural therapy.

- Pharmacotherapy – anti-depressants such as selective serotonin re-uptake inhibitors (SSRIs), selective serotonin/norepinephrine reuptake inhibitors (SNRIs), benzodiazepines, serotonin (5HT) 1 agonists, antihypertensive agents and tricyclic antidepressants (TCAs).

Conclusion

Anxiety disorders are more common in people with ID, many of whom may need professional help to resolve their condition. This help should begin with an assessment and investigations by their GP to identify the relevant symptoms and rule out any underlying physical health condition that could be present, such as an anxiety disorder being caused by a thyroid condition. Treatment may be commenced by the GP and, where required, referral can be made to the specialist mental health ID service in the local area for specialist input.

References

American Psychiatric Association (2000) Diagnostic and Statistical manual of mental disorders (4th ed.). Washington, DC: American Psychiatric Association.

Collacott RA, Cooper SA, Branford D & McGrother C (1998) Behaviour phenotype for Down's Syndrome. *British Journal of Psychiatry* **172** 85–89.

Cooper SA, Smiley E, Morrison J, Williamson A & Allan L (2007). Mental ill-health in adults with intellectual disabilities: prevalence and associated factors. *British Journal of Psychiatry* **190** 27–35.

McDougle CJ, Kresch LE, Goodman WK, Naylor ST, Volkmar FR, Cohen DJ & Price LH (1995) A case-controlled study of repetitive thoughts and behavior in adults with autistic disorder and obsessive-compulsive disorder. *The American Journal of Psychiatry* **152** 772–7.

Royal College of Psychiatrists (2001) DC-LD (Diagnostic criteria for psychiatric disorders for use with adults with learning disabilities/mental retardation). London: Gaskell.

Salkovskis PM (1991) The importance of behaviour in the maintenance of anxiety and panic: a cognitive account. *Behavioural Psychotherapy* **19** 6–19.

Chapter 8: Autism and mental health

By Ilias Partsenidis

Introduction

This chapter looks at autism spectrum disorder (ASD) and associated mental health problems in people with intellectual disabilities (ID). Four case studies illustrate common presentations of mental illness in people with autism and ID.

What is autism?

Autism is a complex condition that arises due to abnormalities in the development of the central nervous system. Although the aetiology of autism remains unknown, it is thought that several genetic and environmental factors play a role. Approximately one in 100 people have autism. It is a lifelong condition. Autism affects social interaction, communication and behaviour. Autism is usually diagnosed during childhood, however some people are diagnosed in adulthood. Currently, there is no medical test that can diagnose autism and autism is therefore diagnosed after a clinical assessment by specialists such as psychiatrists or psychologists.

How does autism affect people?

If we look at the two main diagnostic manuals, the 10th revision of the *International Statistical Classification of Diseases and Related Health Problems* (ICD-10) and *The Diagnostic and Statistical Manual of Mental Disorders, Fifth Edition* (DSM-V), the main features of autism include:

- abnormalities in communication and social interaction such as delay in, or total lack of, the development of language, deficits in non-verbal communication e.g. abnormalities in eye contact and body language, deficits in understanding and using gestures, limited range of facial expressions, stereotyped and repetitive use of language, abnormal social approach and problems with synchrony and reciprocity when holding a conversation, lack of responses to people's emotions, difficulties in developing and maintaining relationships, difficulties adjusting behaviours to adjust behaviour to suit social context, poor integration of verbal and non-verbal communication, reduced sharing of emotions and interests and problems in initiating or responding to social interactions.

- restricted, repetitive and stereotyped patterns of behaviour, interests and activities, including repetitive movements of torso or limbs, lining up or flipping objects, strong attachment to or preoccupation with specific objects, insistence on sameness, extreme distress at changes in daily routines, difficulties with life transitions, hypersensitivity to or unusual interest in environmental sensory stimuli.

People with autism tend to experience the world around them in a different way compared to people without autism. For example, they have cognitive processing difficulties, which means that they can easily become overwhelmed when presented with a lot of information or too many environmental stimuli. Furthermore, they have sensory hypersensitivities e.g. hearing, smell, touch, vision, and hence they can have unpredictable negative reactions to noise, unpleasant smells, bright lights or colours etc. They struggle with lack of structure in their daily lives and they frequently find their environment unpredictable and confusing and may experience daily activities as meaningless (Bakken *et al*, 2016). As people with autism and ID have limited coping strategies when they become overwhelmed by cognitive processing difficulties and sensory overload, this can result in increased levels of distress and agitation.

Coping strategies people with autism use to deal with sensory overload and lack of structure include:

- engaging in and focusing on a specific repetitive behaviour
- avoidance e.g. closing their eyes or running away
- verbal or physical aggression towards others or towards themselves (self-injurious behaviours)
- freezing i.e. they stop engaging in their usual daily activities (Bradley *et al*, 2014).

In view of the above difficulties associated with autism it is not surprising that people with autism, in addition to their ID, can frequently experience common mental health problems as discussed in the following paragraphs.

Anxiety disorders

In view of the multiple difficulties that people with autism and ID experience in their daily life, it is not unexpected that anxiety is one of the most common symptoms experienced by this group of patients. In some of these patients anxiety can be explained within the context of autism, especially if it has been present since the beginning of their lives, however, in other patients within this group, the anxiety symptoms can be or can become so severe that a diagnosis of a specific anxiety disorder can be made, in addition to the diagnoses of autism and ID, at some point in their lives.

People with autism and ID engage in repetitive behaviours and rituals as a coping mechanism when they feel anxious and, in some cases, such behaviours can be so severe that an additional diagnosis of obsessive compulsive disorder (OCD) can be made. When considering a diagnosis of OCD in this patient group we need to look at the impact of their obsessions e.g. fear of dirt/contamination and/or compulsions, e.g. washing their hands repetitively, on their daily lives; for example, we need to look at how much time they spend each day in these activities and if they cause disruption to their routine daily activities.

Furthermore, as people with autism and ID have limited social skills and struggle with social interaction it is not surprising that they often experience social anxiety in their everyday life; however, in some cases the social anxiety is so pronounced and has such a major impact on their daily life that an additional diagnosis of social phobia can be made. Also, some people with autism and ID have specific phobias e.g. dogs, needles etc. which can cause major disruption in their lives.

Mood disorders

Diagnosing a mood disorder in a person with autism and ID can be quite difficult as, firstly, they might not be able to understand how they are feeling e.g. if they are feeling happy or sad, and secondly, they might not be able to communicate how they are feeling e.g. lack of facial expression, incongruent body language, flat affect etc. Furthermore, excessive excitement about special interests, psychomotor overactivity, speech increased in volume and quantity, which can be common features in people with autism, can be mistaken for symptoms of mania. Autism is associated with a general unstable mood that can change rapidly dependent on relatively minor events in the patient's daily life, and this appears to be related to a lack of self-awareness and poor emotional regulation (Carpenter, 2009). In some cases the mood instability is so severe that a diagnosis of bipolar affective disorder can be made. In view of the difficulties people with autism encounter in the their daily lives e.g. due to sensory issues or due to cognitive processing difficulties it is not surprising that some of them will experience low mood as a result and some with be diagnosed with mild, moderate or even severe depression.

Psychotic disorders

Diagnosing a psychotic disorder such as schizophrenia in a person with autism and ID can be a challenge for various reasons. The patient might express rigid and unusual/strange ideas repetitively within the context of autism which may be mistaken for false, firmly held beliefs, i.e. delusions, which are a symptom of psychotic disorder. Also, people with autism might talk about having imaginary friends they have conversations with, which can be misinterpreted as evidence that they are experiencing perceptual abnormalities such as auditory hallucinations. Furthermore, as people with autism find their environment confusing and are unable to understand everything that happens around them, they can become paranoid about others, for example they might think that other people are talking about them, and this can be misinterpreted as evidence of paranoid delusional ideation (Carpenter, 2009). In addition, people with autism who experience increased levels of anxiety, for example due to changes in their routine or due to sensory overload, can potentially engage in bizarre behaviours as a coping mechanism. For example, a young woman who went to Spain on holiday for the first time started removing all the books from the bookcases and all the paintings from the walls in order to cope with her anxiety in her new environment. This might be misinterpreted as a sign of delusional ideation i.e. psychosis.

Attention deficit hyperactivity disorder (ADHD)/hyperkinetic disorder

Diagnosing ADHD/hyperkinetic disorder in a person with ID and autism can be quite difficult as autism – and also ID to some extent – can be associated with poor attention and hyperactivity. Therefore the clinician who conducts the diagnostic assessment must be satisfied that the level of distractibility or restlessness is significantly more severe than would be expected in a person with autism and ID (Carpenter, 2009) and that it is not caused by a mental health or physical health problem, both of which are common in this population group.

Eating disorders

It is not uncommon for a person with autism to be described as a 'fussy eater' and this might have something to do with sensory oversensitivity or ritualistic behaviour. People with autism might have a severely restricted diet as a result, for example eating only chicken and chips all the time, and this can lead to significant nutritional deficiencies over time.

Pica, which is the persistent eating of substances that have no nutritional value, such as paper or soil for example, is more common in people with autism and ID than anorexia or bulimia nervosa. Pica can potentially result in poisoning e.g. eating paint chips containing toxic substances or life-threatening conditions e.g. acute bowel obstruction requiring emergency surgery in a patient who had been eating large amounts of paper. Anorexia is usually more common in people with autism without ID (Carpenter, 2009).

Treatment strategies

It is extremely important to identify and treat the problems caused by the main features of autism before considering any intervention for an associated mental health problem. A multidisciplinary approach is therefore advised:

- Occupational therapy input looking at sensory issues.

- Speech and language therapy input with regard to communication difficulties.

- Behavioural support specialist input with regard to specific challenging behaviours.

- Dietician input.

- Educational and vocational interventions as people with autism really struggle with unstructured time and need to be engaged in meaningful activities during the day.

- Family interventions i.e. educating and supporting families, but also family therapy might be appropriate, for example, when the main problem appears to be the relationship or interaction between the person with autism and ID and a member(s) of their family.

- Medication for managing some of the core features of autism. For example, there is some evidence to suggest that stereotypical, compulsive/repetitive behaviours can be helped with antidepressant medication such as fluoxetine or fluvoxamine, or with antipsychotic medication such as risperidone or aripiprazole (Elvins & Green, 2015). However, we must not forget that medication can have side effects which patients with autism and ID might struggle to identify and report, hence extra caution is advised when prescribing medication for this group of patients.

■ Medication for managing specific mental health problems e.g. depression, psychosis, OCD etc. when a diagnosis of a particular mental health condition is made in somebody with autism and ID.

■ Treatment of associated medical conditions, particularly epilepsy, but also other conditions e.g. gastro-intestinal disorders. (Semple & Smyth, 2013)

Key learning points

■ Autism is a lifelong condition that affects communication, social interaction and behaviour.

■ People with autism and ID encounter extra difficulties in their daily lives due to autistic features such as poor cognitive processing and sensory oversensitivity and this predisposes them to developing mental health problems.

■ Making a diagnosis of a mental health condition in a person with autism and ID can be quite challenging as autistic features can be mistaken for symptoms of mental illness or vice versa.

■ Anxiety and mood instability are very commonly encountered in people with autism and ID but they do not always reach the threshold for a diagnosis of a specific anxiety or mood disorder.

■ A multidisciplinary approach to treating mental illness in people with autism and ID is advised.

Case study: Peter

Peter is a 25-year-old man with mild ID and autism. He has always been an anxious person within the context of his autism diagnosis and he has always had specific routines and rituals e.g. washing his hands twice each time. However, he has been able to manage these difficulties using relaxation techniques and has been able to engage in a variety of daily activities at home and in the community for many years. Over the past couple of months there has been a considerable increase in his daily rituals as he tends to spend up to two hours in the bathroom in the mornings doing his personal care, and then it takes him up to another two hours to get ready to go out. This has had a significant impact on his daily activities as he had been missing all the morning classes at college. Peter insists that he has to shower and get dressed 'in the right way' and although he is well aware that he is missing classes, which is causing even more anxiety, he is unable to get ready in the morning in less than four hours. There is no obvious trigger for the deterioration in his behaviour, however, there have always been complex dynamics in Peter's family.

Peter is referred through his GP to the local team community intellectual disability team where he is assessed by a psychiatrist and a psychologist/behaviour specialist.

He is diagnosed with obsessive compulsive disorder and is started on regular medication. Also, at the same time he receives input from the psychologist. After a couple of months there has been some improvement and although Peter is not back to his normal baseline he is able to attend most of the morning classes at college and is considerably less distressed by his daily rituals.

Case study: Mary

Mary is a 55-year-old lady with moderate ID and autism. She has a weekly timetable of activities she engages in, both at home and in the community, and interacts well with her carers and the other people living with her. Her daily routine, which she has followed for many years, includes going to the local shop to buy her favourite newspaper and to the local café where she has a coffee and a slice of cake.

Over the past couple of months, she has gradually become quite irritable. She has shouted and sworn at her carers and very recently she slapped and kicked one of them. Her sleeping pattern has deteriorated as she struggles to fall asleep and she wakes up two to three hours earlier than usual. She has been refusing meals at times and her carers reported that she has lost some weight. She doesn't engage in most of her usual activities and she has stopped going to the local shop or the local café. When her carers asked her what the problem was she told them to 'go away'. They cannot explain the change in Mary's behaviour as there was no obvious trigger.

Mary is supported by her carers to see her GP and a physical health problem is excluded as physical examination and blood and urine tests are all normal. Mary is then referred to the community learning disability team and is seen by a psychiatrist. Mary is diagnosed with moderate depression and is started on regular antidepressant medication. After a few weeks there is some improvement; the dose of the antidepressant is increased and after a couple of months Mary is almost back to normal. There is no irritability and she is engaging again in her usual daily activities, including going to the local shop and café. Mary will need to continue taking the antidepressant for some time after recovering from this episode of depression and this will be reviewed by her psychiatrist.

Case study: Olu

Olu is a 30-year-old man with moderate ID and autism. For many years he has been observed talking to himself when he is alone in his room and when his carers had asked him who he was talking to, he always said it was his friend 'Tom', who appears to be an imaginary person as Olu doesn't have any friends called Tom. Olu has never appeared to be distressed when he is talking to 'Tom' and he has always engaged in his daily activities without any problems.

However, over the past couple of months Olu has been talking to himself non-stop most of the time, even when he is not alone. He appears to be quite anxious and he has said things that do not appear to make much sense e.g. he would shout, 'danger, danger', 'go away', 'not now'. His carers, who have known him for years, report that Olu has never behaved like this before. In addition, his sleeping pattern has worsened considerably, sleeping only a couple of hours per night, he keeps talking to himself and has been disturbing the other residents at his accommodation. When his carers asked Olu if he could hear people talking to him without being able to see them, he refused to reply and became verbally aggressive towards his carers. In addition, he has been refusing to leave the house saying that he is 'scared' without explaining what he is scared of.

Olu is reviewed by his GP, who examines him and does some blood tests. All the test results are within the normal range and no abnormality is noted on physical examination, hence the GP refers Olu to the psychiatrist of the local community intellectual disability team. The psychiatrist assesses Olu and makes a diagnosis of a psychotic episode and starts him on a regular antipsychotic medication. Over the next few weeks, his carers report that there has been considerable improvement in Olu's presentation as he is sleeping much better, he is talking to himself much less often, he is calmer, and he has been accessing the community without any problems.

Case study: Henry

Henry is a 23-year-old man with moderate ID and autism. Henry's speech has always been quite repetitive and loud and he has always had problems with regard to invading other people's space. Henry can be very affectionate towards people he knows, for example he can hug them tightly without letting them go for a few seconds. He will also touch the hair and face of people that are familiar to him if he likes them. Henry has a weekly schedule of activities both at his accommodation and in the community and he has been engaging with the activities without any problems.

Over the past couple of weeks his carers reported that he appeared to be excessively happy for no obvious reason – he had been trying to hug strangers and touch their hair, he has been taking his clothes off in front of other people and he has been making loud utterances. On one occasion, he took his pants off when he was out in the community and the police were called but took no further action as Henry was persuaded to put them back on and was taken home. In addition, Henry has been sleeping very little and appears to have boundless energy. Despite appearing to be very happy, Henry's carers reported that his mood can change suddenly as Henry became angry very quickly whenever some of his usual daily routines were disrupted due to unforeseen circumstances in the past few days.

His carers took him to his GP who performed a physical examination and did some blood tests, but no abnormalities were detected. As there was no obvious physical health problem, Henry's GP referred him to the psychiatrist at the local community learning disabilities team who diagnosed a manic episode and started him on mood stabilising medication. After a few days there was some improvement and after a few weeks Henry was back to his normal self, enjoying his daily routines without getting into trouble with the police. He continues to take the mood stabilising medication in order to prevent a relapse and he is having regular clinic reviews with the psychiatrist.

References

American Psychiatric Association (2013) *Diagnostic and Statistical Manual of Mental Disorders, 5th edition (DSM-V)*. Washington, DC: American Psychiatric Publishing.

Bradley E, Caldwell P & Underwood L (2014) Autism Spectrum Disorder. In: E Tsakanikos & J McCarthy (Ed) *Handbook of Psychopathology in Intellectual Disability: Research, practice, and policy (Autism and Child Psychopathology Series)* pp237–264. New York: Springer.

Bakken TL, Helvershou SB, Hoidal SH & Martinsen H (2016) Mental illness with intellectual disabilities and autism spectrum disorders. In: C Hemmings and N Bouras (Ed) *Psychiatric and Behavioural Disorders in Intellectual and Developmental Disabilities* (3rd edition) pp132–142. Cambridge: Cambridge University Press.

Carpenter P (2009) Mental Health Aspects of Autism Spectrum Disorders. In: A Hassiotis, DA Barron & I Hall (Ed) *Intellectual Disability Psychiatry A practical handbook* pp85-99. Chichester, West Sussex: Wiley-Blackwell.

Elvins R & Green J (2015) Pharmacological management of core and comorbid symptoms in autism spectrum disorder. In: M Woodbury-Smith (ed) *Clinical Topics in Disorders of Intellectual Development* pp178–200. London: The Royal College of Psychiatrists.

Semple D & Smyth R (2013) *Oxford Handbook of Psychiatry* (3rd edition). Oxford: Oxford University Press.

World Health Organisation (1992) *The ICD-10 Classification of Mental and Behavioural Disorders: Clinical descriptions and Diagnostic Guidelines, Chapter V: Mental and Behavioural Disorders*. Geneva: World Health Organisation.

Chapter 9: Attention deficit hyperactive disorder (ADHD)

By Jane McCarthy & Eddie Chaplin

Summary

This chapter describes the presentation and treatment of attention deficit hyperactive disorder (ADHD) in adults with intellectual disabilities (ID). ADHD is a common condition in children with ID but often goes unrecognised in adults. The presentation of ADHD in adults with ID is often complicated by the presence of other conditions such as autism. In addition, ADHD impacts on a person's achievements and on their social functioning, so hindering their personal relationships. To date there has been no diagnostic tool available to diagnose ADHD in adults with ID, although an assessment tool specifically developed for the purpose is in development. The approach to the treatment of ADHD in adults with ID is same as in the general population, using a combination of both pharmacological and non-pharmacological interventions. This is why it is important to raise the awareness and understanding of ADHD in adults with ID as good treatments are available.

Introduction

ADHD is a common childhood disorder that can persist into adulthood. It affects 3% to 4% of children and 1% of adults. It is a neurodevelopmental disorder as is ID and autism spectrum disorder (ASD), all of which are lifelong conditions affecting several domains of functioning. The age of onset for ADHD within DSM-V (American Psychiatric Association, 2013) is before the age of 12 years. In adults, ADHD commonly occurs with other conditions including ID, anxiety, depression, drug and alcohol use and antisocial behaviour. For children with ADHD, common co-morbid conditions include oppositional defiant and conduct disorders, anxiety and mood disorders, tics or Tourette's syndrome and autism.

A third of children with ADHD go on to have the diagnosis as adults, whereas two thirds show a persistence of symptoms that impacts on their functioning as adults. ADHD can impact on the social, academic and occupational functioning of a person, therefore not just on what they may achieve at school but on their personal relationships as children and adults.

ADHD is three times more common in individuals with ID than in the general population with some studies indicating that up to a third of children with ID are affected by symptoms of ADHD. For those with ASD, up to 50% may be affected with symptoms of ADHD. The prevalence of ADHD is equal in boys and girls for those with ID, which compares to the findings in the general population in which five boys are identified to every one girl. This gender difference may in part be due to less awareness of ADHD occurring in girls.

Studies indicate there is a significant genetic component that influences the risk for developing ADHD. The risk for first degree relatives is four to 10 times the population rate and the prevalence of ADHD among first degree relatives is in the range 20 to 50%. In addition, there are environmental factors associated with ADHD. These include exposure of the foetus to alcohol, nicotine, drugs, high blood pressure, maternal stress during pregnancy, being born preterm and low birth weight. However, these environmental factors (which are associations and not shown to be direct causes) may be modified by genetic factors.

ADHD and ID

ADHD is common in people with ID, with those less able at more risk of showing symptoms. Traditionally, there has not been a focus on ADHD in adults with ID despite it being one of the most common disorders in childhood.

There is increasing evidence to support the diagnosis of ADHD in adults with ID and that this group of the population is at increased risk for the condition (Xenitidis *et al*, 2014). Until recently, the research focused on children with mild ID, confirming an increase of ADHD symptoms in this group (Simonoff *et al*, 2007). The challenge has been to establish how best to apply the diagnostic criteria in people with ID, and others have questioned if ADHD can be diagnosed in children with low IQ. A further complication is that the inattention and associated deficits of executive function in ADHD may result in lower IQ scores, but this will not necessarily indicate ID as defined by the international diagnostic systems (Ek *et al*, 2011). In adults with ADHD, the severity of symptoms has a negative collation with IQ scores. One study examining symptoms of ADHD in adults with ID found that there was greater severity of (adult and childhood) symptoms compared to people with ADHD with no ID. It was also the case that the latter group could expect a greater improvement of symptoms in adulthood than those with ID (Xenitidis *et al,* 2014).

Currently there are no specific rating scales designed to assess ADHD in adults with ID that work with the ICD-10 and DSM-V diagnostic systems. La Malfa *et al* (2008) reported on the use of the Conner's Adult ADHD rating scale in 46 adults with ID, finding an 'ADHD-positive' prevalence of 19.6%. There is also an increasing recognition of the need to screen for the neurodevelopmental disorders as defined by DSM-V to identify when ADHD and ID occur together, especially in at-risk populations such as those in the criminal justice system (McCarthy *et al,* 2015). The key area for future research, therefore, is to develop a validated tool to diagnose ADHD in adults with ID that will lead to the development of studies looking at response to treatment, and so increase understanding of the long-term outcomes in adults with ID and comorbid ADHD.

Diagnosing ADHD

Central to the diagnostic criteria for ADHD in children in DSM-V is a persistent pattern of inattention and/or hyperactivity-impulsivity that interferes with functioning or development as characterised by:

1. Inattention: six or more symptoms (which have been present for at least six months) that are inconsistent with developmental level and that negatively impact directly on social and academic/occupational activities. The individual may: overlook details; have difficulties remaining focused on conversations; seem like their mind is elsewhere; fail to finish tasks; fail to meet deadlines; have problems completing forms; lose items such as keys or phones; be easily distracted and often forgetful in daily activities such as keeping appointment and paying bills.

2. Hyperactivity and impulsivity – at least six symptoms: often fidgets; restless; often 'on the go'; talking excessively; unable to wait turns in a conversation; intrusion into or taking over what others are doing.

For older adolescents and adults (age 17 and above) at least five symptoms are required.

DSM-V notes that although motor symptoms of hyperactivity become less obvious in adolescence and adulthood, difficulties persist with restlessness, inattention, poor planning and impulsivity. DSM-V also stipulates that symptoms are excessive and maladaptive for developmental level, which is a very important issue to consider when making a diagnosis in a person with mild ID compared to a person with severe ID.

The current severity of ADHD is also specified in DSM-V as below:

- Mild – few if any symptoms in excess of those required to make the diagnosis are present, and symptoms result in no more than minor impairments in social or occupational functioning.

- Moderate – symptoms or functional impairment between 'mild' and 'severe' are present.

- Severe – many symptoms in excess of those required to make the diagnosis, or several symptoms that are particularly severe are present, or the symptoms result in marked impairment in social or occupational functioning.

DSM-V states that ADHD can be diagnosed with known genetic syndromes such as fragile X syndrome, velo-cardiofacial syndrome and Down's syndrome.

Assessment of ADHD

There are a number of screening tools available, but it is important to remember that symptoms of ADHD start in childhood, are chronic, and do not fluctuate overtime. The hyperactive and impulsive symptoms do modify more than the attentional symptoms.

Diagnosis is based on a careful assessment, including developmental history and a detailed psychiatric history. The use of informants is helpful specifically in recognising the level of impairment on functioning. There are screening instruments available for identifying adults with ADHD such as the six item World Health Adult Self Report Scale (ASRS). For diagnosis, there are number tools such as the Conners' Adult ADHD Rating scale and Diagnostic Interview for ADHD in adults (DIVA), which is available free on line at www.divacenter.eu. The DIVA has now been developed into a version for use with adults with ID known as DIVA-ID and will soon be available for wider use.

Other symptoms that are commonly associated with ADHD but not necessarily a requirement of the diagnostic systems include procrastination, low tolerance of frustration so seeming on a 'short fuse', and mood lability. Mood lability is very common, with mood changes occurring a number times a day, and low self-esteem is also very common due to earlier experiences of failure and rejection. Adults with ADHD do not settle with age and are often underachievers but will change and/or lose jobs and relationships through being fired or being bored. The clinical picture of ADHD is commonly complicated by frequent comorbid conditions that may occur, making a complex picture of conditions to unravel and treat (Hellings *et al*, 2016).

Parents and carers may report the person with ID to be moody, aggressive or anxious so there may be a response to prescribe medication such as antipsychotics or mood stabilisers. However, this would result in the person not receiving the most appropriate treatment for their ADHD, and therefore missing the opportunity to have much better control of their ADHD symptoms.

Types of ADHD

How ADHD presents will differ by individual. There are three main ways it can present:

1. ADHD where the person is predominantly hyperactive and or impulsive. The person with this will feel the need to move constantly. They may also struggle with making good choices as they become impatient as their impulse control can be affected. Although there may be some issues with inattention, this is not seen as a problem.

2. ADHD where the person is predominantly inattentive and has difficulty paying attention. The person is easily distracted but not usually impulsive or hyperactive. This can often be missed as the person is not seen as disruptive and can even be seen as shy, whereas those in the first group are often seen as disruptive.

3. ADHD, combined presentation. This is the most common type of ADHD, where the person experiences symptoms in both types 1 and 2.

ADHD and other mental disorders

Diagnosing ADHD in people with ID can be challenging as it can be mistaken for a behavioural issue or a mental illness where there is an increase in activity such as hypomania, or where there is a lack of attention paid due to poor concentration, such as depression. However, it is equally important to ensure that symptoms are not better explained by an underlying mental health problem. Some of the ways to distinguish between ADHD and other mental health problems is to look at the presentation in context e.g. chronicity of symptoms, recent stressful life events, severity of symptoms or other medical conditions such as infection.

In addition, ADHD shares some of the symptoms of borderline personality disorder such as impulsivity, mood instability and feelings of boredom.

Treatment

Symptoms of ADHD can be treated effectively in both children and adults. The effects of both stimulant medication and atomoxetine on the core symptoms of ADHD are well established.

Treatment can be broken into pharmacological and non-pharmacological interventions. The focus of treatment should focus on improving symptoms and functioning. Traditionally, those with ID have been excluded from studies of ADHD in the general population as it was felt the symptoms were part of the ID – diagnostic overshadowing. Current clinical practice in treating adults with ID presenting with ADHD is therefore to apply the current evidence available for the non-ID population as described in NICE guidelines for adults with ADHD (NICE, 2008).

Table 9.1 summarises the key treatments for ADHD. The evidence indicates that children with ID and ADHD may not have the same response to psychostimulant medication, such as methylphenidate, as other children.

Table 9.1: Treatments for ADHD

Pharmacological	Non-pharmacological
There are five types of medication licensed for the treatment of ADHD: ■ Methylphenidate. ■ Dexamfetamine. ■ Lisdexamfetamine. ■ Atomoxetine. ■ Guanfacine.	■ CBT. ■ Lifestyle and diet. ■ Behavioural interventions. ■ Psychoeducation. ■ Social skills. ■ Parent education programmes.
(For more information, see NHS Choices: http://www.nhs.uk/Conditions/Attention-deficit-hyperactivity-disorder/Pages/Treatment.aspx (accessed December 2017)	

Pharmacological

Medicines are not intended to be a cure for ADHD but are designed to help with symptoms, for example to make the person more able to concentrate, be less impulsive, feel calmer, and take part in things they would not have been able to before, such as learning. In the UK, all of these medications are licensed for use in children and teenagers and are commonly prescribed as extended release preparations, which have a duration of action of many hours, possibly allowing a one-a-day dose. Atomoxetine is also licensed for use in adults who had symptoms of ADHD.

It is reported that children with ADHD may be more at risk of the side effects from the stimulants as described below. Stimulants may worsen self-injury behaviour so use of non-stimulant ADHD medication may be more suitable.

What side effects can stimulants cause?

Side effects often happen early in treatment and for most people are mild and short-term. Common side effects can include:

- Decreased appetite/weight loss.
- Sleep problems.
- Social withdrawal.
- Rebound effect (increased activity or a bad mood as the medication wears off).
- Tics.
- Stomach aches.
- Mood swings.
- Dizziness.
- Increase in blood pressure or heart rate.
- Bizarre behaviour.
- Growth delay in children.

There are a number of ways side effects can be helped including:

- Changing the dose or time of medicines.
- Trying a different type of medication, for example trying a different stimulant or trying a non-stimulant medicine.

Non-pharmacological

In terms of non-pharmacological treatment, education (psychoeducation) of individuals, carers and parents is often used. In terms of adult treatments, psychological intervention such as cognitive behaviour therapy (CBT) is often used, which helps the person to change the way they think and behave by looking at how they interpret the relationship between their thoughts and behaviours. Some interventions are used both for adults and children such as social skills training, which can incorporate roleplay situations, to show how the person's behaviour affects others.

Another issue often overlooked is diet, as some types of food may worsen ADHD symptoms, for example sugar, food additives and caffeine. There are also some food supplements that may reduce symptoms such as omega-3 and omega-6 fatty acids, although there is currently little evidence as to whether this is effective or not.

Case study: Paul

This is a case example of a failure to recognise ADHD in both childhood and in adult life leading to the diagnosis of a personality disorder in adult life and misuse of alcohol with a devastating impact on the well-being of Paul.

Paul is a 30-year-old man with mild learning disabilities and a diagnosis of emotionally unstable personality disorder. He has had a history of behavioural problems since childhood, including disruptive behaviour, fidgeting, struggling at school and having severe temper tantrums. As a result he has presented as impulsive, disorganised and chaotic throughout his adult life, which has led to multiple presentations to hospital with overdoses and self-harming behaviour, along with a long history of alcohol misuse and accompanying mood instability. Failure to recognise Paul's presentation because of a lack of awareness of ADHD has led to a diagnosis of personality disorder.

Case study: Mark

This case example is an example of making an early diagnosis and providing appropriate treatment.

Mark is 14-year-old boy with moderate to severe ID. He presented with many behavioural difficulties along with restlessness and hyperactivity, which was initially put down to his ID. These behaviours and his presentation caused major difficulties at his special school in terms of engaging and supporting him. On further assessment it was recognised that his hyperactivity and restlessness were much more than expected for his developmental level. Following psychiatric assessment, Mark was diagnosed with ADHD, started on a stimulant and provided with social skills training. Following the initial phase of treatment there was significant improvement in his behaviour and he is no longer being oppositional, is able to participate in family events and to go out to play with his friends.

Case study: David

This is a case example of a person being recognised as having ADHD in childhood but where there was no follow up into adult services to ensure he continued with appropriate treatment. This lack of appropriate treatment is probably contributing to his current presentation.

David is 22-year-old man with mild ID, diagnosed with personality disorder and recognised as having had ADHD in childhood. He has recently been in prison for threats to his ex-partner. In prison, David self-harmed and, due to his continuing vulnerability on release and an increase in his threatening behaviour, he is admitted to an intensive care mental health ward under Section 3 of the Mental Health Act. On the ward he is assaulting staff, damaging property and self-harming by cutting himself with broken objects. He is diagnosed with adult ADHD and commenced on stimulant treatment. On leaving children's services at the age of 18 years, David's ADHD had not been seen as a problem and had not previously been picked up as an adult.

Key learning points

■ ADHD is a common condition in people with ID and can persist throughout adult life.

■ ADHD can be misdiagnosed as personality disorder or mood disorder as they share some traits.

■ There is a need to improve recognition and diagnosis of ADHD in people with ID to improve outcomes in both childhood and adult life.

■ ADHD can have a significant impact on the functioning of a person with ID, including on their personal relationships.

■ There is a good response to treatment so it is important to recognise and diagnose ADHD in a person with ID.

References

American Psychiatric Association (2013) *Diagnostic and Statistical Manual of Mental Disorders (5th Ed)*. Washington DC.

Ek U, Westerlind J, Holmberg K & Fernell E (2011) Academic performance of adolescents with ADHD and other behavioural and learning problems-population-based longitudinal study. *Acta Paediatrica* **100** 402–406.

Hellings JA *et al* (2016) Attention-deficit/hyperactivity disorder. In: RJ Fletcher, J Barnhill and S-A Cooper (Eds) *Diagnostic Manual-Intellectual Disability textbook of Mental Disorders in Persons with Intellectual disability (DM-ID 2)*. New York: NADD Press.

La Malfa G, Lassi S, Bertelli M, Pallanti S & Albertini G (2008) Detecting attention-deficit/hyperactivity disorder (ADHD) in adults with intellectual disability. The use of Conners' Adult ADHD Rating Scale (CAARS). *Research in Developmental Disabilities* **29** 158–164.

McCarthy J, Chaplin E, Underwood L, Forrester A, Hayward H, Sabet J, Young S, Asherson P, Mills R & Murphy D (2015) Screening and diagnostic assessment of neurodevelopmental disorders in a male prison. (2015). *Journal of Intellectual Disabilities and Offending Behaviour* **6** (2) 102-111.

NICE (2008) *Attention Deficit Hyperactivity Disorder: Diagnosis and management* [online]. Available at: www.nice.org.uk/guidance/cg72 (accessed March 2018).

Simonoff E, Pickles A, Wood N, Gringas P & Chadwick O (2007) ADHD symptoms in children with mild intellectual disability. *Journal of the American Academy of Child and Adolescent Psychiatry* **46** 591–600.

Xenitidis K, Maltezos K & Asherson P (2014) Attention-Deficit Hyperactivity Disorder (ADHD). In: E Tsakanikos and J McCarthy (Eds) *Handbook of Psychopathology in Adults with Developmental and Intellectual Disability: Research, policy and practice*. New York, NY: Springer Science.

Website resource

UKAAN is the UK Adult ADHD Network and host an annual congress, provides training and has a number of free resources on the website including assessment tools and publications: www.ukaan.org

Chapter 10: Genetic disorders

By Anne-Marije Prins

Summary

Intellectual disabilities (ID) are associated with both genetic and/or environmental causes. In 25-50% of cases, genetic causes are thought to be present (McLaren & Bryson, 1987). The most common genetic cause of ID is Down's syndrome, while fragile X syndrome is the most common inherited cause. In the majority of cases, however, causal factors are thought to be multifactorial, thus influenced by multiple genetic and environmental factors. Further types of genetic disorders are chromosomal and single gene disorders.

This chapter aims to offer basic knowledge of the complex world of genetic medicine and focuses on specific genetic disorders linked to ID. It will explain the implementation of diagnostics in clinical practice in order to improve patient's and clinician's knowledge of the causes of genetic syndromes as well as possible therapies.

Fundamentals of genetics

Due to advances in genetics and molecular medicine, our knowledge about the role of genetic disorders in people with ID is rapidly growing. There has been a clinical focus on diagnosing possible specific genetic disorders as these advances are likely to help the development of better targeted interventions and possible therapies impacting on mortality, morbidity and quality of life. New diagnostics will allow screening of large numbers of people with ID in the future (Muir, 2000).

DNA (or deoxyribonucleic acid) is a molecule present in the nucleus of each cell in the human body. DNA can be thought of as an 'instruction manual', needed to build and maintain the many different types of cells in the human body. A human's complete set of DNA or genetic material is called a genome. This unique combination of DNA is inherited from our parents. In comparison with other human beings, our DNA matches more than 99% and the remaining 1% is what diversifies people. Chromosomes are thread-like structures of protein and DNA is carried in tightly packed coils located in the nucleus of each cell.

Here are some basics:

- Each human has 23 pairs of chromosomes (therefore 46 chromosomes in total).
- These consist of two sex chromosomes and 44 autosomes (non-sex chromosomes).
- Men have an X and a Y sex chromosome.
- Women have two X sex chromosomes.

The most important function of chromosomes is to carry genes – the functional units of heredity. A chromosome supports an organism's ability to grow and function accordingly by ensuring that DNA is accurately copied and then distributed. Old cells must constantly be replaced by new cells via cell division. During this process it is essential that DNA remains intact and is evenly distributed among cells. A gene is a functional unit of DNA that has a specific 'task' to produce proteins responsible for characteristics of the human body, for instance eye colour. Every person has two copies of each gene, one inherited from each parent. Each cell contains approximately 25,000 to 35,000 genes, and each gene has a specific position on the chromosome.

Mutations: changes in DNA

During cell divisions, errors can occur causing changes to a person's DNA, for instance changes in the number or structure of chromosomes in new cells. Especially in reproductive cells, this may lead to disorders causing cognitive, physical and/or mental health problems. These changes are called mutations and can be described as permanent alterations in the DNA sequence. Mutations can differ in size and can be limited to a part of a gene or a part of a chromosome, or they might affect multiple genes. Research has identified more and more genes and mutations as well as abnormal numbers in chromosomes that can explain specific symptoms or syndromes.

- **Hereditary mutations** are inherited from a parent and are present in almost every cell in the person's body throughout their entire life. These mutations are present in reproductive or germline cells (sperm and egg cells) and are therefore hereditary mutations.
- **Acquired mutations** occur at some time in a person's life and are present in only certain cells. Causes can be environmental, such as sunburn for example, or they can occur if there is a cell division error. These mutations are present in 'somatic' or non-germline cells and can not therefore be inherited.

■ ***De novo* mutations** are mutations that occur just after fertilisation, or only in egg or sperm cells, and may explain how a genetic abnormality can affect all the body cells of a child with no family history of the disorder.

Key terms

Genotype. The genotype is the set of individual's genes, that is, their full hereditary profile.

Phenotype. The phenotype is the set of an individual's actual observable characteristics. A phenotype is influenced by both genotype and environment.

Heritability. Heritability is the proportion of phenotypic variation that can be attributed to inherited genetic factors rather than environmental factors.

Behavioural phenotypes. The behavioural phenotype is the characteristic pattern of social, linguistic, cognitive and motor behaviours consistently associated with a particular genetic disorder. There is a relationship between ID and behavioural difficulties as, for instance, self-injurious behaviours and agitation. Certain behaviours are more common in people with ID than in the general population. These behaviours can be prominent in certain behavioural phenotypes of genetic disorders and can be caused by biological mechanisms, or, if a person with ID has communication problems, in the way they show pain or distress.

Furthermore, gender differences can also determine the level of ID and symptoms. For instance, because females have two X-chromosomes, those with fragile X syndrome have a milder phenotypic expression of the genetic disorder and less severe ID than males. The cause of mortality and morbidity in genetic syndromes in which behavioural phenotypes occur is often complex and some phenotypes have a progressive nature. Clinical advances in understanding behavioural phenotypes can help to find specific therapeutic interventions, improving the quality of life of people with ID as well as mortality and morbidity (O'Brien, 2006).

Genetic disorders

Genetic disorders are commonly subdivided into the following groups:

Chromosomal disorders are caused by changes related to specific chromosomes, for instance deletions, duplications, inversions and translocations. This can subsequently lead to the development of conditions like Down's syndrome in which an individual has an extra copy of chromosome 21.

Monogenetic (or single gene) disorders are caused by a mutation in one single gene. This can occur on one or both copies of the gene on either the sex chromosomes (X or Y linked) or on the autosomal chromosomes. Inheritance of these disorders follows the Mendelian laws of inheritance, as further explained below.

Multifactorial disorders are caused by variations in multiple genes, often in combination with the influence of environmental factors, such as in schizophrenia, obesity and Alzheimer's disease. Most genetic disorders are multifactorial. These disorders do not follow the Mendelian inheritance patterns, but instead 'multifactorial inheritance', as further explained below.

Inheritance

Inherited disorders can 'run in families' as they can be inherited from a person's parents, for instance. There are different kinds of inheritance patterns:

Mendelian inheritance:

- Also named simple inheritance, which follows Mendelian laws of inheritance and is well studied.
- Disorder develops as a consequence of a gene variation.
- A trait can be either dominant or recessive, as for instance with eye colour: brown eyes are dominant over blue eyes. If someone inherits one brown-eye gene and one blue-eye gene they will have brown eyes as this is dominant gene and requires just one gene to be inherited. The blue eye gene is recessive in this case and you would need two copies to inherit blue eyes.
- If someone inherits one faulty recessive gene they can be 'carriers' of a disorder.
- Occurs in monogenetic or single gene disorders.

There are five basic patterns of inheritance for single-gene diseases:

Autosomal dominant inheritance: A child inherits the disorder if they receive one faulty gene located on an autosomal chromosome from a parent. There is a 50% chance they will inherit the illness if one parent has the mutation, and a 100% chance if both have the faulty gene.

Autosomal recessive: A child inherits the disorder only if both parents are carriers of the faulty gene located on an autosomal chromosome. They have 25% chance of inheriting the condition and a 50% chance to become a carrier of the illness.

X-chromosome linked dominant: Only one copy of the faulty gene situated on the X-chromosome is sufficient to cause the disorder when inherited from a parent who has the disorder. This is less common than X-linked recessive inheritance.

X-chromosome linked recessive: Both copies of the faulty gene are required to cause the disorder, meaning that both parents have to be carriers. A girl inherits an X-chromosome from her mother and one from her father, and a boy inherits just one X-chromosome – from his mother. As girls have two copies they are often less affected by the disorder than boys, who have only one copy.

Mitochondrial or maternal inheritance: Genes in the mitochondria (part of human cell that generates power) are inherited by a child from its mother. Faulty genes can cause illness.

Multifactorial inheritance: This is a complex pattern of inheritance where a disorder develops as a consequence of genetic variations in multiple genes in combination with environmental factors, such as lifestyle choices. Specific causes are difficult to identify and focused treatment therefore proves complicated. Multifactorial disorders do often appear to cluster in families, however there is no straightforward pattern of inheritance, as in Mendelian inheritance. A person's risk of inheriting or passing on these disorders is therefore difficult to determine.

Examples of genetic disorders seen in people with ID

Chromosomal disorders

Down's syndrome

Down's syndrome is the most common genetic cause of ID.

- Cause: extra genetic material in chromosome 21 (or trisomy 21)

- Frequency: estimated incidence between 1 in 1,000-1,100 live births worldwide.

- Inheritance: most cases not inherited, although there is a possibility of inheritance of translocation on chromosome 21 from an unaffected parent.

Characteristic features:

- Flat occiput and a flattened facial appearance.
- Low-set, small, and dysplastic ears.
- Epicanthal folds.
- Flat nasal bridge.
- Small nose and small mouth.
- Protruding tongue.
- Short neck.

People with Down's syndrome have an increased risk of the following physical health conditions:

- Hypothyroidism.
- Obstructive sleep apnea syndrome.
- Leukaemia.
- Hearing and vision problems.
- Alzheimer's disease.

Behavioural phenotype divided in areas:
Social:

- Cheerful demeanour.

Cognitive:

- Mild to severe ID.
- Long-term memory difficulties.

Linguistic:

- Language delays, specific difficulties with syntax.
- Relative strength in receptive compared to expressive language.
- Hearing difficulties also negatively impact upon language development.

Motor:

- Hypotonia impacting on motor development.
- Specific motor impairments over fine and gross motor skills reported, such as in balance and flexibility.

Psychopathology:

- Increased risk of hyperactivity, impulsivity and inattentive behaviours.

- Increased risk of depressive and anxiety disorders.

- Increased risk of autism spectrum disorders (but the majority have no problems in reciprocal social interaction).

- Repetitive and obsessive-compulsive behaviours.

- Oppositional behaviours.

- Sleep disorders.

Cri du chat syndrome

This is a rare genetic disorder, but one of the most common syndromes caused by chromosomal deletion. Cri du chat is a non-progressive syndrome.

- Caused by: a deletion on chromosome 5.

- Frequency: incidence between 1 in 15,000-50,000 live-births worldwide.

- Inheritance: most cases not inherited, although 10% inherit a translocation on chromosome 5 from an unaffected parent.

Characteristic features:

- Widely set eyes.

- Small jaw.

- Rounded face.

- Microcephaly.

- Low birth weight.

- Short stature.

- High-pitched cry, which is often described as sounding like a cat.

People with Cri du chat syndrome have an increased risk of gastroesophageal and respiratory problems.

Behavioural phenotype divided in areas:
Social:

- Hypersensitivity to noise.

Cognitive:

- Moderate to severe ID.

Linguistic:

■ Delayed speech and language development, and some never develop spoken language.

■ Receptive language is better than their expressive language.

■ Echolalia.

Motor:

■ Delay in the acquisition of skills requiring mental and muscular activities such head control, sitting up and walking.

■ Repetitive, stereotyped movements, specifically handwringing.

■ Initial hypotonia at birth and hypertonia later in life.

Psychopathology:

■ Agitation.

■ Hyperactivity.

■ Self-injurious behaviours.

■ Obsessional attachment to objects.

Prader-Willi syndrome

■ Caused by: a microdeletion on the paternal arm of Chromosome 15.

■ Frequency: incidence of 1 in 10,000-30,000 people worldwide.

■ Inheritance: it is very rare to be inherited in families and is often a *de novo* mutation occurring at formation of reproductive cells.

Characteristic features:

■ Severe hypotonia.

■ Feeding difficulties.

■ Growth restrictions.

■ Short stature.

■ Narrow forehead.

■ Almond shaped eyes.

■ Triangular mouth.

People with Prader-Willi syndrome have an increased risk of the following physical health conditions:

■ Hypogonadism causing underdeveloped genitals.

■ Delayed puberty.

■ High risk of infertility.

■ Diabetes mellitus type 2.

■ Osteoporosis.

■ Hypothyroidism.

Behavioural phenotype divided in areas:
Social:
■ Possibility of a range of autistic symptoms.

Cognitive:
■ Intellectual disability, often mild to moderate.

Linguistic:
■ Delayed speech development.

Motor:
■ Delayed motor development.

Psychopathology:
■ Insatiable appetite leading to hyperphagia (overeating) and obesity from childhood.

■ Obsessive-compulsive characteristics and self-injurious behaviours like skin picking.

■ Behavioural outbursts, such as temper tantrums.

■ Sleep problems including reduced REM sleep and obstructive apnea.

■ Increased risk of paranoid psychosis.

■ Increased risk of anxiety and depression.

Angelman syndrome

Angelman syndrome is also named 'happy puppet syndrome', and it is non-progressive.

- Caused by: microdeletion on arm of maternally inherited chromosome 15 (70%).
- Frequency: estimated 1 in 12,000 to 20,000 people worldwide.
- Inheritance: rarely inherited, mostly *de novo* mutations.

Characteristic features:

- Feeding difficulties and severe hypotonia in infancy.
- Delayed head circumference growth resulting in microcephaly (not from birth).
- Hypopigmentation – fair hair and skin colour.
- Swallowing disorders
- Coarse facial features: wide mouth and widely spaced teeth.

People with Angelman syndrome have an increased risk of epileptic seizures.

Behavioural phenotype divided in areas:
Social:

- Happy.
- Excitable demeanour with frequent smiling and at times socially inappropriate laughter.

Cognitive:

- ID, often severe to profound.

Linguistic:

- Severe speech impairment, lack of speech is characteristic.

Motor:

- Movement and balance disorders, specifically hand-flapping movements.

Psychopathology:

- Hyperactivity, a short attention span.
- Common to have fascination with water.
- Sleeping difficulties.

Velocardiofacial syndrome (or 22q11 deletion) syndrome

- Caused by: deletion in chromosome 22 (exactly on location 22q11).

- Frequency: estimated 1 in 4,000 newborns worldwide, often underdiagnosed.

- Inheritance pattern: autosomal dominant inheritance, although most cases are *de novo* mutations.

There is a variety in symptoms and the severity of the syndrome, even within families.

Characteristic features:
- Distinct facial features: recessed jaw, tubular nose, flat cheeks, long upper jaw, nasal sounding speech secondary to cleft palate.

- Cleft palate.

- Microcephaly.

People with velocardiofacial syndrome have an increased risk of the following physical health conditions:
- Congenital heart disease.

- Absent or underdeveloped thymus causing immune system dysfunction.

- Hearing loss.

- Hypocalcemia.

Behavioural phenotype divided in areas:
Social:
- Withdrawn, anxious and shy personality.

Cognitive:
- ID, often mild.

Linguistic:
- Hypernasal speech.

- Language delays.

Motor:
- Hypotonia.

- Gross-developmental delay and co-ordination and balance problems.

Psychopathology:

- Increased risk of developing psychiatric disorders such as schizophrenia, mood and anxiety disorders.

- Autistic spectrum disorder (ASD) and ADHD.

Monogenetic/single gene disorders

Fragile X syndrome

- Caused by: mutation on the FMR1 gene, known as the CGG triplet repeat, a 'fragile' site on the X-chromosome.

- Frequency: 1 in 3,600 males and 1 in 4,000 to 6,000 females with full mutation worldwide.

- Inheritance: X-linked dominant pattern.

Fragile X syndrome is the most common cause of inherited ID. The severity of symptoms varies considerably among patients depending on the number of 'repeats' and sexes. Men are more affected than women.

Characteristic features:

- Long and narrow face, large ears, a prominent jaw and forehead.

- Unusually flexible fingers, flat feet.

- In males, enlarged testicles (macro-orchidism) after puberty.

People with Fragile X syndrome have an increased risk of the following physical health conditions:

- Epilepsy (15% males versus 5% females).

- Scoliosis.

- Gastrointestinal disorders.

Behavioural phenotype divided in areas:
The behavioural phenotype in females is a mild variant of that seen in males, with few autistic features and some social anxiety.

Social:

■ Risk of atypical ASD.

■ Social anxiety.

Cognitive:

■ Mild to moderate ID.

Linguistic:

■ Delayed language development, perseveration and echolalia.

Motor:

■ Developmental motor delay related to hypotonia.

Psychopathology:

■ 1/3 of people with Fragile X syndrome develop autism spectrum disorders.

■ Risk of developing ADHD, specifically with hyperactivity.

■ Risk of developing anxiety and mood disorders.

■ Expression of repetitive behaviours.

Multifactorial disorders

Autism is a complex neurodevelopmental disorder with difficulties in three core areas – social interaction and communication – portraying rigid and repetitive behaviours, collectively referred to as autism spectrum disorders (ASDs). The genetics of autism has been studied extensively in recent years. Autism appears to have a high heritability. Recent advances in our understanding of the genetics of autism shows that there appears to be a range in the forms of genetic susceptibility, from a small percentage (5%) of chromosomal disorders such as Down's syndrome, and 5% of single gene disorders such as fragile X syndrome, to more complex interaction of multiple genes and the environment estimated at between 80-85%. Additionally, 10% of cases appear to have *de novo* mutations.

Rutter (2005) stated that ASDs are multifactorial disorders caused by multiple genes and environmental factors. However, Miles (2011) described family studies indicating that autism does not fit the multifactorial model. There therefore appears to be a lack of consensus, proving just how complex ASD is.

Further examples of multifactorial disorders are schizophrenia, obesity and diabetes mellitus.

Genetic testing

Genetic testing is medical testing to explore or exclude genetic disorders. This is often done by taking a blood sample or, in the case of an unborn baby, amniotic fluid or chorionic villus cells (all containing the patient's DNA).

Genetic testing can be a way to determine:

- **Diagnosis:** if there is evidence someone has a specific suspected genetic disorder (prenatal and postpartum).
- **Cause:** if diagnosed with a genetic disorder, testing can find the specific genetic cause.
- **Risk:** if someone is at risk of developing a genetic disorder in the future.
- **Carrier/inheritance:** if someone is a carrier for a certain genetic disorder that can be inherited by their children.

There are several types of genetic tests:

- **Diagnostic genetic tests:** these are used to exclude or confirm a suspected specific genetic condition based on symptoms or features. These can be performed prenatally or later in life, but they are not yet available for all genetic disorders.
- **Carrier tests:** these are used to identify people who carry one mutated gene that, when present in two copies of the gene, causes a genetic disorder. Specifically, these tests can be useful for people who have a family history of a genetic disorder, or for people from certain ethnic groups who are aware of specific genetic disorders, in order to inform them of the potential risk of their child developing a genetic condition.
- **Pre-symptomatic tests:** this is a more controversial type of test as there are no symptoms of a specific disease at the time of testing. This could identify possible genetic mutations that could lead to genetic disorders in the future, often based on a positive family history for genetic conditions such as Huntington disease. Testing could inform someone about their life planning, especially reproductive planning, and help them make decisions about medical treatment options.

- **Prenatal testing:** When there is a family history of a genetic condition, there is an abnormal scan result or increased risk identified from screening test results during pregnancy, then further prenatal tests can be advised, for instance amniocentesis or chorionic villus sampling. This could help parents prepare and decide upon a pregnancy. There is, however, an approximate 1% risk of miscarriage from both procedures.

- **New-born bloodspot test:** Specific screening for new-born babies to identify treatable genetic conditions and so be able to start early treatment, which may reduce the severity of the condition. Examples include sickle cell disease, phenylketonuria and congenital hypothyroidism.

The decision whether or not to have a genetic test can be difficult and therefore genetic counselling by health care professionals is strongly advised in order to educate the patient or their family about possible risks and benefits.

Case study: Peter

Peter is a 42-year-old man with moderate ID who is diagnosed with Down's syndrome. He lives in a residential project that he reports to enjoy, but presented to the psychiatrist's clinic with a number of issues.

He described that his mood had deteriorated as well as his sleep. His support workers reported that Peter often preferred to sleep in a chair, however this would be in the living room where the other residents and the television would further interrupt his sleep. The support workers said that they have tried everything to motivate Peter to sleep in his bedroom and asked for advice.

While discussing the issue with Peter he reported that he could not sleep in his room as his girlfriend would tell him he snored. He also reported having nightmares sometimes and then waking up suddenly. Regarding his preference for sleeping in a chair, he could not elaborate.

With Peter's permission, he was referred to a local sleep clinic to explore the possibility of obstructive sleep apnoea syndrome (OSAS) based on his current presentation of Down's syndrome.

Peter was invited for a polysomnogram (sleep recording) and further observations in the sleep clinic, which he agreed to. He was supported by his support workers and, based on the results, he was diagnosed with OSAS and treatment options were explored with him and his GP.

Analysis

People with Down's syndrome have been found to have a high risk of obstructive sleep apnoea (incidence of 50-100%), but this is often missed, probably due to underreporting and lack of professionals' knowledge about people with Down's syndrome. The increased risk of OSAS is believed to be due to anatomical abnormalities in the palate and tongue, in combination with generalised hypotonia of the muscles, predisposition to obesity, and an immature immune system causing a higher risk of airway infections and gastro-oesophageal reflux disease.

OSAS presents with symptoms of excessive daytime drowsiness, snoring, interrupted breathing/sensation of choking during sleep, morning headaches, waking with dry mouth and sore throat. It can influence someone's physical and mental state significantly. People suffering from OSAS can develop pulmonary hypertension causing cardiac problems, fail to thrive as children, and experience mood disorders and cognitive functioning and behavioural difficulties. This case study thus gives an example of knowing the associations of genetic disorders in people with ID.

Case study: Sophie

Sophie is a 24-year-old woman with mild ID who lives with her mother. Her mother reports that Sophie was 'hearing things' and had developed 'bizarre' behaviour. Her mother said that they had been living next to the same neighbours for years and that they were a very nice family. However, Sophie has all of a sudden begun to dislike them and 'scream at them'. Her mother described Sophie talking to the neighbours while sitting in her bedroom. Sophie has told her mother she can hear them through the walls (which her mother cannot) and she has developed the belief they are trying to kill Sophie and her mother, which is understandably very distressing to Sophie.

On exploring this with Sophie, she was not keen to discuss it, but reported hearing the neighbours through the walls and wanting them to stop as it scares her. She explained she knows they want to harm her and her mother, but does not know why. She asked to move to a new flat to get away from the neighbours. She denied anything has happened to trigger this, but appeared fixed on the idea that the neighbours want to hurt them as she had 'heard them say this'. On reviewing her sleep, Sophie's mother explained that Sophie has reversed day-night and has been afraid of turning on the TV or radio as she believes the neighbours can 'read her mind' through them. She has not tried to harm herself, her mother, or the neighbours, but she has been so terrified of the neighbours she has ran into the street once while passing them.

Sophie's mother explained that her daughter has had these symptoms in the past however cannot remember if she received treatment as she was taking multiple medications at the time for physical health problems. On exploring what these physical health problems were, it was revealed that Sophie had a heart problem, suffered occasional seizures and had 'joint problems' while growing up. Sophie presented with wide set eyes and a long face. There appears to be no clear trigger for this behaviour and a family history is denied by mother.

Analysis

It appeared that Sophie had developed psychotic symptoms; auditory hallucinations and paranoid delusional ideas as well as thought broadcasting and sleep cycle reversal. From the collateral history there appeared to be no clear trigger and no family history, but a possible past history. Further assessment was needed. After this clinic appointment however, she presented with an acute psychotic episode, possibly as part of a schizophrenia diagnosis. (Certain syndromes cause an increased risk of psychosis and even schizophrenia. Among these is 22q11 syndrome or DiGeorge syndrome.)

On reviewing her history, Sophie has a congenital heart condition, possible rheumatoid symptoms and seizures, as well as certain facial features. The psychosis was treated successfully with antipsychotic medication and Sophie and her mother received support and specific genetic counselling to discuss genetic testing exploring/excluding DiGeorge syndrome. Sophie and her mother shared that they wanted to postpone this process at present, however acknowledged that the symptoms for DiGeorge syndrome might match with Sophie's current and past presentation. Schizophrenia, as part of DiGeorge syndrome, is a differential diagnosis that clinicians should keep in mind in this case, which could help explore optimal treatment options.

Key learning points

- A basic knowledge of genetic medicine and different types of genetic disorders.

- The importance of the clinical understanding of behavioural phenotypes and physical health complications linked to specific genetic disorders, which, with advances in therapeutic interventions, can increase quality of life and life expectancy for individuals with behavioural phenotypes.

■ The importance of monitoring the mental health of affected individuals throughout adulthood, owing to the increased likelihood of developing psychiatric disorders.

■ The importance of genetic counselling by health care professionals to provide information to the patient and their family so they can make informed decisions regarding the risks and benefits of genetic testing.

References

McLaren J & Bryson S (1987) Review of recent epidemiological studies of mental retardation: prevalence, associated disorders, and etiology. *American Journal of Mental Retardation* **92** (3) 243–254.

Miles J (2011) Autism spectrum disorder: a genetics review. *Genetics in Medicine* **13** (4) 278–294.

Muir (2000) Genetic advances and learning disability. 176 12–19.

O'Brien G (2006) Behavioural phenotypes: causes and clinical implications. *Advances in Psychiatric Therapy* **12** 338–348.

Rutter M (2005) Aetiology of autism: findings and questions. *Journal of Intellectual Disability Research* **49** 231–238.

Chapter 11: Neuropsychiatric disorders including epilepsy

By Rob Winterhalder

Summary

Patients with a variety of neurodevelopmental and neurological disorders are at risk of developing additional psychiatric or behavioural disorders. The relationship between these disorders is complex and can involve shared pathophysiology, genetic and epigenetic factors, iatrogenic side effects and psychosocial factors. This chapter focuses on the presentation, investigation and management of neurodevelopmental and neurological conditions, which are strongly associated with comorbid psychiatric disorders.

Introduction

It is important to realise that the classic symptoms seen in functional psychiatric disorders such as anxiety, depression, hallucinations, delusions etc, can also occur in medical conditions which affect the brain. Psychiatric disorders have traditionally been divided into organic and functional disorders, although this distinction is, up to a point, artificial.

Organic cerebral disorders are caused by recognisable medical conditions which affect the structure and/or functioning of the brain – when they present with psychiatric symptoms or syndromes, they are referred to as neuropsychiatric disorders. Functional psychiatric disorders, such as schizophrenia, obsessive compulsive disorder, bipolar affective disorder etc, are not caused by recognisable medical conditions, although undoubtedly there is a strong biological component, such as genetic factors, a history of obstetric or developmental problems etc, and it is possible to demonstrate subtle abnormalities on structural and functional neuroimaging. However, they are considered 'functional', as they are not due to overt, gross brain pathology or dysfunction. See Box 1 for causes of neuropsychiatric disorders. Dementias are reviewed in chapter 4.

Box 1: Causes of neuropsychiatric disorders

- Parkinson's disease.
- Multiple Sclerosis.
- Cerebrovascular accident (CVA).
- Traumatic brain injury.
- Epilepsy.
- Brain tumours.
- Metabolic disorders.
- Autoimmune disorders
- Neuroendocrine disorders
- Dementia e.g. Alzheimer's disease, lewy body disease, etc.
- Iatrogenic.
- Central nervous system infections.
- Delirium – multiple causes.

Clinical presentation

The underlying medical condition causing a neuropsychiatric condition may be acute or chronic, and affect a localised area of the brain or be widespread. Acute presentations affecting most of the brain are of sudden onset over hours or days, with symptoms of disorientation, impaired consciousness, hallucinations etc, as seen in delirium. Chronic, widespread presentations evolve over months and years, with short term memory loss, personality change, hallucinations etc, but in clear consciousness, as seen in dementia.

Localised lesions on the other hand, such as a brain abscess, tumour or cerebrovascular accident (CVA) – or 'stroke' – give rise to signs and/or symptoms that reflect the area of the brain affected, for example personality change with frontal lobe lesions and memory deficits in temporal lobe damage. Depending on the nature of the responsible medical condition, the resulting brain damage and/or dysfunction may be temporary and reversible, or permanent.

Neuropsychiatric syndromes present, by definition, with psychiatric symptoms, and are usually accompanied with cognitive impairments and neurological signs/symptoms, either early on in the presentation or developing over time.

The main neuropsychiatric symptoms seen in clinical practice are anxiety, apathy, depression, hallucinations, delusions, behavioural problems, personality change, delirium and cognitive impairment (Miyoshi *et al*, 2015). They can be accompanied by neuropsychological symptoms affecting language, cognition and behaviour, as well as neurological signs affecting motor and sensory function, reflexes, co-ordination etc.

Assessment and investigations

As in other branches of medicine, an accurate history is of the utmost importance in making the correct diagnosis. Patients with ID are by definition cognitively impaired, and also often have impaired communication, which makes it difficult for them to describe their subjective experiences. Carers therefore have a vital role in helping provide some, or all, of the history – it is very important to give the clinician accurate timescales regarding, for example, medication changes, new or worsening symptoms etc.

The clinician will then complete a full physical examination concentrating mainly, but not exclusively, on the neurological and cardiac systems. Finally, investigations will be arranged ranging from blood tests, urine analysis and chest X-rays, to electroencephalography (EEG) and neuroimaging.

Neuropsychiatric disorders

The following conditions have been chosen either because of their association with ID, as with seizure disorders (epilepsy), or because they are sufficiently common in the general population that they are also likely to be encountered in individuals with ID, such as Parkinson's disease and acute confusional state (delirium). Tourette's syndrome, a neurodevelopmental disorder, has also been included as it can sometimes be confused with behaviours and movements seen in autism.

Epilepsy

Epilepsy is the recurrent tendency to have seizures. An epileptic seizure is the observable and reportable clinical symptoms due to a sudden paroxysmal, synchronous and repetitive discharge of cerebral neurones. The symptoms will depend on where the discharge started, how far it has spread and, to some extent, how long it went on for. Epileptic seizures in an individual tend to be stereotyped and are usually brief.

In broad terms, there are two main types of seizure that are distinguished by where the changes in brain activity begin: 'generalised' seizures involve the whole brain from the beginning (and consciousness is therefore lost), while 'focal' seizures start in just one area of the brain, but may then spread.

Generalised seizures

Generalised seizures are further divided into:

Absence seizures: sudden onset; last a few seconds; patient appears blank, unresponsive and stares; body posture is retained; rapid recovery. In atypical seizures, eyelids may flutter and the head nod.

Tonic-clonic seizures: limbs stiffen, patient may cry out, fall (tonic phase); followed by rapid, rhythmical jerking of limbs and head, which then slows down and stops (clonic phase). Breathing may be laboured, face becomes blue, tongue or cheek may be bitten. Possible incontinence. Headache and sleep often follow. May last up to a few minutes.

Tonic seizures: limbs stiffen, patient usually falls backwards; injuries to the back of the head are common. Brief.

Atonic seizures: sudden loss of muscle tone, patient usually falls forward; facial injuries are common. Quick recovery. Very brief.

Myoclonic seizure: a single sudden very brief jerk, usually of the arms and upper body. If there is more than one jerk, they are not rhythmical. Often occur upon waking up. Patient may fall if severe.

Focal seizures

Focal seizures are further divided into 'simple', where consciousness is preserved, and 'complex', where consciousness is impaired. Consciousness involves both full responsiveness to stimuli and recall of the events. The symptoms of a focal seizure depend on the region of the brain where the discharge started. Seizures originating from the temporal lobes can present with a sudden intense fear, a rising sensation in the stomach, a strange taste or smell, staring, lip smacking, automatic undressing, picking at clothes etc. Frontal lobe seizures, which often arise during sleep, may present with head or eye version to one side, tonic or clonic movements of a part, or parts, of the body including adopting a 'fencing' posture, repeated movements such as rocking, pedaling or pelvic thrusting, and dysphasia.

If the neuronal discharge spreads to include both cerebral hemispheres, the seizure develops into a tonic-clonic seizure (secondary generalisation).

Any seizure that lasts 30 minutes or longer, or intermittent seizures that last 30 minutes or longer without the patient recovering between each seizure constitutes 'status epilepticus'. Convulsive (e.g. tonic-clonic) status epilepticus is a medical emergency.

The International League Against Epilepsy (ILAE) has recently updated the classification of epileptic seizures – this includes a review of seizure terminology and additional 'new' seizure types such as myoclonic-atonic, myoclonic absences etc. Fisher (2017) gives more detailed descriptions of the various seizure types.

Box 2: Aetiology of epilepsy

- Genetic causes:
  - Metabolic disorders e.g. phenylketonuria.
  - Structural e.g. tuberous sclerosis.
  - Some primary generalised epilepsies.
  - Mitochondrial disorders.
- Developmental disorders e.g. neuronal migration defects.
- Intrauterine injury/anoxia.
- Perinatal injury/anoxia.
- Infection e.g. encephalitis, meningitis.
- Vascular.
- Tumour.
- Dementia.
- Metabolic e.g. hypoglycaemia.
- Toxic e.g. alcohol.
- Autoimmune disorders.
- Brain trauma.

Epilepsy and intellectual disability

In ID, the prevalence of epilepsy increases in parallel with the degree of ID, i.e. up to 50% in profound ID. Up to 30% of individuals with autistic spectrum disorder develop epilepsy, usually by the age of 10 years. The risk of developing epilepsy is greater if ID is present, rising from 5–10% in Asperger's Syndrome to 30% in classic autism. There is a complex relationship between epilepsy, autism and ID in tuberous sclerosis – autism only occurs when temporal lobe tubers are present and when there is epileptic activity in the temporal lobe. The development of autism often correlates with the onset or worsening of epilepsy.

There are many other ID syndromes that are associated with a particularly high risk of epilepsy. Rett's syndrome, mainly due to a mutation of the MECP2 gene on the X chromosome, is usually seen in girls and associated with epilepsy in 90% of cases. In Down's syndrome, there are three heightened periods of onset: infancy – infantile spasms; 3rd decade – tonic clonic seizures and 4th/5th decade – myoclonic seizures associated with the onset of dementia.

Epilepsy and psychiatric disorder

Most studies, but not all, have demonstrated higher rates of affective and psychotic disorders in patients with ID and epilepsy, compared to the general population. The literature remains unclear on whether the level of IQ in patients with epilepsy is a protective or risk factor for developing a severe psychiatric disorder (Winterhalder & Ring, 2014).

It is important to distinguish between transient psychiatric symptoms, occurring in isolation and of relatively short duration – for example, seconds or minutes – and sustained periods of psychiatric illness lasting days, weeks or months. Traditionally, psychopathological states occurring in epilepsy have been classified based on the timing of the psychopathology in relation to the epileptic seizure (Betts, 1998).

Box 3: Terminology: seizure stages and psychopathology

Prodromal: before the seizure

Ictal: during the seizure – 'aura' (focal seizure); non-convulsive status (absence or partial)

Post-ictal: after the seizure

Inter-ictal: unrelated to the seizure; changes in seizure frequency (including forced normalisation)

(Prodromal, ictal and post-ictal are also referred to as 'peri-ictal')

There is a complex relationship between psychiatric medication and antiepileptic drugs (AEDs). AEDs may alter the drug levels of some psychotropic drugs, while some psychiatric drugs can affect the levels of AEDs. This can lead either to toxicity or a reduced therapeutic effect with breakthrough seizures or psychopathology. AEDs also cause a variety of side-effects, including psychiatric and cognitive symptoms; in turn, most types of psychotropic medication can lower the seizure threshold.

Prodromal phase

The prodromal phase may last from a few minutes to several days and culminates in a seizure. On recovery, the prodromal symptoms are no longer present. Symptoms include changes of mood with withdrawal, irritability disinhibition, agitation etc. occurring in clear consciousness.

Ictal episodes

'Auras', which are in fact focal seizures, tend to last from a few seconds to a few minutes and terminate (or generalise e.g. to tonic-clonic convulsions with loss of consciousness). The content of the aura depends on the location of the focus, as mentioned above, and can include intense fear or lowering of mood, hallucinations in various modalities – auditory, gustatory, etc.

'Automatisms' involve states of clouded consciousness, in which posture and muscle tone is retained and simple or complex movements are performed without the patient being aware, such as repeated dressing and undressing.

'Twilight states' also result in impaired consciousness, but instead of motor and behavioural manifestations, the patient has abnormal subjective experiences, such as peculiar emotions and memories. Twilight states are usually due to non-convulsive, complex focal status, although occasionally they may be post-ictal.

'Fugues' are very uncommon, but involve a less severe impairment of consciousness, and can last hours or days during which the patient may wander away while appearing 'alert and aware', but will have no recollection afterwards of the event.

While tonic-clonic status epilepticus is a medical emergency, there are other types of status epilepticus that are non-convulsive, for example resulting from prolonged absence or partial seizures. These episodes of status can last hours or days, and are usually associated with impaired consciousness, although this may be subtle. The patient may present with confusion, irritability, affective change, hallucinations or delusions.

Post-ictal episodes

Post-ictal depressive symptoms are fairly common but short-lived, but there is often confusion. 'Twilight states' lasting hours or even days are often accompanied by restlessness, and the patient may even react violently to trivial stimuli.

Post-ictal automatisms occur when recovery of full consciousness lags behind resumption of motor activity after a seizure and involves repetitive, stereotyped behaviours such as pulling at clothes, buttons etc. Rarely, and usually in patients with gross brain damage, dangerously violent behaviour lasting several minutes may occur (the epileptic furore).

Post-ictal paranoid and/or hallucinatory states may occur, often following a lucid period of several days after the seizure. It is not yet known whether or not impaired consciousness needs to be present for these symptoms, but regardless, this state tends to subside over several days (occasionally weeks).

Inter-ictal episodes

Psychosis: Risk factors in patients with epilepsy for developing an inter-ictal psychosis include a family history of psychosis, early onset of epilepsy, complex partial seizures – especially those originating from the temporal lobe – and borderline intellectual functioning. These disorders arise independently of a seizure and can become chronic, lasting years. They occur in clear consciousness and consist of paranoid delusions and hallucinations similar to those seen in schizophrenia. These disorders differ from schizophrenia in that personality is preserved, there are no negative symptoms, especially flattening of affect, catatonic symptoms are absent, and the course tends to be more benign and variable.

Affective and anxiety disorders: There is no convincing evidence for a significant increased risk of bipolar affective disorder, but major depressive disorder is probably under-recognised and under-treated. Inter-ictal anxiety is, not unsurprisingly, frequent, but actual anxiety disorders are fairly uncommon.

Dementia: Dementia is associated with epilepsy and may be more common in those with significant ID. Dementia itself can cause epilepsy due to the underlying progressive neurodegenerative process. People with severe brain damage, including those with ID, are more likely to have epilepsy and dement earlier, presumably due to having less 'cognitive reserve'. Finally, patients with severe epilepsy may experience on-going cognitive decline, due to the uncontrolled seizure activity.

Changes in seizure frequency: A rapid increase in seizure frequency, particularly with hardly any time for recovery between each seizure, can lead to a clinical picture resembling delirium. Interestingly, an abrupt reduction or complete cessation of seizures, for example following the introduction of a new antiepileptic drug (AED) or epilepsy surgery, may lead to the emergence of a condition called 'forced normalisation' lasting days or weeks, during which the patient may experience severe depression or psychosis. The term originates from the fact that the seizures have been 'forcibly suppressed', and the EEG has 'normalised'.

Non-epileptic seizures

Seizures are not always due to epilepsy – they can, for example, be due to hypoglycaemia or heart conditions. Or they may be due to psychological causes – several terms describe this type of seizure – 'psychogenic', 'dissociative' and 'non-epileptic attack disorder'. Prospective recording of events, including written descriptions, can be very helpful in reaching a diagnosis. Videotelemetry will usually confirm or refute the diagnosis.

Table 1: Differentiating epileptic from psychogenic seizures

Feature	Epileptic seizure	Psychogenic/ behavioural
Onset	Sudden	May be gradual
Retained consciousness in prolonged seizure	Very rare	Common
Pelvic thrusting	Rare	Common
Flailing and thrashing	Rare	Common
Asynchronous limb movement	Rare	Common
Rolling movements	Rare	Common
Movements waxing and waning	Rare	Common
Cyanosis	Common	Unusual
Tongue biting and other injury	Common	Less common
Stereotypical attacks	Usual	Uncommon
Duration	Seconds or minutes	Often many minutes
Gaze version	Rare	Common
Resistance to passive limb movements or eye opening	Unusual	Common
Prevention of hand falling on face	Unusual	Common
Induced by suggestion	Rarely	Often
Post-ictal drowsiness or confusion	Usual	Often absent

Factors associated with psychogenic seizures include adult onset, bizarre and dramatic eye-witness descriptions, provocation by stressful events such as bereavement or recurrent hospitalisation, and they do not respond, or may even worsen, when treated with AEDs. They are more common in females, particularly if they have suffered a traumatic childhood including sexual abuse in particular. Patients often have a history of unexplained physical symptoms, deliberate self-harm, or co-morbid psychiatric disorder. Neurological examination is normal, as is the patient's EEG and neuro-imaging (any abnormalities do not explain the patient's presentation).

Case study: Epilepsy

A 25-year-old man with severe ID and epilepsy due to anoxia at birth had been seizure-free for five years on levetiracetam and carbamazepine. His family history was unremarkable apart from a history of mood disorder in his mother and sister. Staff noticed that at times he appeared lethargic and his concentration was poor. He was taken to the GP who arranged blood tests which revealed low sodium levels (which is associated with carbamazepine). The carbamazepine was withdrawn over three months and his sodium levels normalised. Initially he seemed to have more drive and ability to concentrate and he remained seizure free. He then started to become more withdrawn with loss of interest, tearfulness, reduced appetite and insomnia. He was diagnosed with clinical depression and responded well to an antidepressant (mirtazapine was chosen as it is less likely to cause low sodium levels compared to SSRIs) and individual psychological therapy.

Carbamazepine has both antiepileptic and mood stabilising properties. It had been treating or masking an undiagnosed mood disorder. Although SSRI antidepressants in general are not particularly epileptogenic, they too can lower sodium levels, and citalopram in particular may be slightly more epileptogenic than the other SSRIs.

Parkinson's disease

Parkinson's disease is classically a progressive neurological disorder caused by degeneration of dopaminergic neurones in the *substantia nigra*. It is characterised clinically by bradykinesia (slowness of movement), tremor, rigidity and postural instability. Non-motor symptoms can be even more distressing than the motor symptoms, and psychiatric disorders are commonly associated with this condition (Kummer & Teixeira, 2009).

The reasons for the increased risk of psychiatric disorder in Parkinson's disease are multifactorial. The onset of Parkinson's disease is in mid to late adult life – a time of increased susceptibility to depression and intellectual decline. The psychological sequelae of Parkinson's disease can be more distressing and disabling than their motor symptoms. Florid psychiatric conditions may also be due to the underlying disturbance in neuro-transmission.

Parkinson's disease is not the same as 'Parkinsonism', which is a term often used to describe a group of motor side-effects secondary to certain medications such as antipsychotics. The side-effects include tremor and rigidity etc., which are similar to those seen in Parkinson's disease but are usually bilateral from the beginning and reversible on discontinuing the offending drug.

Anxiety and affective disorders

Generalised anxiety, agitation, panic attacks and phobic disorders can occur in up to 40% of cases of Parkinson's disease. The prevalence of depression is also estimated to be about 40%. Symptoms include dysphoria, sadness, irritability, pessimism about the future and suicidal ideation. There tends to be no relationship between the degrees of depression or anxiety, for instance, and the duration or severity of motor disability.

While these psychiatric disorders are sometimes an understandable psychological response to having a severe, chronic and progressive disorder, they are considered to be often due to the underlying neurobiology of this degenerative disorder. Equally, while apathy is also common in Parkinson's disease, it tends to be a direct consequence of the pathophysiology of the disorder rather than a psychological/psychiatric state. Finally, these conditions can be secondary to treatment side-effects. For example, anticholinergic drugs such as procyclidine can cause anxiety states (and cognitive dysfunction including delirium).

Psychosis

Up to 30% of patients with Parkinson's disease will develop hallucinations, particularly visual, within the first five years after diagnosis. Patients may also develop delusions, and these psychotic symptoms are considered one of the most disabling and distressing symptoms of Parkinson's disease. While the association between psychosis and Parkinson's disease was recognised in the pre-levodopa era, psychotic symptoms are the most common psychiatric side-effect of anti-parkinsonian medication. Dopamine agonists are most likely to cause psychotic symptoms, followed by anticholinergic drugs, and then levodopa preparations. Therefore, where appropriate, the dopamine agonist should be reduced or withdrawn first, if the patient is on several anti-parkinsonian drugs. However, there is a risk of a deterioration in control of the motor symptoms. Unfortunately, with the exception of clozaril (and a new agent, pimavanserin), most antipsychotic drugs risk exacerbating the underlying motor disorder.

Dementia

Two thirds of Parkinson's patients show some cognitive impairment on average 3.5 years after diagnosis, while 10% will have developed dementia.

Impulse control disorders

These are seen particularly in patients taking dopamine agonists and other types of anti-parkinsonian medication. Behaviours include addictive gambling, binge eating or shopping, repetitive acts, purposeless behaviour and hyper-sexuality.

Sleep disturbance

Two thirds of people with Parkinson's disease have sleep disturbance, including excessive day time somnolence, fragmented nocturnal sleep, insomnia, hypersomnia, parasomnia and REM sleep behaviour disorder.

Case study: Parkinson's disease

A 56-year-old lady with moderate ID of unknown aetiology and with no significant past psychiatric history slowly developed a tremor at rest and a poor sleep pattern. Her family were unconcerned initially because they thought it was simply part of the 'ageing process'. Two years later, the tremor had worsened and she was experiencing balance problems with falls. She was referred to a neurologist who diagnosed Parkinson's disease and commenced her on levodopa. While her tremor improved, she started to behave out of character – screaming, appearing agitated and refusing to sleep in her bedroom. When taken into her room she would become scared and point to the corner and say, 'dog', as she moved back towards the door. She was diagnosed as having a drug-induced psychosis and the dose of levodopa was reduced. Her psychotic symptoms resolved.

Some drugs have a wide range of potential psychiatric side-effects. Levodopa may cause a confusional state and disorientation, anxiety and depression, hallucinations and delusions, insomnia and a dopamine dysregulation syndrome.

Tourette's syndrome

Tourette's syndrome (TS) is a complex developmental disorder of childhood onset, characterised by motor and vocal tics, which tend to improve in most patients during adulthood. Motor tics can consist of blinking, mouth twitching, shoulder shrugging, sudden head or arm movements etc. Vocal tics can include clearing of the throat, coughing, grunting, barking, shouting, sniffing or, infrequently, swearing. Tics can be simple or complex – a simple tic affects one or just a few parts of the body e.g. blinking the eyes or a grunt, whereas a complex tic involves many parts of the body or saying words e.g. jumping or swearing. There is a sensation of tingling or tension before a tic, and the movement makes the sensation disappear. Patients can make a conscious effort to supress the tic for a while, but at the cost of mounting tension – eventually the tic will break through, and the tension disappears.

TS is associated with ADHD (Kerbeshian & Burd, 1992). It is also associated with obsessive compulsive disorder and specific neuropsychological deficits, but there is no increased risk of ID (Burd *et al*, 2005). The precise cause of TS is unknown, but at least some cases are likely to be due to a genetic mutation, as the disorder often runs in families. This condition is thought to be linked to problems in the basal ganglia in the brain, which help regulate body movements.

The motor and vocal tics seen in TS can sometimes be mistaken for autism. It is important to remember that the individual with TS will not have impairment in social relationships, verbal/non-verbal communication, nor have a restricted repertoire of interests, as seen in autism. They are empathic and have an intact 'theory of mind'. The stereotypies seen in autism are not accompanied by mounting tension and patients do not voluntarily suppress the movements.

Acute confusional state (delirium)

Delirium is an organic brain syndrome characterised by a reversible, transient, impairment of cognitive function with impairment of consciousness, which is often worse in the early evening or at night. There are many causes of delirium – often there may be more than one condition present, particularly in very ill and/or elderly people.

In *hyperactive delirium* patients are over-aroused, restless, agitated and may be aggressive; *hypoactive delirium* is characterised by withdrawal and quiet, excessive sleep.

It is important to distinguish delirium from dementia and functional psychiatric disorders such as schizophrenia and depression, although these disorders may co-exist.

Box 4: Common causes of delirium

- Heart failure.
- Hypoxia due to severe respiratory disease.
- Acute Infection – pneumonia, urinary tract infections, meningitis, encephalitis, sepsis etc.
- Medication – anticholinergics, AEDs, lithium, digoxin, steroids etc.
- Endocrine disorders, e.g. diabetes mellitus, hypo/hyperthyroidism etc.
- Metabolic disorders, e.g. hyper/hypocalcaemia, hyponatremia etc.
- Dehydration.
- Vitamin deficiency – thiamine, vitamin B12 etc.
- Constipation (particularly in the elderly).
- Kidney failure.
- Liver failure.
- Alcohol or drug abuse, or withdrawal.
- Cerebrovascular disorders – haemorrhage or infarction.
- Trauma – head injury.

Symptoms include:

- impairment of consciousness
- reduced concentration and attention
- disorientation
- incoherent thought
- perplexity
- hallucinations – particularly visual
- motor disturbance
- delusional ideas – often of a fragmented persecutory nature
- mood – suspicion, fear, anxiety.

Case study: Delirium

A 64-year-old lady with mild ID, Down's syndrome, mid-stage dementia and morbid obesity, moved to a new service provider because of an increase in her care needs. At times she was oppositional and unco-operative, particularly regarding her personal care and fluid intake. Later, over a period of a few days, she became much more agitated, screaming and threatening staff who she thought were trying to poison her. Blood tests by the GP revealed only mild dehydration. Physical examination was difficult due to her limited co-operation and her obesity. Over the next 48 hours her sleep pattern became fragmented and she developed visual hallucinations – particularly in the evening she could see a clown in the corridor, which terrified her. On reviewing her case again, the GP and staff realised that she had not been opening her bowels sufficiently and an abdominal X-ray revealed severe constipation. Laxatives and a more rigorous approach to maintaining her hydration led to a full recovery.

Severe constipation can cause delirium, particularly in the elderly. In this case, a poor diet and dehydration led to constipation and ultimately delirium in a patient who was vulnerable due to her age and pre-existing dementia.

Management

The treatment of psychiatric disorders secondary to medical conditions often involves treating the underlying medical condition e.g. thyroxine replacement in a patient presenting with hypothyroidism and depression. However, sometimes the psychiatric disorder needs to be treated in its own right with appropriate psychiatric medication.

It is important to recognise that sometimes treatment of a psychiatric disorder may cause or aggravate various neurological conditions, for example several neuroleptics and antidepressants may worsen seizure control by lowering the seizure threshold. Equally, the medicines used to treat a medical condition may be the cause of an emergent psychiatric disorder, such as levodopa used to treat Parkinson's disease, which may cause depression or psychosis. Ideally the offending drug should be withdrawn or the dose reduced.

In the case of epilepsy-related psychiatric conditions, prodromal events may respond to a review of the patient's medication in an attempt to improve seizure control. Ictal events such as auras do not require additional treatment as they are short lived. Non-convulsive status will require rescue medication such as clobazam, if the patient is able to swallow safely. Alternatively, buccal midazolam can be considered within community settings. Prolonged post-ictal states, lasting days, may require treatment with benzodiazepine medication. If unsuccessful, particularly in terms of paranoid and/or hallucinatory states, neuroleptic medication is occasionally indicated.

Inter-ictal episodes are treated with psychotropic medication – as most psychotropic drugs can reduce the seizure threshold and therefore worsen seizure control, great care is required in choosing an appropriate drug. Antidepressants such as moclobemide and mirtazapine are fairly safe choices, as are most of the SSRIs. Neuroleptic drugs that appear to be safe include amisulpiride and haloperidol. In the case of 'forced normalisation', particularly due to the introduction of a new AED, it may be necessary to reduce the dose, which will allow seizures to re-emerge but with a subsequent improvement in the patient's mental state.

The management of delirium requires treatment of the underlying medical disorder. It is also important to reassure the patient and not worsen their confusional state. Carers should remain calm and communicate with the patient in short, simple sentences. The patient should remain in a quiet room with low-level lighting to reduce the risk of experiencing distressing illusions or hallucinations. Attention should be paid to ensuring adequate hydration and nutrition, control of pain etc. It is important to note that sedatives often make the delirium worse, and should therefore be used in exceptional circumstances only. Low doses of antipsychotic medication may need to be given to help with frightening hallucinations or paranoid delusions, or extreme agitation.

Conclusion

When a patient presents with emergent psychiatric symptoms or a change in behaviour, a high index of suspicion is required, particularly when the patient also has associated neurological and cognitive abnormalities. Knowledge of the patient's past medical history and medication, especially any recent changes, can help point to a neuropsychiatric condition. While investigations such as blood tests may help confirm the diagnosis, obtaining an accurate history is of paramount importance, and carers often have a vital role is supplying this information.

Key learning points

■ Psychiatric symptoms such as hallucinations, delusions, depression etc. can occur in medical as well as in psychiatric conditions.

- A combination of cognitive, neurological and psychiatric signs/symptoms is suggestive of an underlying neuropsychiatric disorder.

- Drugs may cause adverse psychiatric side effects – it is important to note any relationship between emergent or worsening psychopathology and commencing a new drug, or changes in its dose.

- An awareness of the psychiatric complications associated with various medical (and particularly neurological) disorders will lead to an earlier diagnosis and treatment of a co-morbid psychiatric disorder.

- Treating one component of a neuropsychiatric condition may worsen another aspect e.g. treating depression with an antidepressant may worsen seizure control. Sometimes a compromise must be reached to optimise the patient's quality of life.

References

Betts T (1998) *Epilepsy, Psychiatry and Learning Difficulty.* London: Martin Dunitz.

Burd L, Freeman RD, Klug MG & Kerbeshian J (2005) Tourette syndrome and learning disabilities. BMC *Paediatric* **5** (34).

Fisher RS, Cross HJ, D'Souza C, French JA, Haut SR, Higurashi N, Hirsch E, Jansen FE, Lagae L, Moshé SL, Peltola J, Roulet Perez E, Scheffer IE, Schulze-Bonhage A, Somerville E, Sperling M, Yacubian EM & Zuberi SM (2017) Instruction manual for the ILAE 2017 operational classification of seizure types. *Epilepsia* **58** (4) 531–542.

Kerbeshian J & Burd L (1992) Epidemiology and co-morbidity. The North Dakota prevalence studies of Tourette's syndrome and other developmental disorders. *Advances in Neurology* **58** 67–74.

Kummer A & Teixeira AL (2009) Neuropsychiatry of Parkinson's disease. *Arquivos de Neuro-Psiquiatria* **67** (3b) 930–939.

Miyoshi K & Morimura Y et al (2010) Clinical manifestations of neuropsychiatric disorders. In: K Miyoshi, Y Morimura & K Maeda (Eds) *Neuropsychiatric Disorders* pp1–14. Japan: Springer.

Winterhalder R & Ring H (2014) Epilepsy. In: E Tsakanikos & J McCarthy (Ed) *Handbook of Psychopharmacology in Intellectual Disability* pp 95-107. New York: Springer-Verlag.

Chapter 12: Offending behaviours and risk assessment

By Max Pickard & Andy Inett

Summary

This chapter discusses behaviour that is highly dangerous or that is likely to cause significant harm to others. It will address the principles and problems of how to assess risk, and how to manage those risks (including the interface with the criminal justice system (CJS)).

Introduction and principles

Risk has always permeated health and care services at every level, and for good reason. However, this emphasis on risk assessment and management is not without its critics. Perhaps the most important criticism is that it has led to services that are far too risk averse, paralysed from taking risks due to fears over responsibility and accountability.

Case study: Tim

Tim is a man in his 30s with mild intellectual disabilities (ID). He also has dysexecutive syndrome, meaning he has quickly changing, powerful emotions, such as a quick temper, and he often flies into a rage. The staff at his care home struggle with him, with almost daily conflicts and arguments arising about taking his medication, and they try to keep him storming out of the house and disappearing for a day or more at a time. There are frequent incident reports of violence and restraint. Interestingly, when he does storm out of the house, he always returns unharmed, in good health and calm.

After consultation with mental health services, Tim was taken off his medication and home staff no longer prevented him from leaving leave the house if he wanted to leave – in fact, they sometimes encouraged him to leave. He was, however, offered some basic 'safety net' advice and given a mobile phone with pre-programmed contact numbers.

After this, the number of incidents dropped to under one a month. Tim continued to leave the home and always returned safely. It was agreed that, while he was not absolutely 'safe' in the community, the risks of letting him out were a lot less than trying to control him.

This case example demonstrates a few important principles about risk. First, services should take a 'positive risk taking approach'. This means that carefully considered risks should be taken in order to help people live a meaningful life – it is not acceptable to consider the prevention of risk as the primary (or indeed the only) goal of a service.

Tim's case also demonstrates a point about absolute and relative risk. Absolute risk is the risk of something happening (usually within a certain time span, such as risk of reoffending five years after finishing a prison term). Relative risk is how likely it is that something will happen in comparison to the risk of it happening to the general population. For instance, a man who has previously tried to kill himself will always be at increased relative risk of committing suicide. However, provided he is not acutely mentally unwell and has had no major stresses in his life, the absolute risk is still (probably) very low. It is important not to worry so much about increased relative risk, but instead focus on the absolute risk.

Risk assessments should not be reduced to categories such 'low', 'medium', and 'high' risk. Instead there are several dimensions to consider. For instance:

- What is the probability of something happening? (Usually in the context of something undesirable.)

- What will actually happen? (I.e. What might be the impact of the event?)

- Who is likely to be the target?

- Under what circumstances is the event likely to happen? (I.e. what might the triggers be?)

Case study: John

John is a man with moderate ID and schizophrenia. He generally takes medication that controls his mental illness, but if he doesn't he can become very paranoid. He has developed a particular erotic fixation with a child who walks past his house every day on his way to school, and has been found at the window masturbating while waiting for the child. He expressed a wish to have sex with the child but when interviewed about this he doesn't really have any plan or understanding about how to do this.

In this case there is a very high risk (probability) of a sexual offence taking place (indecent exposure). There is a lower risk, but still raised, of a more serious sexual offence (such as rape). The target is very likely to be the child with whom he has a fixation (although other children and vulnerable adults are also at increased risk). Any offence is likely to occur around the morning or mid-afternoon when children commute to and from school (although again, the risk is not completely confined to this). It is probable that if he does not take his medication and becomes increasingly paranoid, the risks of both sexual assault and violence increase, but the risk is hard to quantify.

Risk assessment

Historically, clinicians have tended to use their clinical judgement alone to determine whether an offending patient presented a high or low risk of recidivism, with mixed results. This led to an over reliance on statistical predictions of risk. Although such measures have received criticism for lacking validity, some actuarial tools have shown that there is in fact good predictive validity when used with offenders (Harris, 2016; Stephens *et al*, 2018). Structured professional judgement tools, such as the HCR-20 (Douglas *et al*, 2014), utilise risk factors based on sound empirical evidence, yet incorporate both historical and current clinical factors and also allow for clinical judgment of the presence and relevance of such items for each individual case. The HCR-20 has been shown to have good validity with offenders with ID, and guidance has been offered on how to adapt tools when applying them to LD populations (see Boer, 2010).

Risk management

Principles derived from the Structured Professional Judgement approach should inform risk management plans, with a clear focus on monitoring, supervision, treatment and victim safety planning, and should also take the person's strengths and protective factors into account.

Robust risk management plans should follow a bio/psycho/social model, focusing on biological factors (such as treatment with medication), psychological factors (such as personality type, insight and attitudes), and social factors (such as housing, finances and social support).

In offenders with ID there is often a reliance on external factors for key risk-management strategies, such as high levels of monitoring or staff support. This is due to potential difficulties with retaining information and internalising coping strategies from treatment due to cognitive limitations, leading to a reliance on staff to prompt the use of relapse-prevention strategies. High levels of impulsivity and deficits in consequential thinking are also common in this population. Risk is often therefore managed most effectively by a robust residential or supported service with staff who are risk aware and trained in risk management, who can offer support with firm behavioural boundaries.

Common problems in ID leading to offending

Received wisdom has historically suggested that being diagnosed with ID increases criminality, although more recently it has been accepted that they actually display lower levels of antisocial behaviour than mainstream populations. Lindsay *et al* (2013) examined which factors predicted referrals to ID forensic services and found that witnessing violence in childhood, along with additional diagnoses of personality disorder and/or ADHD, were the strongest predictors of future forensic problems.

A great deal has been written about the factors that increase risk of offending in mainstream populations, and these often cite the following:

- Having a history of violence/anti-social behaviour.
- Chaotic/abusive/neglectful childhood experiences.
- Relationship problems.
- Employment problems.
- Substance misuse.
- Attitudes that support offending.
- Poor engagement with treatment/supervision.
- Presence of mental disorder/anti-social personality disorder.
- Lack of insight.
- Impulsivity.

Many of these risk factors apply to offenders with ID and are exacerbated in some cases, with more pronounced difficulties with problem solving, empathy, maintaining perspective, impulsivity and poor consequential thinking.

Sexual offending

Mainstream theories of sexual offending focus on the role of conditioning through early life experiences and difficulties with self-esteem, intimacy and attachment – difficulties that often affect people with ID disproportionately. Some ID-specific theories have emerged, one of which is the concept of 'counterfeit deviance' that suggests that sexualised behaviour in people with ID may be driven by deficits in sexual knowledge and a lack of appropriate intimate relationships. However, more recent research has thrown doubt on this theory, suggesting that men with LD who sexually offend do not necessarily have poorer sexual knowledge than other men with LD. Other mainstream theories that have been applied to sex offenders with ID include the 'Good Lives Model' (Aust, 2010), Browne and Finkelhor's model of child sex offending (1986), and the self-regulation pathways model (Langdon *et al*, 2007). Sex offenders with ID tend to adopt pathways that reflect approach goals, employing approach/explicit and approach/automatic pathways, i.e. explicitly planning offending and engaging in well-rehearsed scripts of behaviour (see Lindsay (2009) for a review).

In mainstream forensic settings, cognitive behavioural therapy (CBT) based programmes have shown to reduce sexual offending significantly. This has led to ID forensic services adapting such programmes (i.e. Lindsay, 2009), but the Sex Offender Treatment Services Collaborative programme (SOTSEC-ID) has the most extensive evidence base. This is a 50-session, manualised programme that focuses on sex education, offence analysis, victim empathy and relapse prevention, using simplified models, videos, basic roleplays and pictorially enhanced materials. While there are no published randomised control trial data for adapted groups, the SOTSEC programme used pre- and post-data to show improvements in attitudes towards sex offending, victim empathy and sexual knowledge in 46 ID offenders. Low levels of recidivism were also noted during a six-month follow up (see SOTSEC ID, 2010).

Case study: Chris

Chris is a 30-year-old man with mild ID and autism who lives in a supported living flat. He has a history of inappropriate sexual behaviour towards younger children while at school and his early life was characterised by neglect, which led him to be taken into care. He has struggled to find employment and has had many short-term intimate relationships, characterised by conflict. He goes out regularly and drinks large amounts of alcohol. He views women as sex objects and thinks it's acceptable to approach them in pubs and make sexual comments or touch them inappropriately.

He recently started a new job in a café. Soon after, a young woman also started working there who he was attracted to, and he sent her naked pictures of himself via social media. He was subsequently arrested and placed on a Sexual Harm Prevention Order by the courts. This means he should have no unsupervised contact with females under the age of 16, and that he will be regularly visited by police officers from the VISOR unit, who could check his internet-enabled devices upon request. A breach of this order would be classed as a sexual offence, with a maximum five-year prison sentence, and result in him being placed on the sex offender register.

There were concerns previously that Chris felt there were no negative consequences to his behaviour, as the previous response from the CJS had not been robust. This led to him justifying his sexual behaviour, and minimising its severity.

He agreed to attend the 50-week adapted sex offender treatment programme run locally by NHS and probation psychologists. He engaged well. He learnt to develop problem-solving strategies to manage his impulsivity, and gained some insight into the risky thoughts and feelings that led to his offending and the risky situations he put himself in such as drinking too much alcohol. He developed his own 'New Life Plan', which was adapted to meet his communication needs, and is making good progress in remaining offence-free at his supported living placement.

Fire setting

Fire setting may be a maladaptive coping mechanism, with fire setters presented as a psycho-socially disadvantaged group who set fires as a result of difficulties with interpersonal relationships, lacking the skills to assertively deal with problems. They may use fire setting to express strong feelings, escape from adverse situations or to avoid demands. Murphy and Clare (1996) highlighted that expressing anger is a key motivation for fire setters with ID.

At present, the evidence base for adapted treatment for ID fire setters focuses on a small number of small sample based studies, although programmes are being adapted that follow a CBT approach, focusing on fire education, developing interpersonal and social skills, managing emotions and attitudes that support fire setting, and helping relapse prevention.

The relationship between offending and mental illness

Certain psychiatric illnesses have a particular relationship with offending although what that relationship is may not always clear or well understood.

Perhaps the clearest relationship is between psychotic illnesses (such as schizophrenia) and violence. In the general population, it is estimated that these illnesses treble the chance of violent events (although it is still not clear if this is the case in people with ID and schizophrenia). It is important to note that the absolute risk of violence is still low, and that a diagnosis of schizophrenia is much more risky to the sufferer than to the general public (suicide rates are very high). Evidence suggests that paranoid symptoms and delusions of being controlled (together termed 'threat-control override symptoms') are the particular features of untreated schizophrenia that are associated with the risk of violence. Well controlled, asymptomatic schizophrenia is unlikely to pose any significantly increased risk.

The relationship between other mental illness and offending is less clear. Manic episodes (as part of bipolar disorder) can lead to impulsive and disinhibited behaviour. Equally, certain dementia-type illnesses can lead to disinhibited and/or challenging behaviour. Autistic spectrum disorder poses particular problems with offending. As noted above, a lack of empathy can lead to offending behaviour, and although there is still some controversy about the relationship between autistic spectrum disorder and empathy, it is probably fair to say that many people with autism have, at the very least, problems recognising other people's emotional states. In addition, although rare, the 'special interests' of people with autism can involve offending (for instance, poisoning or bondage).

Attention deficit disorder is believed to be linked to offending in large population studies, although the reasons for this relationship are not clear. In attention deficit disorder there is increased impulsiveness and affective instability (for instance, quickly and easily becoming angry), which are obvious areas of concern. People with attention deficit disorder are also believed to find boredom exceptionally toxic, and thus often engage in 'high stimulus' behaviours, which might include offending behaviour, or they may seek out situations and environments that are risky and thus lead to offending (or, equally, being the target of offences).

Legal frameworks and the criminal justice system

So, if a person with ID offends or is at risk of offending, what can be done? Offending or challenging behaviour is not in itself a mental illness and while some interventions can be offered, there is no 'cure'.

The CJS should be involved in most serious offences, but it is important to recognise that the involvement of the CJS does not mean that somebody will end up in prison, or even in a secure hospital. The CJS has many other options at its disposal, such as the probation service or suspended sentences, that can help prevent offending in the future. It can thus be unhelpful to try and 'spare' a person with ID from the CJS as it may be depriving them of a useful intervention.

The other reason for involving the CJS (initially the police) is to protect people with ID. Mental health services (or social services or care providers for that matter) are not experts in the investigation of facts, and nor should they be put in a position of being judge, jury and executioner.

Prison is an option in some cases. The 'No one knows' initiative in 2008 found that seven per cent of the UK prison population met the criteria for a diagnosis of ID. However, people with ID who do enter the CJS may be vulnerable. They may struggle to understand simple legal procedures, such as being read their rights, they may be suggestible during interviews, and be ill-equipped to understand the process of a trial and going to court.

The Bradley Report (Lord Bradley, 2009), a government-funded examination of the experience of people with ID within the CJS, uncovered poor identification of ID in custody, a lack of training and poor inter-agency working. The report led to some improvements in practice, such as an increase in police custody liaison mental health teams, and an increased number of adapted resources explaining criminal and court procedures to people with ID.

Case study: William

William is a 60-year man with a fairly severe ID who lives in a care home with no unescorted access to the community. He has been prescribed an anti-libidinal drug for decades. There are reports from about 40 years ago that he sexually assaulted a minor, but the records are patchy and the case was never processed through the CJS. As such it is impossible to know what happened, if anything, and his risk assessment and management is therefore extremely difficult, if not impossible. A presumably well-meaning decision to spare him the oversight of the CJS means that he may well have had to endure decades of unjustified restrictions to his liberty, plus needless and probably harmful medication.

It is important to note that in the wake of the revised Mental Health Act (2007), the Winterbourne View scandal, political direction, and the subsequent closure of many beds, the landscape of mental health admission has changed dramatically over recent years. Admitting somebody with ID to a psychiatric hospital in the absence of treatable mental illness for challenging behaviour is still technically possible, but will quite rightly be under heavy legal and service scrutiny, and it can only ever be even considered in the most extreme of cases. The criteria of 'least restrictive option' and 'therapeutic purpose' mean that admission in these cases is often hard to justify legally (as well as clinically or ethically).

Detention under the Mental Health Act is usually under what are termed the 'civil' sections of the act, namely section 2 (admission for one month, primarily for assessment) and section 3 (admission for six months, primarily for treatment, which can be renewed indefinitely). However, there are additional sections of the Mental Health Act that can be imposed by a court of law. These are used by a court when a crime has been proven to be committed but the individual requires mental health treatment. The main 'forensic' sections used are section 35 (where an individual is detained in hospital for assessment and the case is subsequently reviewed by the court to determine if this is appropriate), and section 37 (detention in hospital for assessment and treatment). In addition, those detained under section 37 can also have a section 41 applied (named 'Section 37/41'), which is used for very severe and dangerous offences such as murder.

The Mental Health Act only applies to people within a psychiatric hospital. It has no value or legality (normally) to people in the community. However, on discharge from hospital, when under a section of the Mental Health Act, a community treatment order can be used. In essence this 'suspends' the Mental Health Act and the patient will have conditions written into their community treatment order (for instance, to attend a psychotherapy group, take medication, or submit to urine drug screening). Breaking these conditions allows the Mental Health Act to be reinstated at the discretion of the treating clinicians, and an individual can be quickly detained back in hospital.

Community treatment orders are not without criticism, however. For instance, although there is no clear evidence that they reduce hospital admissions or serious incidents, they effectively decrease the liberty of an individual and they are still used as a legal framework for care of people with mental disorder in the community.

Summary and learning points

- People with ID can commit serious offences and, in most cases, the CJS should be involved when they do (or are under suspicion).

- People with ID are sometimes imprisoned for serious offences, but, particularly with more severe ID, other options are available (including detention in a secure mental health hospital).

- Risk assessments are often challenging but can be approached in a structured way by multi-disciplinary assessment, sometimes using standardised rating instruments.

■ Risk management does not mean risk elimination, but rather trying to work out the least risky strategy.

■ Risk management should, ideally, involve the person with ID and all parties involved in their care and safety.

References

Aust S (2010) Is the Good Lives model of offender treatment relevant to sex offenders with a learning disability? *Journal of Learning Disabilities and Offending Behaviour* **1** (3) 33-39.

Boer D (2010) Suggested adaptations to the HCR-20 for offenders with Intellectual Disabilities. In: Craig L, Lindsay WR & Browne KD (Eds) *Assessment and Treatment of Sexual Offenders with Intellectual Disabilities: A handbook*. London, Wiley and Sons.

Browne A & Finkelhor D (1986) Impact of child sexual abuse: a review of the research. *Psychological Bulletin* **99** (1) 66-77.

Douglas KS, Shaffer C, Blanchard AJE, Guy LS, Reeves K & Weir J (2014) *HCR-20 violence risk assessment scheme: Overview and annotated bibliography*. HCR-20 Violence Risk Assessment White Paper Series, #1. Burnaby, Canada: Mental Health, Law and Policy Institute, Simon Fraser University.

Harris GT, Rice ME & Quinsey VL (2016) *Violence Risk Appraisal Guide-Revised, 2013: User Guide*. Data Services, Queen's University Library.

Langdon PE, Maxted H, Murphy GH & SOTSEC ID (2007) An exploratory evaluation of the Ward and Hudson Offending pathways model with sex offenders who have intellectual disabilities. *Journal of Intellectual and developmental disabilities* **32** (2) 94-105.

Lindsay WR (2009) *The Treatment of Sex Offenders with Developmental Disabilities: A practice workbook*. London: Wiley and sons.

Lindsay WR, O'Brien G, Carson D, Holland AJ, Taylor JL, Wheeler JR, Middleton C, Price K, Steptoe L & Johnston S (2013) Pathways into services for offenders with intellectual disabilities: Childhood experiences, diagnostic information and offense variables. *Criminal Justice and Behaviour* **37** (6) 678–694.

Lord Bradley (2009) *The Bradley Report* [online]. Available at: http://webarchive.nationalarchives. gov.uk/20130123195930/http://www.dh.gov.uk/en/Publicationsandstatistics/Publications/ PublicationsPolicyAndGuidance/DH_098694 (accessed April 2018).

Murphy GH & Clare ICH (1996) Analysis of motivation in people with learning disabilities who set fires. *Psychology, Crime and Law* **2** (3) pp153–164.

Sex Offender Treatment Services Collaborative – Intellectual Disabilities (SOTSEC-ID) (2010) Effectiveness of a group cognitive behavioural treatment for men with intellectual disabilities at risk of sexual offending. *Journal of Applied Research in Intellectual Disabilities* **23** (6) pp537–551.

Stephens S, Newman JE, Cantor JM & Seto MC (2018) The Static 99R predicts sexual and violent recidivism for individuals with low intellectual functioning. *Journal of Sexual Aggression* **24** (1) 1-11.

Chapter 13: Challenging behaviour

By Alice Nicholls and Terence Davidson

Summary

This chapter explores the meaning and context of the term 'challenging behaviour' when it is applied to people who have intellectual disabilities (ID). Ways of assessing challenging behaviour are discussed with reference to case studies, including how such assessments are used to inform psychological and environmental interventions.

Introduction

People with ID sometimes behave in ways that put them and others at risk of harm, including aggression, self-injury and property destruction as well as social withdrawal and self-neglect. Such behaviour can be difficult to understand and manage and, as a result, can be described as 'challenging behaviour'. The most widely used definition of challenging behaviour is that of Emerson (1995):

'Culturally abnormal behaviour(s) of such an intensity, frequency or duration that the physical safety of the person or others is likely to be placed in serious jeopardy, or behaviour which is likely to seriously limit use of, or result in the person being denied access to, ordinary community facilities.'

Between 5% and 15% of people using services for people with ID engage in challenging behaviour (NICE, 2015). Rates are higher for young people (those under 30) and among those in hospital settings. People with autism, sensory impairments, sensory processing difficulties and other mental health problems (including dementia) may also be more likely to engage in challenging behaviour.

Context of challenging behaviour

People with ID are discriminated against as a group of people. They are less likely to have jobs, get married or have children, and they are more likely to live in poverty. They are less likely to have regular contact with friends or family, and are more likely to be neglected and abused by other people. They have a lower life expectancy and are very much more likely to die of preventable causes.

This same discrimination and lack of understanding can result in people with ID being supported inappropriately. This can increase the chance that some people will develop challenging behaviour, and the negative impact of some responses to challenging behaviour can make it more likely to happen again.

Figure 1: The cycle of challenging behaviour and inappropriate support

Inappropriate support

There are several different aspects of support that can increase the risk of someone challenging those supporting them. Different places tend to have different rules for how people are expected to behave, and sometimes these rules are not written down or clear to people with ID. For example, screaming and jumping up and down would be considered challenging behaviour in most social care day services, and yet it would also describe the behaviour of almost everyone at a rock concert. This means that if an environment or supporter has unreasonable rules about what they expect of people, it is more likely some behaviour will be defined as challenging.

Behaviour is also more likely to be described as challenging if the person can't explain why they have done something. If someone can say, 'I'm sorry, I'm having a bad day and I got carried away', people are more likely to be understanding about them having broken a social rule. This means that the behaviour of people without ID is almost never called 'challenging behaviour', even if the things they do are identical to those with ID.

It is almost always other people who say that someone's behaviour is challenging. The extent to which people decide to call the behaviour of other people challenging is often affected by their beliefs about why the person has acted in a certain way. It is thought that people's behaviour will be labelled as challenging if other people think the person is totally in control of their behaviour and that it will not change. In families and social care settings it may be that the culture of the environment has the greatest impact on how individual carers understand the behaviour of people with ID.

The 'culture' of a setting has been described as the manner in which people let each other know 'what we do around here'. The culture of a setting is predominantly established by those leading the service, which is not always the manager or other people with formal authority.

Culture and leadership are also important factors in terms of whether those in an environment feel capable of managing and helping people with challenging behaviour. The Tizard Centre has looked at many years' of research and best practice and identified the following standards for environments capable of supporting those at risk of developing challenging behaviour (Denne *et al*, 2013).

In a capable environment, people are:

- liked and frequently interacted with in meaningful ways
- supported in rich communication environments
- supported to participate in meaningful activities
- supported consistently and given support to understand and predict events
- supported to maintain relationships with family and friends
- offered experiences that lead to meaningful choices, which are clearly communicated
- supported to try new experiences, develop skills and increase independence
- supported in dignified ways to care for and look after themselves and their health
- supported in acceptable physical environments
- supported by skilled and mindful carers
- receiving support that is delivered and arranged within a broader understanding of challenging behaviour that recognises (among other things) the need to ensure safety and quality of care for both individuals and carers.

The social care context does not always help supporters provide this kind of environment, and this in turn increases the likelihood that people with ID will develop challenging behaviour.

This can be affected by government policy decisions. For example, a large majority of people with ID now live in supported accommodation. In theory, this should allow people to choose where they live, and with whom, and enable them to receive personalised support. In reality, however, there may be little choice available and people often end up being supported in the same way as everyone else, often by staff who have not had adequate training and who are not being supported to learn and develop. It can also be affected by local factors such as commissioning, availability of care providers and the functioning of local specialist health and social care teams.

Psychological impact

The way in which people respond to challenging behaviour can have a negative impact upon people with ID, and actually make it more likely that they will challenge those supporting them again.

A good example is the prescription of anti-psychotic medication even though research has identified that there is little evidence that this is an effective treatment for challenging behaviour (Sheehan *et al*, 2015). It can also cause side effects, such as weight gain and other physical health problems, which can in turn increase the risk of challenging behaviour.

People who present with challenging behaviour are also sometimes moved to out-of-area placements, or even admitted to specialist hospitals. This can limit their contact with family and friends, as well as with local health services. People in out-of-area placements also seem to be more vulnerable to abuse by others. This might include inappropriate restrictions or a deprived environment, but it can also include deliberate harm, which the person is less likely to be able to report.

Even if people are not moved to out-of-area placements, they can still have their access to the local community restricted as a result of their challenging behaviour. This can lead to a lack of social contact and a lack of meaningful activity, and by definition represents a reduction in a person's choices about how they spend their time. Such restrictions are sometimes even imposed by people supporting them as a punishment for what they perceive as inappropriate or challenging behaviour.

Attracting the label of challenging behaviour can have negative consequences for how a person is seen by others and how they see themselves. These changes to a person's reputation can lead to further discriminatory treatment by others, and the changes to a person's identity can make them feel hopeless and negative about the future.

Case study: John

John is 45 years old and has a severe degree of ID and autism. John lived in a residential service for 18 years where, when not at day services or in the community, he would spend most of his time in the communal areas of the residential service flapping his hands and tearing up newspapers. John would frequently ask one of the team of staff about what was happening that day using some idiosyncratic Makaton and spoken language, and they would be able to answer his question quickly using accessible language.

Following a change to the commissioning policy in his local area, John was moved to a newly built supported living service. In the new service, John was supported 1:1 some of the time in his own flat, with staff not easily accessible at other times of the day. Although John would continue to engage in hand flapping and paper tearing when staff were present, he started to grab staff when they prepared to leave his flat. It became more difficult for staff to leave the flat, and one day a member of staff shouted, 'No, John!' at him when he grabbed their arm. John pushed and kicked this staff member who was hurt and unable to work for several weeks.

Following a serious incident review it was decided that John had to leave the new service. He was moved to a different residential service in the neighbouring county where, in order to manage risk, they started locking his door and rarely supporting him to access the community. John's grabbing of staff became more frequent and intense and John was referred to a psychiatrist who prescribed antipsychotic medication, even though they acknowledged there was no evidence of a serious mental illness.

John remains at this out-of-area placement. The grabbing is the same and so are the restrictions upon his life. John has no contact with his old housemates or staff, and he almost never leaves the house. John has gained weight and, because of the psychiatric medication, he has to have regular blood tests, which he finds highly anxiety provoking. John is allocated a duty care manager so a different person visits to review his placement each year and it is recommissioned, unchanged.

Assessment

The assessment of challenging behaviour seeks to understand the person's reasons for engaging in the behaviour that is causing concern (the target behaviour). The target behaviour should be clearly described using the following criteria:

1. **Topography:** What it looks like.
2. **Frequency:** How often it happens.
3. **Duration:** How long it lasts.
4. **Intensity:** The impact of the behaviour.

Taking time to define the target behaviour ensures that everyone working with the person is clear on what they are monitoring and assessing. It also provides a baseline for later comparisons.

Case study: Holly

Holly was referred to local services for people with mental health and ID by her key worker at her residential home. The referral stated that Holly was 'constantly smearing faeces all over herself, risking the physical health of others around her and limiting her ability to access the community'. At assessment, the staff team met with the clinical psychologist and defined the target behaviour:

Topography: Staff agreed the target behaviour was Holly inserting her left index finger into her anus, retrieving a pea-sized amount of faeces and wiping it across the chest panel of her t-shirt.

Frequency: Staff disagreed on the frequency of the behaviour; their responses varied from none to three times a day, to two to five times a day. They agreed on an average of three times per day.

Duration: Staff agreed that the duration of the incident seemed to vary depending on how easy Holly found it to get a sample of faeces, ranging from 10 seconds to three minutes, most commonly (90% of the time) the incident took about one minute from start to finish.

Intensity: Holly had no known infectious disease, only smeared on herself, and used her right hand to open doors and turn on taps. She was willing to go with a member of staff, wash her hands and put her t-shirt in the washing machine, meaning no one else had physical contact with the faeces. There was some risk to Holly's dignity and the potential for the emotional distress of others as they sometimes saw her bottom. The most disruptive consequence of the target behaviour was the time it took to clean up after the incident. By the time staff had supported Holly to clean her hands and put her top in the washing machine, Holly had usually missed the bus to the day centre and taken 30 minutes of staff time at one of the busiest times of day.

Outcome: Once the target behaviour had been defined, staff appeared less confused about what they wanted help with, less concerned about infection control risks and described feeling relieved that someone was listening to them and taking their concerns seriously.

Assessment should include a holistic overview of all aspects of the person's family, social, emotional and medical life, including their interests, likes and dislikes, identifying any unmet needs, even if they are not obviously related to the behaviour of concern.

Functional analysis

All behaviour serves a function, although it may be outside of the person's awareness. The function may be any one or a combination of the following:

- **To gain access to preferred activities or objects:** For example, going out or having a bath, being given food or a clean t-shirt.

- **To gain social attention:** The behaviour may elicit a response from others. This response might be desirable to the individual, even if it is a negative response. For example, getting one-to-one attention to clean up after creating a mess.

- **To gain sensory stimulation:** The behaviour may give the person an internally pleasing sensation or remove an unpleasant internal sensation or pain, for example head-banging to distract from the pain caused by an ear infection or smearing faeces because the texture feels nice.

■ **To escape or avoid a situation:** The behaviour of concern might result in the person being removed from an unpleasant situation, for example hitting a passenger on a noisy over-crowded bus to get removed from the bus, or smearing faeces to avoid going to a day centre.

There are several ways to investigate the function of the target behaviour, which are more accurate when used in combination. Three of the most common methods are outlined below:

1. **Informant interviews:** Semi-structured interviews such as the Functional Assessment Interview (O'Neill *et al*, 1997) can be conducted with staff and family groups, asking questions to identify factors that make the target behaviour more and less likely to occur. It helpfully phrases the question as 'what you would do if you wanted to guarantee the behaviour would occur and what would you do if you were trying to avoid it'. Informants are not always able to answer all of the questions but their responses help to build an understanding of the behaviour.

2. **Behavioural recordings:** Traditional ABC forms ask staff or family members to record what was going on immediately before the behaviour occurred (antecedent), exactly what happened when the behaviour occurred (behaviour) and what happened immediately afterwards (consequence). This description can help inform hypotheses regarding the triggers and/or motivators for the behaviour. If staff are already collecting the information on incident forms there is no need to introduce a new form as the information can be collated from existing records. Plotting the frequency of incidents by day of the week, time of day and staff members present, can also stimulate further helpful questions. For example, if there are a disproportionate number of incidents on a Monday it might be worth asking more about what happens on a Monday. If incidents peak at 12pm it might suggest that hunger, waiting for food or crowding (e.g. in a busy dining room) is contributing to the problem. If the target behaviour is particularly associated with one member of staff then further investigations might be needed: it could suggest that there is an interpersonal problem between that member of staff and the client; that the member of staff is particularly good at recording on incident forms; or that they work a lot of shifts.

3. **Observations:** It is of course very helpful when clients are able to converse with the person assessing them, to talk about their likes and dislikes, their thoughts and feelings, and about the behaviours of concern. Unfortunately, for many clients with ID presenting with concerning behaviour, this is not an option and in these cases direct observation of the client and interacting with them using their own communication system, where possible, will enrich the assessment in a way that is very difficult to achieve with third-party information alone. As

an external person meeting the client for the first time, the assessor may notice things that people who work with them every day have become desensitised to or have dismissed as part of the client's personality. The assessor can note how being around the client, the staff and other service users makes them feel, which can help generate hypotheses about how the client, staff and other service users feel in relation to each other. Aside from general observations about the client and their environment, these sessions can also be an opportunity to witness the behaviour of concern first hand and record further ABCs for analysis. If the presence of the observer causes a change in the behaviour of concern, the reasons for this should be carefully considered as part of the assessment.

Information captured by the assessment may lead to potential explanations which can then be tested like scientific hypotheses. For example, if the behaviour of concern is occurring shortly before meal times and results in the client receiving food, one hypothesis might be that the client is reacting to hunger and their behaviour is reinforced by receiving food. This could be tested by offering the client lunch half an hour earlier for a week and looking at the frequency of incidents over that week. If the frequency of incidents declines then the hypothesis is supported, if the frequency remains the same, it would suggest that there is an alternative explanation, requiring further assessment.

An alternative explanation may be that the client finds the anticipation of food too exciting and they are unable to self-regulate their level of arousal. This could be tested by introducing an arousal-reducing activity or removing some of the environmental stimulation before meals times and examining whether this has any impact on the frequency, duration or intensity of the behaviour of concern.

Sometimes functional assessment does not result in a simple 'the client does x because of x' formulation. Often, target behaviours have served many functions over the course of the person's life or they are the only way they have been able to regulate their emotional, mental or physiological state. In these cases, assessment tends to result in a list of the following:

- **Setting events:** events that make the behaviour more likely.

- **Warning signs:** signs that the behaviour is likely to occur.

- **Antecedents:** events that occur immediately before a behaviour and that might trigger an incident.

- **Behaviours of concern:** the client may have a list of target behaviours that get used in a chain, interchangeably or as a hierarchy, where the behaviour deployed depends on the level of their distress, or how long their needs have gone unmet.

- **Function(s):** what the person gains or avoids through their behaviour.

- **Protective factors:** anything that makes the behaviour less likely to occur or helps to reduce the frequency, duration or intensity of an incident.

Positive behaviour support

Positive behaviour support (PBS) interventions seek to remove or reduce the individual's need to engage in the target behaviour. Intervention plans are made up of the following components:

- **Ecological changes:** making changes to the environment, activities and treatment of the person to avoid or reduce setting events. For example, if hunger and thirst are known setting events, the person could be offered drinks and snacks at more regular intervals. If a setting event is boredom, the person could be offered more frequent changes of staff, activities or location.

- **Positive programming:** teaching the individual skills so that they can meet or communicate their needs in a less harmful way. For example, teaching the person another way of getting or asking for a snack, showing them an alternative way of ending an activity, event or interaction.

- **Focused support:** supporting the person in a predefined way to help them avoid the behaviour of concern at times or within situations that have been identified as high risk.

- **Situational management:** reacting to early warning signs or the behaviour of concern itself, as soon as they occur, in a way that makes the situation as safe as possible, as quickly as possible.

Case study: James

James is a 25-year-old man who lives in a small group home. He was referred for banging his head and scratching his face with his nails. His parents reported that he had engaged in these behaviours since he was about three years old but that the frequency and intensity had increased since he left home and went to live in the group home six months ago. A thorough assessment was conducted and the following formulation agreed between staff, parents and the clinical psychologist.

Setting events
- Having gone to bed late the night before.
- Being woken up early by the man in the next room.

- Hunger.
- More that about three people in the room at once.
- Meal times.
- Noisy environments.

Antecedents

- Waiting for dinner to be served.
- Another resident making a loud, high pitched vocalisation.
- Being told to sit down and wait at the dining table.

Warning signs

- Rocking.
- Closing eyes.
- Holding face with hands.

Behaviour

- Scratching face with fingernails.
- Banging head on table.

Consequence

- Pain.
- Other residents go quiet.
- Staff encourage James to leave the dining room and sit in the lounge.
- If during meal time, James is given his food in the lounge.

Functions

- James gains sensory stimulation from pain, which overrides or distracts him from feelings of overstimulation.
- Escapes from environmental stimulation by quietening other residents and by being moved to a quiet room.
- Avoids further stimulation by being moved to a quiet room.
- Gains recognition of distress and a caring reaction from staff.

This formulation resulted in the following positive behaviour support plan being developed in collaboration with staff, family and the clinical psychologist:

Ecological changes

- Staff shifted James' evening routines so that he was ready for bed by 10pm every evening.
- James moved bedrooms so that he was living next door to a quiet resident.
- James was offered a snack mid-morning and mid-afternoon.
- James was served all his meals in the quiet room.

Positive programming

Staff identified a small quiet room that was not being used by any of the other residents and started to encourage James to go into this room whenever they noticed his early warning signs. They made sure the quiet room was only for James' use and left a healthy snack and a drink in there for him. After a few weeks, James started signing for the quiet room and taking himself there in response to his own early warning signs.

Focused support

Staff altered the way they supported James around meal times. They stopped disturbing James from his activity until his dinner was ready for him in the lounge, and only then would a member of staff would go and sign 'dinner', and James would follow them to the quiet room where they would sit quietly together. If James indicated he was hungry before his meal was ready, staff showed him on the clock when his dinner would be served. If, following this information, James started to show his early warning signs, he was offered a healthy snack.

Situational management

If James began to rock, close his eyes, rest his hand on his face, scratch his face or bang his head, he was encouraged to move into the quiet room where there was a snack and a drink available to him.

The outcomes of a PBS intervention can be measured through changes in frequency, intensity and duration as captured by behaviour recordings and incident forms. The client, their staff and their family may have more subjective feedback on how they feel their quality of life and the behaviours of concern have changed, and there may be other positive changes, such as an increase in community based activities, or a decrease in visible signs of the behaviour such as bruising on the head or scratches on the face.

When the desired changes do not occur it is important to check the extent to which the PBS plan has been carried out. It may have included recommendations that were not possible within the current home. Any barriers to the successful implementation and maintenance of the PBS plan should be discussed with staff and, where possible, more realistic plans drawn up. If, despite adherence to the plan, the behaviours of concern have not decreased, further assessment and formulation may be required.

Key learning points

- Discriminatory attitudes towards people with ID can result in them being supported in unsuitable environments.

- This can increase their chance of developing challenging behaviour, which in turn can lead to further inappropriate treatment.

- This vicious cycle can have a very significant impact upon the health and quality of life of people with ID.

- All behaviour is motivated by *gaining something pleasant* or *avoiding something unpleasant*.

- Assessment of challenging behaviour seeks to understand the person's reasons for engaging in the behaviour of concern.

- Positive behaviour support seeks to prevent the behaviour of concern occurring by meeting the person's needs in alternative, proactive ways.

References

Denne LD, Noone SJ, Gore NJ, Toogood S, Hughes JC, Hastings RP, Allen D, Baker P and McGill P (2013) Developing a core competencies framework for positive behavioural support: issues and recommendations. *International Journal of Positive Behavioural Support* **3** (2) 24–31.

Emerson E (1995) In: *Challenging Behaviour: A unified approach* (2007). Royal College of Psychiatrists, British Psychological Society, Royal College of Speech and Language Therapists.

NICE (2015) *Challenging Behaviour and Learning Disabilities: Prevention and interventions for people with learning disabilities whose behaviour challenges* [online]. Available at: https://www.nice.org.uk/guidance/ng11 (accessed January 2018).

O'Neill RE, Horner RH, Albin RW, Sprague JR, Storey K & Newton JS (1997) *Functional Assessment and Program Development for Problem Behavior*. Pacific Grove, CA: Brooks/Cole Publishing.

Sheehan R, Hassiotis A, Walters K, Osborn D, Strydom A & Horsfall L (2015) Mental illness, challenging behaviour, and psychotropic drug prescribing in people with intellectual disability: UK population based cohort study. *British Medical Journal* **351** doi: https://doi.org/10.1136/bmj.h4326.

Chapter 14:
Personality disorder and deliberate self-harm

By Andrew Flynn

Case study: Chloe, part 1

Chloe is 19 years old and has mild intellectual disabilities (ID). She has been taken to her local A&E department after cutting her wrist superficially with a piece of glass from a broken bottle. Chloe tells the doctor that she had an argument with a support worker earlier in the day about going shopping. Shortly after this, she says she heard a voice in her head telling her to hurt herself. The doctor notices a number of similar, though older, scars on her arms. Chloe confirms that she has often self-harmed, commencing after she went into the first of a series of foster placements in her early teens because of her mother's 'drinking and bipolar disorder'. She tells him she does it when she is very upset and it helps to get rid of the 'bad' feelings. When Chloe first arrived in A&E she appeared sullen but her mood has brightened considerably while her cut is being tended to. She starts to ask the doctor questions about his job as well as more personal questions such as whether he has a girlfriend or any pets. When he mentions about her returning home, Chloe says that she won't go back and that she will kill herself if she does. The doctor isn't sure if Chloe is 'really suicidal' and calls the duty psychiatrist because of the voices in her head and the history of repeated deliberate self-harm.

Three months ago, Chloe moved to a small residential service for people with ID. She has had a number of similar moves in the past. Although things went well at first, lately the staff have been struggling with her emotional needs. Chloe's mood is changeable and she gets angry easily. She demands a lot of their time and frequently complains of physical health problems even though her GP says there is nothing wrong. This is the second time she has hurt herself in a month and they have already asked her social worker to find somewhere 'more appropriate' for her to live. The duty psychiatrist believes that Chloe has a 'personality disorder' and that her self-harm is impulsive and not representative of suicide risk. He has to work quite hard to reassure the member of staff who is with Chloe. She thinks Chloe should really be in hospital and only reluctantly agrees to take Chloe home.

Introduction

In the case study above, the duty psychiatrist has diagnosed a complex mental health condition called 'personality disorder', often abbreviated to 'PD'. Although a number of distinct PDs have been described, Chloe's is the form that most often presents in states of crisis to mental health and social care services. Although formerly, in ICD-10, it would have been called 'emotionally unstable PD', the term 'borderline PD' is also frequently used. Recurrent impulsive acts of deliberate self-harm in the form of cutting, taking overdoses and, occasionally, ligature tying, are commonly associated with the diagnosis of borderline PD, but the condition is also associated with a variety of other important complaints. These include hearing voices, physical health problems for which no cause is found ('somatisation'), substance misuse, unstable relationships, suicidal threats, short-lived but intense shifts to negative mood states (frequently described by patients as 'mood swings'), as well as anger and aggression.

PD is increasingly recognised in people with ID, particularly in those with milder degrees of impairment (Flynn *et al*, 2002). However, while recognising and diagnosing the condition is one thing, responding to it poses a set of special challenges. At the heart of these challenges lies one consistent observation in a field otherwise rife with uncertainties: the capacity of people with PD to induce negative sentiments in others.

The concept of 'normal' personality

What is a 'normal' personality? We would probably say that if personality is not a physical thing, then it is a *psychological* thing. We would also probably agree that it relies heavily on the brain (but is not the same thing), and that it has an innate, genetic aspect as well as an aspect acquired through upbringing and life experience. Traditionally, the innate component is called 'temperament' and the acquired component, the one that grows over time, is called 'character'. Together, temperament and character develop through childhood into a 'personality' – a concept that is both biological and psychological in nature (Svrakic *et al*, 2002) . It was once thought that the mature personality stayed more or less unchanged once it was established in adulthood, but recent research indicates that it retains a capacity for a degree of change throughout the lifespan.

The term 'personality' refers to the enduring ways in which an individual engages with the world around them. Everyone has a personality and everyone's is different. Some people are habitually shy while others might be more typically social and out-going. Some people are very even-tempered, others given to passionate displays of emotion. Some are of us find it easy to see the best in others while others take longer to trust people. Some of us are perfectionists who like to plan ahead and have things tidy and in order, while others of us are content to lead messier lives and leave things till the last minute. Although several hundred personality traits are recognised, evidence suggests that any individual personality can, in fact, be characterised in terms of a much smaller set of overarching personality traits known as *neuroticism, extraversion, openness, agreeableness* and *conscientiousness*.

- **Neuroticism:** sensitive/nervous *vs* secure/confident (emotional stability).

- **Extraversion:** solitary/reserved *vs* outgoing/energetic (sociability).

- **Openness:** consistent/cautious *vs* inventive/curious (engagement with novelty).

- **Agreeableness:** friendly/compassionate *vs* analytical/detached.

- **Conscientiousness:** efficient/organised *vs* easy-going/careless (orderliness).

These traits (or 'factors') are *dimensional* so that a person may sit anywhere between two extremes, from 'high' to 'low'. They are also independent of one another, meaning that a person's position on one factor says little about where they will be on any of the others. So-called 'normal' (or 'adaptive') personalities lie somewhere between the extremes of each of these dimensions and reflect flexible tendencies rather than rigid constraints. So, for example, even quite extraverted people are able to stay quiet during a concert, even though they may well be the loudest to cheer at the end. Personality (the dynamic sum of our traits), therefore, does not operate in isolation but works within the social and physical environment around us at any given moment to produce behaviour.

Personality x situation = behaviour

This simple model of personality plays an important role in our understanding of the actions of others. We are used to forming judgements of someone's character (a closely related idea) based on our knowledge of them, and we use these judgements to make predictions about how they will be in a given situation. Such judgements are also used to understand an individual's personal responsibility for their behaviour. In other words, does someone behave in a certain way because of the sort of person they are, or because of the circumstances they find themselves in? This is important when we consider negative or problematic behaviours shown by others. If we decide, for instance, that Chloe's self-harm is due to some difficult or upsetting event she has been through, we might well feel sympathy for her and appreciate her distress as real, and perhaps justifiable. On the other hand, if we think her self-harm is just a reflection of, say, her excessive need for attention (a personality-type attribution and a commonly held explanation for deliberate self-harm) we may quickly find ourselves feeling resentful and angry towards her. The tendency to attribute negative behaviours to personality rather than situation has been termed the **fundamental attribution bias**.

Personality, coping and mental health

If we think of personality traits as representing psychological 'needs' of one sort or another, we begin to build a framework for understanding the genesis of at least some mental health and behavioural problems. When our needs are not met we experience a state of *dissonance* that either motivates action to address the need (e.g. by tidying up, visiting a friend) or activates other coping strategies to reduce our emotional discomfort. We might, for example, reassure ourselves that the mess can wait until later if we can't fix it now, or that, if our friend isn't in, he will be home later and we can phone them then.

These coping strategies might not always make the tension we experience dissipate entirely, but they help us to tolerate it, at least for a while. If our unmet need is too great or persists for too long, our initial discomfort may grow into distress, a state of emotional arousal that, if intense enough, may adversely affect the way we think and act. Thinking may become more concrete (or 'black and white'), self-centred and short-sighted, and actions take on an impulsive quality that we might later regret. Consuming alcohol, shouting at people to leave us alone, driving too fast, rebound relationships and spending money on things you don't really need are all examples of impulsive actions that many people will recognise having done at some time in their lives when faced with a crisis.

For most people most of the time, these behaviours – sometimes referred to as instances of *emotion-focussed coping* – are infrequent and self-limiting, arising only under special circumstances of duress called *life events* (such as a failed romantic relationship, a bereavement or a job loss) and usually not entailing significant or lasting harm. Occasionally, however, they can be more damaging and lead to other problems such as damaging an important relationship, losing a driving licence, accrual of debt and the development of conditions such as depression. This is the basis of the 'stress-vulnerability model' of mental disorder.

Our personalities, therefore, contain not just our strengths but also our potential weaknesses. These weaknesses may only become apparent when we are challenged by circumstances that we cannot easily reconcile with our own particular patterns of psychological need. It is unusual for most of us to find our coping resources overcome to the point where we engage in harmful impulsive acts or develop mental health problems, but occasionally this may happen. Usually we do so successfully, in which case we may have learnt an important lesson about ourselves and be equipped to deal with such situations in the future. The most valuable of our coping responses is the ability to reflect and discuss our problems and, when they occur, explore the difficult emotions that accompany them. For individuals with good communication skills and supportive social networks, most life crises are dealt with informally by talking to friends, family or colleagues. An openness to engage interpersonally in this way is also a facet of adaptive personalities. Together with the capacity to tolerate distress without resorting to impulsive acts, it is a core aspect of our resilience to stress.

Personality disorder

For some people, the vulnerabilities contained within their personalities lie much closer to the surface and are triggered easily and frequently. People with personality disorder (PD) are in some way 'unbalanced', unresponsive or inflexible to context, or extreme in their expression. So, for example, someone unusually high in the trait of conscientiousness may struggle to cope with even minor changes in their life. Indeed, many of the emotional difficulties experienced by people with autistic spectrum disorder, a condition that is not in itself usually regarded as a form of PD, can be understood in just this way. Someone unusually high in the trait of neuroticism may react excessively to an upsetting event and suffer levels of distress that make it hard for others to support or reassure them.

Self-harm and 'mentalisation' in PD

Learning to recognise and talk about unpleasant emotional states is the central task in most forms of counselling and psychotherapy. The cognitive process underlying this activity has recently been termed 'mentalisation' (Bateman & Fonagy, 1999) and relies both on neurodevelopmental factors and the development of a secure attachment to reliable parental figures or other caregivers to develop. Children raised in circumstances of emotional, physical or sexual abuse, or where caregivers are unresponsive or insensitive to their needs (perhaps because of alcohol or drug misuse or the effects of serious mental illness), are at special risk for PD and harmful impulsive behaviours. Problems with mentalising are now believed to be a core deficit in borderline and emotionally unstable forms of PD and lie behind the acts of self-harm and other challenging behaviours shown by individuals like Chloe.

Mentalisation as a cognitive skill has not been studied in the context of ID although problems with language development and the capacity for complex or abstract thought that constitute part of the disability itself may represent a special risk factor for impulsive behaviour disorders, even in cases of otherwise stable upbringing. Mentalisation involves the accurate recognition of emotional and psychological states in others, and the use of these to make sense of their behaviour and respond to it. It is closely related to the idea of *theory of mind* as well as the concepts of empathy, psychological mindedness and reflection.

Case study: Chloe, part 2

Manager:	Chloe, why did you hurt yourself this morning? You must have been feeling pretty bad.
Chloe:	I was feeling really angry.
Manager:	How are you feeling now?
Chloe:	A bit better.
Manager:	Do you know what you were feeling angry about?
Chloe:	I wanted to go out to the shops but Suzanne said no.
Manager:	Why did she say that? You usually get on well with her, don't you?
Chloe:	I think she was very busy this morning. She looked a bit stressed.
Manager:	Is that why she said no then?
Chloe:	Probably. Well, now I think of it, she didn't exactly say no.
Manager:	Can you remember what she did say?
Chloe:	She said that if I could hang on we could go later on.
Manager:	And you couldn't wait?
Chloe:	I think I was in a bad mood already. I was thinking about my mum and whether I'll get to see her soon. Shopping takes my mind off it.
Manager:	I understand. Do you miss your mum a lot?
Chloe:	When I think about her I get upset sometimes and think no one likes me. Do you think Suzanne will still want to work with me?

With the manager's support, Chloe can talk about events earlier in the day. Note that in doing so she moves beyond just recounting but refers to states of thinking and feeling, both in herself and, importantly, in Suzanne. The manager's questions are posed so as to encourage such responses. As Chloe talks, she moves from an 'egocentric' position towards a more *empathic* one, a psychological shift sometimes called 'decentring'. She is also able to recognise how her state of feeling now is distinct from that of earlier, although she doesn't volunteer much about it on this occasion. Finally, as Chloe explores the event, she recalls more detail (Suzanne not actually saying 'no') and her perspective changes. She is able to guess how Suzanne was feeling and how she might be feeling now. Her interpretations of Suzanne's states of mind are provisional, however: she says 'probably'. This is another feature of accurate mentalisation: an appreciation of the fundamental opacity of mental states in others: although we might have an intimate knowledge of our own minds, we can never know for definite what someone else thinks or feels.

Finally, Chloe gives us a clue to what lies behind some of her behaviour – the fact that she misses her mum and how events in the here-and-now bring that to mind. We now understand Chloe differently, and perhaps we now feel differently towards her too.

Contrast this with the conversation that might have occurred with Suzanne that morning:

Chloe: I want to go to the shops.

Suzanne: I'm really busy at the moment. We can go later.

Chloe: I want to go now!

Suzanne: Well, that's not possible.

Chloe   [beginning to shout, hands balling into fists]:
                    You can't stop me! You lot are always doing this.

Suzanne: I'm not going to talk to you if you shout at me like that.

Chloe: You're horrible to me. No one here likes me. I hate you!

Suzanne   [tone rising, crossing arms]: That's not an appropriate way to talk.
                    Please, go away and let me finish my work.

Chloe: I want to kill myself!

Suzanne   [sounding irritated]: Please don't threaten me like that. Go away
                    and calm down, please.

This exchange is narrowly focused and makes little use of mental state language. As she becomes angry, Chloe interprets the staff as 'hating her'. This is an extreme, concrete and very generalised statement with a strong persecutory aspect. At times such thinking can take on a delusion-like quality. Indeed, transient stress-related psychotic episodes (including voice-hearing) are well-recognised in patients with borderline and related PDs.

The encounter occurs against a backdrop of escalating arousal, evident not just in Chloe but in Suzanne as well. It is a spiral that has been initiated by Chloe, but as things progress Suzanne's own ability to think is under threat. She finds herself resorting to a 'professionalised' form of communication, indexed by the words 'not appropriate' and the commanding tone of her voice and posture. She terminates the encounter by pushing Chloe away. We hear later, as Chloe reflects, about the significance of rejection in her life and get a further clue to the nature of her self-harm.

As with any ability, the capacity to mentalise varies between individuals and it also fluctuates within an individual. It is undermined, for example, by intoxication or fatigue or noise or the need to juggle competing demands. It is also eroded by high arousal levels such as when feeling threatened. The recognition and modulation of arousal states is a major issue in supporting people with PD at times of emotional crisis. Mental health professionals will often refer to this as *de-escalation*, with the discussion Chloe subsequently has with her home manager, during which she is encouraged to reflect on an incident, is a good example of *de-briefing*.

The challenges of supporting people with PD

People with borderline PD elicit complex emotional responses in those around them. It is a harsh irony of the condition that sufferers crave relationships, idealise them when they are first established, but soon begin to act in ways that that place them under severe strain. Rejection is watched for and almost expected at every turn and, when it is suspected, behaviours such as suicidal threats or self-harm are deployed in a desperate attempt to save the relationship. These behaviours naturally erode the relationship further and may ultimately destroy it.

Main (1957) described the effects of PD in a nursing team in a psychiatric hospital in his seminal study, *The Ailment*. In this study, the nurses found the emotional demands of their work at times overwhelming. The patients had adverse effects on staff morale, particularly when initial optimism gave way to frustration and feelings of failure when patients failed to improve. Main (1957) described that this can manifest in a process he called *splitting*, which occurs when there are quite different attitudes towards a patient's behaviour among members of a staff team, accompanied by strong differences of opinion about how to respond. Polarisation of opinion emerges, with some staff wanting to see the best in the patient and work with them despite all the challenges, while others become alienated and disengaged from them. Attributions such as 'attention seeking' and 'manipulative', or problems labelled as 'behaviour', are indicators of these negative feelings, as is a view that the patient is 'in control' of their behaviour. The theme of *controllability* is a recurring one in cases of recurrent self-harm in PD. Sufferers are often seen as choosing to behave as they do, with the intention of manipulating or controlling other people. PD patients therefore tend to be held accountable for their actions in a way that is not usually the case, for example, in schizophrenia.

Self-harm can be distressing to witness and can have profound emotional effects on those who see it. This may extend to frank revulsion, and result in efforts by staff to distance themselves from the person harming themselves. For nursing and support staff this can cause a unique conflict in professional values: between, on the one hand, the duty to provide care and protect from harm and, on the other, the understandable wish not to 'give in' to manipulation and risk encouraging it further. Under such circumstances it is hard to adopt and sustain a balanced view for long and it comes as little surprise that staff in Chloe's home, unfamiliar as they are with the spectrum of challenges she poses, would like her to move on.

Care staff do not simply have negative feelings towards PD-related behaviours, but these are made worse by the fact that these behaviours are *induced* as part of the caring relationship. In fact, what these patients really had in common, beyond their symptoms and behaviours, was an ability to bring about conflicting and potentially damaging emotional and behavioural reactions in caregivers (Flynn, 2014). This induction process takes place, at least initially, at an unconscious level, outside the conscious awareness of both the patient and the staff themselves. Main (1957) described a vicious circle in which patients inducing emotional states in others, evoking counter-therapeutic behavioural responses that rekindle symptoms and behaviours in the patient and so on. The attempts of professionals or other caregivers to support sufferers with PD may, in fact, contribute to making it worse.

How can people with PD be helped?

It used to be thought that little could be done to help people with borderline PD; that the outlook was uniformly poor and that efforts at treatment were, for the most part, futile. However, more recent research in the general population – research in which PD patients have been followed up over a number of years, suggests that recovery rates can be substantial even if some difficulties do persist. Such improvement may take several years to emerge. There are a number of specialist treatment models, particularly psychotherapeutic models that may bring forward the time to recovery substantially. However, these are also long-term interventions with patients typically in both group and individual therapy for in excess of two years. The inability to communicate verbally, for example, is a significant limiting factor in therapies that place a strong reliance on talking, particularly in the format that conventional therapies operate with. It is nonetheless the case, however, that people like Chloe can still communicate effectively with clinicians and support workers who are used to simplifying language, allowing time for responses, using accessible examples, avoiding jargon and who are prepared to be flexible in the length and timing of sessions.

Recent evidence now suggests that although specialist therapies offer some advantage over more generic or supportive forms of therapy, this advantage turns out to be relatively small, and that effective work relies on the therapist's flexibility, consistency, reliability, empathy, curiosity (the interest in discovering another's perspective; a stance of 'not knowing') and non-judgemental acceptance to build a 'therapeutic alliance'. Therapeutic alliance, however achieved, is recognised as a key prognostic factor in the treatment of PD and related conditions, with an understanding of mentalisation as a key perspective that helps this to be achieved. In this context, Chloe's debriefing discussion with her home manager after her self-harm represents a brief therapeutic intervention delivered by an informed non-specialist from, in this case, a social care background. The availability of such 'on the spot' interventions – provided repeatedly and patiently over a prolonged period – will expand Chloe's ability to mentalise and start to develop the sort of internal controls over her emotions that she failed to acquire earlier in life.

Encouraging Chloe to reflect in a mentalised way, however, is only half of the story. We have seen how the emotional responses of staff may exacerbate disturbance. Teams benefit not just from theoretical training in PD but also from the provision of ongoing support, supervision or consultancy. This helps them to identify and address unhelpful conflicts within their team as well as to talk about the emotional impact of their work. Much as it does for Chloe, this encourages a mentalising attitude within the team that allows them to take a more sophisticated view of the problems that someone like Chloe presents, and to respond in less 'reactive' ways.

Working at the level of the care team in itself, even without any specific focus on Chloe, may, in fact, be surprisingly effective. Singh *et al* (2009) trained the staff team of a challenging behaviour service in the use of mindful meditation and found that, over the following months, levels of aggression decreased significantly. Mindfulness (a practice of adopting psychological distance from one's own emotional states through meditation) overlaps with mentalisation, although may be better seen as *supporting* mentalisation. It is likely that it helped staff respond in calmer or more thoughtful ways in the face of challenging behaviour through modulating their own arousal levels.

What about medication?

The role of medication in PD remains uncertain. Some patients seem to respond very well to treatment with antipsychotic, antidepressant and mood stabilising medications, while others appear to gain little sustained benefit. The diagnosis of PD is not a reliable guide in itself as to what will work for whom in the field of psychopharmacology. On the occasions when medication is helpful in people with PD (with or without and intellectual disability), it is not always clear how they achieve their effects. For example, it is unclear whether they act on the PD itself or they target symptoms of a separate (or co-morbid) mental health condition. It can be difficult to spot episodes of treatable mental illness in this group or to attribute symptoms such as hallucinations to the PD itself rather than to, for example, an emerging psychosis. Clinicians in ID services are already familiar with the idea of diagnostic overshadowing (the bias of attributing psychiatric symptoms or behaviours to the ID itself rather than another cause) in the course of their routine work, but they may be less so in cases of PD, and complicating mental illnesses can easily be missed or disregarded as a result.

Finally, there is also evidence from genetic and other research that at least some cases of borderline PD may represent atypical presentations of mental illnesses for which well-established and potentially effective drug treatments exist. Chloe's story – that her mother suffered with bipolar disorder – is a common one, for example. Not only can severe bipolar illness have the potential to cause severe parenting disruption but it is also highly heritable, with its symptoms, like those of PD, often emerging in adolescence. Although Chloe does not have typical bipolar mood changes, her own mood instability may be partly driven by the same underlying process. This does not in itself negate the diagnosis of PD but rather provides another tool to help understand its causes and symptoms.

Conclusions

In 2009, NICE published its first guidelines for the treatment of borderline PD based on the prevailing state of evidence. It made reference to people with ID and that, where applicable, the guidelines refer to this population also. The guidelines do not, however, include advice on adaptations for people with communication and cognitive problems. Flynn (2014) takes a closer look at the applicability of the diagnosis in this group of people and examines some controversies in the field, such as the uncertain boundary between PD and mental illness. It also reviews the different forms of psychotherapy recommended for the condition as well as the role of medication. Flynn (2012) discusses in detail the challenge of adapting psychotherapies for people with ID and the importance of staff support and consultancy.

The *Handbook of Mentalisation-Based Treatment* (Allen & Fonagy, 2006) provides an in-depth yet accessible and engaging introduction to the field. *The Ailment* (Main, 1957), however, remains the seminal text and captures the emotional challenges faced by staff in a thoughtful and resonant way. It shows how open discussion in the setting of a facilitated staff supervision group can mitigate against splitting and the other harmful dynamics brought about in the course of working with PD patients.

Key learning points

- The diagnosis of PD can apply to some people with ID, especially those with milder ID.

- The diagnosis can often be very helpful for staff to understand why some people engage in extreme behaviours.

- Medication has uncertain effects in PD.

- Psychotherapy for the person with PD can be helpful, especially when it encourages a mentalising approach.

- Staff must always consider whether their responses to people with PD are being 'induced' by them unconsciously.

- Staff must be vigilant to consider whether unhelpful responses to people with PD, such as 'splitting' in care teams, are making things worse.

References

Allen JG & Fonagy P (Eds) (2006) *Handbook of Mentalisation-Based Treatment*. Chichester: Wiley.

Bateman A & Fonagy P (1999) Effectiveness of partial hospitalization in the treatment of borderline personality disorder: A randomized controlled trial. *The American Journal of Psychiatry* **156** 1563–1569.

Flynn AG (2012) Fact or faith? On the evidence for psychotherapy with adults with intellectual disability and mental health needs. *Current Opinion in Psychiatry* **25** 342–347.

Flynn A (2014) Personality Disorders and Intellectual Disability. In: E Tsakanikos and J McCarthy (Eds) *Handbook of Psychopathology in Intellectual Disability: Research, practice and policy*. New York: Springer.

Flynn A, Matthews H & Hollins S (2002) Validity of the diagnosis of personality disorder in adults with learning disability and severe behavioural problems. *British Journal of Psychiatry*. **180** 543–546.

Main T (1957) The Ailment. *The British Journal of Medical Psychology* **30** 129–145.

NICE (National Institute for Health and Clinical Excellence) (2009) *Borderline personality disorder: Treatment and management. Clinical guideline 78* [online]. Available at: https://www.nice.org.uk/guidance/cg78 (accessed January 2018).

Singh NN, Lancioni GE, Winton ASW, Singh AN, Adkins AD & Singh J (2009) Mindful staff can reduce the use of physical restraints when providing care to individuals with intellectual disabilities. *Journal of Applied Research in Intellectual Disability* **22** (2) 194–202.

Svrakic DM, Draganic S, Hill K, Bayon C, Przybeck TR & Cloninger CR (2002) Temperament, character, and personality disorders: etiologic, diagnostic, treatment issues. *Acta Psychiatric Scandinavica* **106** 189-195.

Chapter 15: The impact of life events and abuse on the mental health of adults with intellectual disability

By Hugh Ramsay & Philip Dodd

Summary

For all of us – people with intellectual disabilities (ID) and those without – life events can be positive and empowering, or they can be negative and traumatic. However, people with ID are more susceptible to negative life events and have fewer skills to protect themselves from their effects. This chapter explores the frequency of negative life events for people with ID and their effects on mental health. It considers how best to assess for them, and what management approaches may be helpful in addressing the effects of negative life events on mental health.

Background

Life events may be defined as a major event that changes a person's status or circumstances. Everyone therefore experiences these events to varying degrees. Negative life events are causally associated with a range of physical and mental health problems in the general population. Given that individuals with ID are exposed to more negative life events than average, including abuse (Jones *et al*, 2012) and typically have fewer psychological or social resources to cope with these events, this population would be expected to show increased negative mental health associations. This chapter explores the effects of negative life events, including abuse, on the mental health of adults with ID, aiming to clarify a number of key questions: what life events might be important in adults with ID?

How common are these events? What types of mental health problems and challenging behaviours are associated with these events? Does this association reflect correlation or causation? Finally, what should we do about these events as clinicians, both in terms of assessment/management and health promotion, including building psychological resilience?

What negative life events are significant for those with ID?

As is the case for the entire population, life events for people with ID may be positive or negative. Negative or adverse life events vary in severity from mild and predictable to severe and unpredictable. At its most extreme, adverse life events may be considered traumatic, with trauma defined in the DSM-V as 'exposure to actual or threatened death, serious injury, or sexual violence' (American Psychiatric Association, 2013).

It is well recognised that life events, including bereavement, unemployment and serious financial problems, can lead to mental health problems in certain vulnerable individuals. Given their vulnerabilities, the impact of adverse life events has been particularly well-studied in people with ID. Adverse life events can be categorised as arising from intimate relationships (e.g. divorce), parenting experiences (e.g. neglect), family environment in childhood (e.g. an ill family member, abuse), peer violence and community violence. Studies in people with ID have generally considered these broad areas, but particular life events are more common or significant in people with ID. These include vulnerability to family environment events such as bereavement (Dodd *et al*, 2005), vulnerability to sexual abuse (Turk & Brown, 1993) and exposure to peer violence (Jones *et al*, 2012). Each of these events are significant in themselves, but their secondary consequences can also be particularly devastating for people with ID. For example, parental bereavement may more significant where there is a lack of broad social supports or where it is associated with move from the family home.

How common are adverse life events?

Adverse life events, including traumatic events, are common among people with ID. The most common of these are: a move of house (22%), problems with a close friend, neighbour or relative (12%), and the death of a first degree relative (9%) (Tsakanikos *et al*, 2007). Other common adverse life events include serious illness of a close relative (8%), unemployment (7%), and problems with police or authorities (7%). These rates are relatively similar to those reported in general population samples, though the effect of the events may differ.

Some more severe adverse life events, such as exposure to violence (Jones *et al*, 2012), are known to be more common among people with ID. These increased levels of violence are evident in specific domains, such as in higher rates of intimate partner violence, higher chances of being the victim of violent crime and higher rates of general interpersonal conflict. One study found high rates of adverse family violence experience (87%) and violent attack later in adulthood (50%) (Catani & Sossalla, 2015), with family violence particularly strongly associated with post-traumatic stress disorder (PTSD). Other forms of violence are generally rare but reasonably common in those with ID, for example physical restraint (Hulbert-Williams *et al*, 2014). In addition to physical violence, people with ID experience much higher rates of sexual abuse than the general population.

Life events and abuse

General associations

Correlations between life events and a range of mental health problems have been noted in a number of studies. For example, Hastings *et al* (2004) found that those with ID who have experienced at least one negative life event in the previous 12 months were more likely to be diagnosed with an affective/neurotic disorder, but not to be diagnosed with an organic or psychotic disorder.

Associations with number and types of life events

There is evidence that the association between life events and mental health problems differs both by number and type of life event and by type of mental health problem. For example, examining a sample attending a specialist ID mental health service in the UK, different numbers of life events were associated with different problems (Tsakanikos *et al*, 2007) and, while at least one life event was associated with personality disorder, depression and schizophrenia, at least two and at least three life events were associated with personality disorder, depression and adjustment reaction. It is important to note that these associations are cross-sectional and it is therefore not possible to determine the direction of causality.

There have been attempts to examine specific life events and their associations with certain mental illnesses (Tsakanikos *et al*, 2007) and indeed there are specific life events associated with specific mental health problems, although not necessarily in a causal relationship. For example, unemployment, problems with authorities, sexual problems and major financial problems are associated with personality disorders, but not adjustment reactions, while loss or theft of a valuable item and separation or divorce are associated with adjustment reactions but not personality disorders. This study also found that moving house or residence was associated with schizophrenia.

Interestingly, a number of outwardly very serious life events were not associated with any mental health problems in this study, including the serious illness of a close relative, serious illness or injury of the person themselves, the break-up of a steady relationship or retirement from work. This study does, however, highlight the limitations with inferring causation from correlations (Tsakanikos *et al*, 2007). For example, personality disorder features can give rise to poor decision-making in the areas of alcohol, legal issues and employment.

There are two specific life events have been more extensively researched in people with ID – childhood abuse and bereavement. Given its sensitive nature and the fact that it is often undisclosed, childhood abuse, particularly sexual abuse, may not be adequately considered in broader studies of adverse life events. Catani and Sossalla (2015) found extremely high rates (87.5%) of childhood abuse had been experienced by adults with ID. This included 12.5% experiencing childhood sexual abuse in their family. In this context, it is unsurprising that a high proportion of this sample (25%) reached cut-off for a DSM-IV PTSD. In addition, a high proportion of the sample showed clinically significant depressive symptoms.

The study concluded that sexual abuse in people with ID has broadly similar effects to those seen in the general population, leading to a wide range of psychopathology. It has been harder to separate out this range of psychopathology, particularly when it comes to measuring symptoms of PTSD in those with severe and profound ID, but it does appear similar to the general population.

Bereavement has also been studied more extensively than other specific life events. People with ID experience high rates of complicated grief and there is reason to hypothesise that this population are at greater risk of pathological grief responses than the general population (Dodd & Guerin, 2009).We know that people with ID are more likely to have a limited understanding of death (MacHale *et al*, 2009). In addition to complicated grief, bereavement appears to be associated with a number of specific difficulties, particularly higher rates of affective and neurotic symptoms in people with ID (MacHale & Carey, 2002). However, many of these symptoms are common to normal grief, making it difficult to draw firm conclusions.

Association with types of mental health problems

In terms of specific mental health problems, life events appear to be more associated with mood and neurotic disorders than with other types of disorders including psychosis.

PTSD is, by definition, associated with traumatic life events, but its associations in people with ID have been harder to measure. There are a number of reasons for this including the lack of specific diagnostic criteria and difficulty in clarifying some of the symptoms seen in PTSD, such as flashbacks and nightmares around the trauma. There is little reason to expect that observations of higher rates of PTSD in adults exposed to childhood violence would not also be present in adults with ID, even when they have more difficulty in describing the symptoms.

Evidence for causality between life events and mental health problems

Much of the research on life events and mental health problems has been cross-sectional. This makes it difficult to determine if people who have mental health problems are more likely to encounter negative life events or if negative life events cause mental health problems. Though the evidence is limited, it appears reasonable to consider that life events are a risk factor for mental health problems in those with ID in the same manner as they are for the general population.

There have been some efforts to clarify this using longitudinal studies specific to ID populations. Even after controlling for earlier psychological problems, life events precede, and are significantly associated with, later psychological problems (Hulbert-Williams *et al*, 2014). Interestingly, this study did not find that psychological problems are significantly associated with subsequent life events.

Do negative life events impact more on those with ID than on others?

Adverse life events might be expected to impact to a greater extent on people with ID than those without ID due to factors such as reduced cognitive coping mechanisms. Indeed, higher intelligence has been shown to be protective in the case of PTSD. Social factors that protect against negative life events are also less present in the lives of adults with ID, for example they have fewer social supports and higher risk peer networks. Martorell *et al* (2009) found that traumatic experiences were significantly associated with mental disorders even after controlling for life events in general. However, life events were not significantly associated after controlling for traumatic experiences. This suggests that it is the event combined with the reaction to it that likely causes the psychiatric outcome.

Assessment

In some cases, the individual may be able to clearly relay any negative life events once they are asked. For others, screening for negative life events when assessing an adult with ID and mental health problems may provide insights. Some life events, such as childhood abuse, are strongly associated with specific disorders, such as depression and PTSD. Other life events are important as more general risk factors. 'Life event' checklists can be a valuable aid in assessment. This is particularly true where the tool was developed for an ID population and therefore screens for events that might not be regarded as significant in other populations. For example, moving house or the death of a non-first-degree relative may not be considered significant in other groups but are important for many individuals with ID. In addition, a high index of suspicion in the presence of symptoms suggestive of trauma is appropriate, especially where the individual cannot describe the trauma.

For some individuals, the pattern of symptoms, for example avoidance behaviour or signs of hyper-arousal (e.g. agitation, self-injurious behaviour), may point towards a negative life event experienced as a trauma.

Management

Awareness of the significant effects of adverse life events on adults with ID is the first step towards appropriate management. While there is a significant lack of specific research on the management of trauma-related mental health problems in people with ID, particularly PTSD, there is no reason to expect large differences from the general population.

Psychological and social interventions to address trauma and life events are effective for people with ID. Certain approaches are also useful in building resilience before potential traumas or adverse life events occur. For example, there is evidence that social support may promote resilience, and this may be particularly important where an individual has already experienced a number of adverse life events. Such social support has the potential to prevent an adverse life event giving rise to trauma.

Education approaches, targeting individuals themselves, staff and family, have a significant role to play in reducing risks and additional harms. For example, educational approaches can reduce the risk of negative events taking place and can be useful in addressing knowledge gaps that can contribute to difficulties after negative life events. Staff education and support is also important in providing best support to individuals with ID, particularly those with more significant impairments.

Case study: Childhood trauma and adult PTSD

A woman with a moderate ID and Down's syndrome lived with her family until she was aged 45. At that point she moved very quickly into residential services due to serious concerns around her home welfare. Her father had abused alcohol and was violent towards her, but he had died many years ago. Her mother had severe mental illness and was observed to be aggressive with her daughter. The woman with ID had never been treated for mental illness but presented in residential services with recurrent nightmares, intrusive memories of home traumas and occasional behavioural disturbance around food. She was diagnosed with PTSD and commenced psychotherapy along with SSRI medication. She showed some improvement but some difficulties persisted, likely due to the chronic nature of her life experiences.

Case study: Bereavement and psychotic disorder

A young man with a mild ID of unknown cause first presented to mental health services after the death of his mother. He presented with paranoid delusion, believing that his family were monitoring him and that he was being followed. A full assessment and collateral history suggested he had presented as paranoid for a number of years, but had been able to manage a job and had a high degree of independence. This changed with the death of his mother, who had always given him a lot of support. His remaining family were unable to support him in the same way and the death of his mother therefore led to a gradual increase in paranoia to the point of psychosis. He engaged well with the ID mental health team and commenced medication while attending a day service. His paranoia gradually improved and he was further supported with on-going community mental health nurse support at home.

Case study: Needle phobia

A young woman with a moderate ID of unknown cause presented to mental health services following verbal and physical aggression when staff tried to bring her to the hospital for a routine blood test. Assessment suggested that she had a needle phobia following on from an emergency hospital admission that was poorly explained to the woman. A behavioural management strategy was put in place to gradually address her fears. This involved visits to the local health clinic rather than the hospital, building in positive experiences alongside this and a clearer explanation of blood tests. Alongside this, a social story was developed to explain the process of blood testing. Ultimately, she was able to go to the health clinic for routine blood tests.

Key learning points

■ Adverse life events are common in adults with ID.

■ Adverse life events are associated with a range of psychopathology in adults with ID, but particularly PTSD and neurotic and affective disorders.

■ Childhood abuse, including sexual abuse, is extremely common among those with ID and should be considered whenever a person with ID presents with mental health problems.

■ Bereavement can have a disproportionately large effect on adults with ID, likely due to limited understanding of the concept of death and poor social support networks.

■ Assessments of the mental health of adults with ID should always consider and enquire about adverse life events, both recent and in childhood.

■ Management approaches to mental health problems related to adverse life events and trauma are similar to those used in the general population.

References

American Psychiatric Association (2013) *Diagnostic and Statistical Manual of Mental Disorders, 5th Edition (DSM-5)*. Arlington, VA: APA.

Catani C & Sossalla IM (2015) Child abuse predicts adult PTSD symptoms among individuals diagnosed with intellectual disabilities. *Frontiers in Psychology* Doi: 10.3389/fpsyg.2015.01600.

Dodd PC, Dowling S & Hollins S (2005) A review of the emotional, psychiatric and behavioural responses to bereavement in people with intellectual disabilities. *Journal of Intellectual Disability Research* **49** (7) 537-543.

Dodd PC & Guerin S (2009) Grief and bereavement in people with intellectual disabilities. *Current Opinion in Psychiatry* **22** (5) 442–446.

Hastings PR, Hatton C, Taylor JL & Maddison C (2004) Life events and psychiatric symptoms in adults with intellectual disabilities. *Journal of Intellectual Disability Research* **48** (1) 42–46.

Hulbert-Williams L, Hastings R, Owen DM, Burns L, Day J, Mulligan J & Noone SJ (2014) Exposure to life events as a risk factor for psychological problems in adults with intellectual disabilities: A longitudinal design. *Journal of Intellectual Disability Research* **58** (1) 48–60.

Jones L, Bellis MA, Wood S, Hughes K, McCoy E, Eckley L, Bates G, Mikton C, Shakespeare T & Officer A (2012) Prevalence and risk of violence against children with disabilities: a systematic review and meta-analysis of observational studies. *Lancet* **380** (9845) 899–907.

MacHale R & Carey S (2002) An investigation of the effects of bereavement on mental health and challenging behaviour in adults with learning disability. *British Journal of Learning Disabilities* **30** (3) 113–117.

MacHale R, McEvoy J & Tierney E (2009) Caregiver perceptions of the understanding of death and need for bereavement supports in adults with intellectual disabilities. *Journal of Applied Research in Intellectual Disabilities* **22** 574-581.

Martorell A, Tsakanikos E, Pereda A, Gutierrez-Recacha P, Bouras N & Ayuso- Mateos JL (2009) Mental Health in Adults With Mild and Moderate Intellectual Disabilities. *The Journal of Nervous and Mental Disease* **197** (3) 182–186.

Tsakanikos E, Bouras N, Costello H & Holt G (2007) Multiple exposure to life events and clinical psychopathology in adults with intellectual disability. *Social Psychiatry and Psychiatric Epidemiology* **42** (1) 24–28.

Turk V & Brown H (1993) The sexual abuse of adults with learning disabilities: results of a two year incidence survey. *Mental Handicap Research* **6** (3) 193-216.

Chapter 16: Medication

By Omaima Daoud, Shama Parveen & Asim Naeem

Summary

This chapter explores the role of psychotropic medications in people with intellectual disabilities (ID). It includes an overview of the key factors to consider regarding their use; using medication for challenging behaviour; using PRN (as required) medications; and the different classes of psychotropic medications, including their indications and side-effects. Four case studies highlight the complexities regarding the use of medications in people with ID, incorporating additional learning points for readers.

Introduction

The prevalence of mental illness is higher in individuals with ID compared to the general population. Up to half of people with ID will have significant mental health problems at some point in their life (Hassiotis *et al*, 2000), with anxiety and depression being particularly common, and the prevalence rates for schizophrenia up to three times greater compared to the general population (Smiley, 2005). It is not therefore surprising that the use of psychotropic medications in people with ID is greater than in the general population.

People with ID also have higher rates of physical health problems. Difficulties in communication, atypical presentations and barriers in accessing services can result in these comorbidities being under-diagnosed (Buckles *et al*, 2013). Behavioural and emotional difficulties are also more common in people with ID and can greatly increase the costs of providing care. There have been concerns raised regarding the overuse of long-term psychotropic medication in the absence of comorbid mental illness, and under-utilisation of effective alternative therapies (Deb *et al*, 2009). These issues were particularly highlighted by the events at the independent hospital Winterbourne View.

It is important to separate the appropriate use of psychotropic medications in the management of diagnosed mental illness in people with ID from the concerns that arise from their long-term use in people with challenging behaviours alone (where no underlying mental illness has been found). This can help avoid depriving individuals with ID of available treatment for a diagnosed mental illness. The use of short-term (or 'as required') psychotropic medication may also be clinically appropriate as part of a crisis management package to avoid placement breakdown where intensive and high-quality behavioural interventions are either not immediately available or have been ineffective (Glover *et al*, 2014).

Key factors to consider in the use of psychotropic medications in people with ID?

1. There are a range of factors that can make it more difficult to diagnose mental illness in people with ID, and in some cases it can be missed. Box 1 highlights the specific complexities that result in under-diagnosis.

Box 1: Barriers to diagnosing comorbid mental illness in people with ID

■ Difficulty in expressing symptoms due to limited or altered verbal communication and/or social skills.

■ Some symptoms (e.g. self-talk) may be considered age-appropriate for the level of ID.

■ Diagnostic overshadowing (assuming a change in behaviour or presentation is due to the underlying ID and/or autism, and not considering mental or physical illness as a cause).

■ 'Atypical' presentation of symptoms of mental illness e.g. hearing voices presenting as head-banging or other self-injury; depression presenting with predominant anxiety symptoms or aggression.

■ Overlapping symptoms e.g. obsessional rituals in autism with obsessive-compulsive disorder; autism and social phobia.

■ People with ID can often have a combination of symptoms based on the complex interaction of mental illness, physical illness and environmental factors. Some primary physical illnesses (e.g. hypothyroidism) can also present with secondary mental illnesses (e.g. depression).

■ Standardised rating scales may not factor in the individual heterogeneity (differences) of people with ID (e.g. risk factors from their past life experiences, their specific cognitive profiles and/or means of communication).

Case study: Julie

Julie is a 50-year-old lady who lives with her sister and parents in their family home. She has severe ID and diabetes mellitus, and she is due to have a hysterectomy for the treatment of complicated fibroids. She presented with a six-month history of apparent loss of interest in activities she previously enjoyed (e.g. listening to music and watching TV), irritability and some weight loss. Her family had noticed that she was interacting less with them. There was no evidence of any acute infections or of her being in any pain.

Her presentation appeared consistent with a depressive episode, and the option of antidepressant medication was discussed with her parents. A capacity assessment was conducted and it was decided that she did not have the capacity to consent regarding such medication. A best interest decision was made to prescribe her antidepressant medication, which was recorded in the notes. As she was due to have the hysterectomy soon, it was thought that medication should be started after the surgery.

Julie made a good recovery from surgery and her parents reported that she had improved a lot. She was less withdrawn, more interactive and had started to engage with her previous interests. Use of the Glasgow Depression Scale (carer's version) did not indicate depression. Her mood appeared to have improved although there was some occasional irritability. It was deemed that she did not require antidepressant medication and would be further reviewed in a month. At the next review, Julie's parents reported that she was back to her normal self. The team was able to discharge the patient back to the care of the GP.

In this case, it was found that Julie had become anaemic secondary to fibroids, and that this had resulted in her becoming more tired, lethargic and irritable, rather than her having a true endogenous depression.

This case highlights the following learning points:

■ Due to difficulties with communication, people with ID can present with 'atypical' presentations of physical illness, some of which can be mistaken for mental illness or 'behavioural difficulties'. Physical symptoms of tiredness had resulted in Julie no longer interacting as well as previously, and attempts to re-engage her led to her becoming irritable.

■ Unless the clinical situation warrants more immediate intervention, 'watch and wait' is a valid management strategy. This can help to reduce the risks of unnecessary prescribing of psychotropic medications.

■ It can be helpful to draw up a collaborative medication management plan, with appropriate time-frames, as part of the 'best interest' process.

2. Another factor to consider regarding the use of psychotropic medications with people with ID is that most of the licensed indications for medications are based on research done on the general adult population, without ID. In these studies, certain groups tend to be excluded, including people with ID, people with a combination of health problems (as these can act as 'confounding variables'), those on multiple medications, and sometimes the elderly. This can be due to some of these population groups lacking capacity to consent to research studies. Most of the evidence-base for the effectiveness of these medications is therefore extrapolated from the general population data. Provided a medication is licensed for use in a particular type of mental illness (e.g. bipolar affective disorder or generalised anxiety disorder), it does not require a specific additional license for its use in someone with ID. However, it is essential that the clinical reason or indication for prescribing a particular medication is clearly stated. Where there is an occasion of prescribing a psychotropic medication for an unlicensed indication it is important to document the reasons for this.

3. It is also common for people with ID to have at least some difficulties with their communication. Before prescribing a medication, adapted communication methods such as Easy Read leaflets and/or pictures may be needed.

4. Some people with ID do not have capacity to consent to treatment with psychotropic medications, as in the case study above, which can also raise significant ethical issues. In such cases, the medication is prescribed in their best interests under the Mental Capacity Act (2005) (MCA). This should be recorded in the patient's notes, and shared with the carers/family members responsible for administering the medication.

5. Some psychotropic medications need regular blood monitoring (e.g. lithium), which can be frequent (e.g. clozapine requires initial weekly blood tests). This is necessary to monitor for potentially serious side-effects (e.g. neutropenia, or reduced white cell count, and thereby difficulties fighting infections, in the case of clozapine). When prescribing these medications, the prescriber has to consider the frequency of necessary blood tests, and whether the person with ID could tolerate this. The increased use of some newer anticonvulsant medications (to treat epilepsy) in people with ID, such as levetiracetam, has been due to them not requiring routine blood test monitoring.

6. People with ID may be on more than one psychotropic medication and/or multiple medications to treat physical health problems. This is known as 'polypharmacy'. It is important to consider the potential interactions among these medications.

7. The use of psychotropic medications should not be viewed as an alternative to psychological therapies. In some cases it may be necessary to start medications to decrease baseline anxiety or depressive symptoms to allow psychological therapeutic work to commence subsequently.

There are a number of additional specific factors to consider when prescribing psychotropic medications in people with ID, listed in Table 1.

Table 1: Specific prescribing considerations for people with ID

Prescribing factor	Example
Medication concordance	People with autism may refuse to take a particular medication if it changes in appearance (size/shape/colour/writing on the tablet) e.g. if the medication prescribed is changed from 'branded' to 'generic'.
Medication efficacy	Some types of anticonvulsants (to treat epilepsy) need to be specifically brand-prescribed due to their altered pharmacokinetics (i.e. how quickly/slowly they are absorbed into the body).
Dose	It is preferable to start medications at low doses and make dose increases gradually ('start low, go slow'). However, evidence suggests that psychotropic medications for people with mental illness and ID are effective at the same doses as for those without an ID, and that there is no clear evidence that they have more side-effects (Frighi *et al*, 2011). It is likely that any pre-existing physical health problems in people with ID may make some side-effects appear worse.
Physical form of medication	Some people with ID have dysphagia (swallowing difficulties) and may require liquid preparations rather than tablets. This can also occur in the later stages of dementia in people with ID.
Maintenance, monitoring and withdrawal of medications	Increased community support on starting or altering drug doses, especially if a patient is on multiple medications. Regular monitoring of treatment response, side-effects and exploring continuation/discontinuation issues (at least every 3-6 months).
Good documentation	Clinical indications (e.g. type of mental illness) for prescribing psychotropic medications should be clearly documented.

Using psychotropic medications for challenging behaviour

A significant proportion of people with ID can display behaviours that challenge. Challenging behaviour is a socially constructed, descriptive concept and not a diagnosis in itself. It makes no suggestions about the aetiology of the cause of the behaviour. The behaviour can have a range of possible underlying causes, including underlying (or associated) mental illness, physical health problems, communication difficulties, long-standing, impaired behaviours that have been learnt, environmental changes, or a combination of any of these. While it is not always associated with mental illness, it can be a primary or secondary manifestation of it (Xeniditis *et al*, 2001).

Off-label prescribing of a range of psychotropic medications (in particular antipsychotics) to manage challenging behaviour that is not associated with mental or physical illness often arises in the context of clinicians having to manage acute disturbances in community placements. In these situations, the need for immediate action to help prevent placement breakdown (Glover *et al*, 2014) may necessitate its use. The significant reduction in specialist assessment and treatment units for people with ID, the reduction in mainstream general psychiatry beds, and the paucity of urgent respite placements are likely to continue to exacerbate these difficulties.

NICE (2015) recommends that antipsychotic drugs only be considered to manage behaviour that challenges if:

- psychological or other interventions alone do not produce change within an agreed time

- treatment for any co-existing mental or physical health problem has not led to a reduction in the behaviour

- the risk to the person or others is very severe, such as due to violence, aggression or self-injury.

It also recommends that narrative accounts of improvement in symptoms should be supplemented by objective rating scales (e.g. HoNOS-LD).

Case study: James

James is a 30-year-old man with severe ID and autism living in a residential home. He has limited verbal communication skills and presented with a six-week history of new challenging behaviours in the form of intermittent scratching and thumping of his chest. During this time he also started to refuse certain food and drink items. There were concerns that he was becoming increasingly dehydrated, especially as the weather became hotter. GP review excluded any infections.

Unfortunately, James collapsed in the home, resulting in an emergency admission to the local acute hospital. He was admitted to the general medical ward where blood investigations showed that he was severely dehydrated, but in the absence of any infective cause. He was commenced on I.V. fluids and then given a graded regime of increased oral fluid and food. However, the episodes of intermittent chest thumping recurred, and he again started refusing some food items. Staff on the ward also noticed that James appeared to have become more withdrawn and irritable, and his sleep cycle was disturbed (with him having difficulty getting off to sleep and frequently awakening). A referral was made to the mental health ID team for advice on the potential addition of medication to improve James's mood and decrease his anxiety.

The psychiatrist was able to see James with his keyworker from the residential home, who had been on leave during the time of the initial admission. He was able to confirm that both the food/fluid refusal and chest thumping were new behaviours and out-of-character for James. He was able to verify that the food refusal did not occur with all foods/drinks; James happily consumed Wotsit crisps and milk; and the chest thumping occurred more after meals and at night.

In view of James's presentation, the psychiatrist recommended a gastroscopy (OGD) to rule out gastrointestinal (GI) reflux or peptic ulceration as a cause for the challenging behaviour. A best interest meeting was held in view of James not having capacity to consent to this invasive procedure. The gastroscopy revealed the presence of a peptic ulcer and GI reflux. James was subsequently started on lansoprazole (an acid-blocker treatment for peptic ulcers). Within a few days the chest thumping stopped and James started to eat a greater variety of foods. He also appeared brighter in himself. He was discharged back to his placement after a few days of full recovery.

In this case, James's chest thumping challenging behaviours were secondary to an undiagnosed peptic ulcer and GI reflux disorder. He was hitting his chest area after certain meals due to pain, in the same way people may rub a body part if it starts hurting following a knock or injury. The symptoms were worse if James lay down flat e.g. at night time.

This case highlights the following learning points:

- The importance of taking a good longitudinal history from reliable informants (e.g. carers who know the patient well).

- Thinking 'outside the box' can help professionals correctly identify pain symptoms in people with severe ID.

- Specialist ID mental healthcare professionals play an important liaison role with mainstream services.

The different classes of psychotropic medications

Antipsychotics

There are two broad classes of antipsychotic medications: first generation (typical or 'older' antipsychotics) and second generation (atypical or 'newer' antipsychotics). Typical antipsychotics (e.g. chlorpromazine, haloperidol) generally cause more extrapyramidal side-effects such as hand tremors, arm/leg stiffness, altered gait, restlessness or abnormal movements of the face or tongue. It is more common to use atypical antipsychotics (e.g. olanzapine, risperidone, aripiprazole) as these have less of these 'motor system' side-effects. However, they can cause side-effects such as weight gain and metabolic syndrome (e.g. changes to glucose metabolism).

Antipsychotics are licensed for treating schizophrenia, bipolar mood disorder and other psychotic illnesses. Some are also licenced for short-term use in severe anxiety symptoms. Clozapine is used for treatment-resistant schizophrenia and needs regular (weekly) blood monitoring due to the potentially serious side-effect of neutropenia (reduced white blood cell count).

Case study: Steven

Steven is a 25-year-old man with moderate ID, autism and schizophrenia. He lives in a residential home and has some verbal communication skills. He had a relapse of psychotic symptoms two months ago. These symptoms had resolved quickly with a small increase in his antipsychotic medication (risperidone). He now presented with a two-week history of being unable to sit still, poor concentration and disturbed sleep. No physical cause was identified for his new symptoms, and there had not been any acute changes to his environment or routines.

Following psychiatric examination, it was discovered that Steven had developed akathisia (motor restlessness) secondary to the dose increase in risperidone. The dose was reduced back down to the previous maintenance level, with close monitoring and follow-up for any relapse of psychotic symptoms. Steven's akathisia resolved without psychotic relapse.

This case highlights the following learning points:

■ Akathisia is a recognised extrapyramidal side-effect of antipsychotics. It can be particularly distressing to someone who is unable to fully describe what is happening to them.

■ For cases of akathisia, it is important to explain the rationale behind decreasing antipsychotic medication in a person with ID whose symptoms can mimic severe anxiety/agitation.

■ In some people with ID, atypical antipsychotics can cause extrapyramidal side-effects even at moderate range doses.

Antidepressants

Antidepressants are licensed for use to treat depression and some also have a license for use to treat a range of anxiety disorders (e.g. panic disorder, obsessive-compulsive disorder, post-traumatic stress disorder). The commonest types of antidepressants used in people with ID are SSRIs (selective serotonin reuptake inhibitors, such as citalopram, sertraline, fluoxetine), mirtazapine, venlafaxine and trazodone. Most of these can have gastric side-effects (e.g. nausea) with the exception of mirtazapine. Some people with ID may still be on older-style antidepressants such as tricyclic antidepressants, which have more cardiac (heart) side-effects and can also cause sedation. All antidepressant types take a number of weeks to work most effectively ('lag treatment effect'). Some people may experience a temporary initial increase in anxiety when started on such medications.

Specific anxiolytics

These are usually the benzodiazepine group of drugs (e.g. diazepam, lorazepam) and are used to treat anxiety disorders. They have addictive potential so should be used with caution and for short time periods only. They are also anticonvulsants and so can be helpful in people with ID who have comorbid epilepsy or vulnerability to seizures.

Mood stabilisers

This group includes medications such as lithium, sodium valproate and carbamazepine. They are used to treat bipolar mood disorder. Some atypical antipsychotics (e.g. olanzapine) also have significant mood stabilising effects. Lithium has a 'narrow therapeutic window', which means the toxic dose (at which serious side-effects can occur) is very close to the therapeutic dose. Regular blood testing is needed to check lithium levels. Sodium Valproate can cause deformity to unborn babies, so female patients of childbearing age need to be carefully monitored.

Case study: Jane

Jane is a 40-year-old lady with moderate ID, autism and bipolar mood disorder who lives in a residential home. She presented with a six-week history of restlessness, pacing, over-talking and poor sleep. She had difficulty maintaining her concentration in her usual interests as she got easily distracted. She had been intermittently hitting out at staff. She had been on long-term sodium valproate and low dose olanzapine. On review by her mental health ID team, the olanzapine was slowly increased up to its maximum dose. Unfortunately, this resulted in worsening of her symptoms. She also failed to respond to a switch of antipsychotic medication from olanzapine to risperidone.

In view of the apparent 'treatment resistance', her team reviewed her diagnosis. It was felt that Jane may be presenting with an agitated depression rather than a manic relapse. The antipsychotic medication was therefore stopped and trazodone (an antidepressant with additional anxiolytic effects) commenced. Jane made a good recovery with this switch.

This case highlights the following learning points:

- In people with ID, an agitated depression may mimic manic symptoms. Antidepressant treatment, as opposed to antipsychotic, is needed in such cases.
- Some antidepressants have dual effects (i.e. they can help manage both depression and anxiety symptoms).
- In cases of 'treatment resistance' to medication it is important to review the diagnosis as an initial step.

Hypnotics

This group of medications (e.g. zopiclone, promethazine) are used for sleep disturbance. Some people with ID and autism who have persistent sleep cycle difficulties may be on melatonin longer-term.

Anticonvulsants

These are used to treat epilepsy, and include sodium valproate, lamotrigine, levetiracetam and carbamazepine. Some of these medications are also used as mood stabilisers. Pregabalin is also licensed for use in generalised anxiety disorder. Antiepileptic medications can interact with many other medications by altering their breakdown in the body via liver enzymes.

ADHD (attention deficit hyperactivity disorder) medications

These are 'stimulant' medications (e.g. methylephenidate, atomoxetine, dexamfetamine) and are mainly used to treat children with severe and persistent symptoms of ADHD. Such medications sometimes need to be continued into adulthood.

Anti-dementia drugs

These are covered in Chapter 4: Dementia and old age.

The use of PRN (as required) psychotropic medications

PRN medications are used to treat either episodes of severe anxiety (with benzodiazepines or antipsychotics) or sleep disturbance (with benzodiazepines or Z-drugs/hypnotics e.g. zopiclone). Benzodiazepines, such as diazepam or lorazepam, may sometimes be used to reduce anxiety that some people with ID experience before necessary health investigations such as blood tests or CT scans. The principles of good prescribing of such PRN medications include:

- Setting clear indications that are easy to follow by all care staff e.g. 'use medication X if symptoms of anxiety persist for more than 60 mins despite environmental calming methods', rather than 'use if severe anxiety' – 'severe' can be interpreted differently by various staff.

- Monitor response of target symptoms to PRN medications (e.g. duration of sleep, frequency of self-injury).

- Use the lowest effective dose.

- Review the need for PRN medications, including options for withdrawal.

Key learning points

■ The use of psychotropic medication in the management of diagnosed mental illness should follow the same principles in people with ID as for the general population.

■ The decision to use psychotropic medication should be based on a 'person-centred' management plan, taking into account a range of prescribing factors.

■ The indications for using psychotropic medications should always be clearly documented, including the need for ongoing review and monitoring for efficacy and side-effects.

■ Adapted communication methods (e.g. Easy Read leaflets or pictures) may be necessary in discussing the role of medication with people with ID. If someone lacks the capacity to consent, the decision to use medication needs to be in the person's best interests.

■ In the absence of mental illness, the use of psychotropic medication should be part of a management plan that includes psychological and/or other behavioural interventions.

■ People with ID are more likely to have 'atypical' symptom presentations, which can result in failure to treat an underlying mental or physical illness with the correct medication(s). It can also result in 'atypical' presentations of side-effects from medications.

References

Buckles J, Luckasson R & Keefe E (2013) A systematic review of the prevalence of psychiatric disorders in adults with intellectual disability, 2003–2010. *Journal of Mental Health Research in Intellectual Disabilities* **6** 1181–207.

Deb S, Kwork H, Bertelli M, Salvadr-carulla L, Bradley E, Torr J & Barnhill J (2009) International guide to prescribing psychotropic medication for the management of problem behaviours in adults with intellectual disabilities. *World Psychiatry* **8** (3) 181–186.

Frighi E, Stephenson MT, Morovat A, Jolley IE, Trivella M, Dudley CA, Anand E, White SJ, Hammond CV, Hockney RA, Barrow B, Shakir R & Goodwin GM (2011) Safety of antipsychotics in people with intellectual disability. *British Journal of Psychiatry* **199** (4) 289–295.

Glover G, Bernard S, Branford D, Holland A & Strydom A (2014) Use of medication for challenging behaviour in people with intellectual disability. *British Journal of Psychiatry* **205** (1) 6–7.

Hassiotis A, Barron B & O'Hara J (2000) Mental health services for people with learning difficulties. *BMJ* **321** 583–584.

NICE (2015) *Challenging Behaviour and Learning Disabilities: Prevention and interventions for people with learning disabilities whose behaviour challenges (NG11)* [online]. NICE. Available at: http://www.nice.org.uk/guidance/ng11 (accessed January 2017).

Smiley E (2005) Epidemiology of mental health problems in adults with learning disability: an update. *Advances in Psychiatric Treatment* **11** 214–222.

Xeniditis K, Russell A & Murphy D (2001) Management of people with challenging behaviour. *Advances in Psychiatric Treatment* **7** 109–116.

Chapter 17: Psychological interventions

By Emma Rye, Jo Anderson and Anna Bodicoat

Summary

This chapter describes some of the most widely used forms of psychological therapy and explores the ways in which adaptations need to be made to ensure these are appropriate for people with intellectual disabilities (ID). We focus on individual, group and family work, as well as systemic work with staff teams. We also share some thoughts about how a psychologist might decide which approach to use with a particular client.

What works for whom?

After an assessment has been completed, the clinical psychologist (or other psychological practitioner) will develop a psychological formulation. A formulation is a description of a person's difficulties, which includes an explanation of the possible causes of these, in the context of the person's life and history. This is based on the information gathered in the assessment and is informed by psychological theories. The formulation will then be used to decide what psychological intervention would be most helpful.

In the UK, the first NICE (National Institute for Clinical Excellence) national guidance on the prevention, assessment and management of mental health problems in people with ID was produced in September 2016. This included a very short section on psychological interventions with limited advice as to which approaches might be most helpful. This is because, compared to other areas of mental health, there is limited robust evidence as to which psychological treatment would be most helpful for specific conditions.

In some cases, a range of approaches could be helpful. For example, individual therapy with the client, group therapy, work with the whole family or staff team might all be equally helpful in addressing a person's distress. The clinical psychologist would therefore usually discuss the options with the person – if they are able to engage in such a discussion – and/or their carers in order to decide which would be the most suitable. For some clients, both direct work with the person with ID and indirect work with the staff team may be offered.

Once an assessment is completed, it is sometimes decided that no intervention is required. It may be that a formulation is developed during the assessment which helps the referred person – and the people around them – to better understand their thoughts, feelings and behaviour. Together, it may be agreed that what had previously been viewed as a problem is in fact an understandable response to life events. In these cases, hopefully, everyone leaves the assessment feeling better about themselves, and less worried.

Adaptations for adults with ID

Most psychology interventions that were developed for adults without ID can be used for adults with ID, however adaptations will need to be made to account for the person's difficulties. These adaptations might include keeping verbal and written language as simple and concise as possible, and providing additional support to understand outcome measures and therapy documents. Sometimes non-verbal creative techniques, such as drawing, can also help. Allowances may also be required for difficulties understanding time and numbers, for example having a 'calendar countdown' of sessions written out for the person, and not trying to establish exactly when or how many times something happened, if this is beyond the person's ability. It might be helpful to adapt the duration of sessions to account for the person's ability to concentrate. However, many people with ID are able to engage in therapy sessions for an hour every week. A person's support network (e.g. family, support staff, care management, other professionals) may need to be involved in supporting the intervention for both logistical and therapeutic reasons. However, this would need to be considered with the person's views, ability to consent, and best interests in mind. It is sometimes helpful to work alongside colleagues such as speech and language therapists, occupational therapists, nurses or other professionals.

People with ID might not have the experience of being listened to, due to living in busy residential homes; they may have had repeated experiences of loss due to high staff turnover, or being in care (Mattison & Pistrang, 2000). For these reasons they may need more time to develop a trusting therapeutic relationship.

Some people with ID may be able to access mainstream psychological services rather than a specialist ID service. However, reasonable adjustments would need to be made in line with government policy (Department of Health, 2001; 2009).

In addition to these issues, people with ID may have learned to agree with professionals, or to acquiesce even if they do not actually agree or understand, perhaps as a way of masking their ID or of being liked and accepted (Finlay & Lyons, 2002). In any work with someone with ID, professionals will need to be mindful of the possibilities of acquiescence – or suggestibility – and adapt by asking questions in different ways or stating out loud that it is ok for the person to disagree.

Individual therapy

Table 1 lists some of the most widely used forms of therapy; some of these approaches may be used in either group or individual settings.

Table 1: Forms of therapy
Acceptance and commitment therapy (ACT)
Cognitive behavioural therapy (CBT)
Compassion focused therapy (CFT)
Dialectical behaviour therapy (DBT)
Interpersonal therapy (IPT)
Psychodynamic psychotherapy
Narrative therapy
Eye movement desensitisation and reprocessing (EMDR)
Mentalisation based therapy
Mindfulness based cognitive therapy
Art psychotherapy
Drama psychotherapy

This chapter now focuses on two of the above approaches as used in individual therapy: cognitive behavioural therapy and psychodynamic psychotherapy. It then moves on to cover group work and systemic work with families and staff.

Cognitive behavioural therapy

CBT is based on the understanding that someone's thoughts (cognitions) are directly connected to their mood, which in turn is connected to their behaviour. In CBT the therapist works collaboratively to elicit the person's thoughts and develop a shared understanding about why they felt a certain emotion and thus acted in a given way. Repeated conversations with the individual in therapy aims to help them to notice their own thinking patterns that lead to them experiencing negative emotions, and then enacting unhelpful behaviour. Once these patterns are identified, the person is encouraged to try to break any 'vicious cycles' by either changing their behaviour or challenging their thinking.

This form of therapy is often adapted for people with ID by representing thoughts, feelings and actions visually, and drawing these out on paper in front of the person. Once this is done in several sessions and the person is able to recognise the patterns, the therapist will gently make suggestions about ways of challenging the thoughts or of changing the behaviour. Behavioural experiments, or other 'homework' tasks, are often used as a concrete method of helping the person take control over their situation. It might be agreed to invite a trusted carer to offer support in completing these tasks in between therapy sessions, as in Sarah's case study.

Case study: Sarah

Sarah lives in her own flat and has care staff visit her twice a day to help her manage her bills and paperwork and to prepare her meals. She was referred to a psychologist to help with anxiety and panic attacks. In particular, her anxiety was stopping her from going out into the community unaccompanied, other than to the local shop and back. During CBT it was identified that Sarah had had a bad experience when she first moved to her flat, when she took the wrong bus and became lost. She was unable to work out which bus she needed to get back and had a panic attack while on the bus. She felt humiliated by this experience, and although a fellow passenger helped her in the end she felt that others were laughing at her.

CBT helped Sarah to recognise that when going out she had thoughts like, 'I won't be able to cope', 'I'm going to get lost' and 'Everyone will know I am scared'. The link was made between these thoughts and Sarah's anxiety, and then to her behaviour which was to avoid going out at all.

The therapist helped Sarah to challenge some of her thoughts by building evidence of times that she had gone out and had coped well, as well as helping her to think of alternative thoughts she could tell herself. These were written down on cue cards that Sarah kept in her wallet so she could look at them whenever she was out. The therapist also worked with the carers to complete a behavioural experiment. They followed a graded plan with a carer initially going with Sarah on a bus journey, then walking a short distance behind her and sitting separately to her on the bus. After a few weeks Sarah was able to walk to the bus stop and travel into town by herself. CBT had helped Sarah to build her confidence and see a shift in her thinking patterns, which also gradually reduced her anxiety.

Psychodynamic psychotherapy

In psychodynamic psychotherapy, the therapist helps the person to understand their current difficulties in the context of their earlier experiences. The therapist gradually works with the person to start to understand the links between the ways in which the person interacts with people in their current life, and their childhood relationships with their mum, dad, or whomever cared for them in their early years. The therapist pays particular attention to the way the person relates within the therapeutic relationship in the therapy room. This helps the therapist to understand how the person relates to others, which facilitates the development of a psychodynamic formulation. This then enables the therapist to establish what to focus on in the therapy. Reflecting on aspects of the therapeutic relationship also gives an opportunity to give the person feedback about how they are relating in the room, which helps them to make sense of difficulties in other relationships outside the therapy room. As the person learns more about the part they play in difficulties in their adult relationships, they can start to approach these differently and to develop more fulfilling and less damaging relationships (Sinason, 2010).

Group work

Many people who present to mental health services are struggling with problems that are common to other people with ID. It can often be more helpful to offer these people an intervention in a group setting so that there is the opportunity to learn that others are going through the same experiences, or have had similar experiences and have survived.

The experience of being in a group setting for someone with ID can be especially powerful as it may be the first time that they are encouraged to support others through difficulties and to give advice, while also being listened to and being able to share in the group as an equal member. This can be empowering in a way that didactic approaches are not.

Group work can come in various different forms. Some groups aim to specifically address one need, for example in anger management, anxiety, or skills development groups. These would tend to follow a clear structure each week with subject matter defined by the group facilitators. They would consist of psychoeducation initially to help the group to understand how the problem developed and how it is maintained, before then focusing on teaching the group members a variety of coping strategies or skills.

Other groups are less structured and aim to provide a safe space for people to talk about a shared difficulty. Hearing-voices groups do this by encouraging people with auditory hallucinations to acknowledge their experiences without judgement. This can help group members to feel less isolated and to provide support for one another as to how to cope with their voices, rather than how to remove them.

Psychotherapeutic groups also follow a less rigid structure, being led by what the group members wish to talk about. The role of the facilitators here is to ensure that the group remains psychologically safe and that emotions are contained. The group is then able to discuss issues such as past trauma and abuse, and to think together about how these are connected to current difficulties in the group members' relationships and lives outside the group. For some group members, this will be the first opportunity they have had to discuss their painful feelings about having ID. Verbalising hitherto unspeakable things and being supported to do so by those who understand them is an important part of the healing process.

Case study: Scott

Scott had experienced physical and verbal abuse and bullying as a child and had ended up in care. He had learned to cope with his psychological distress by keeping busy. When his dad died, however, memories of childhood trauma came flooding back and he started experiencing night terrors and panic attacks. After an assessment with a clinical psychologist he was offered a place in a psychodynamic psychotherapy group. The group met for an hour and a quarter every week for a year. There were seven other people with ID in the group: men and women of a wide age range. Scott initially felt too ashamed to talk about his childhood experiences of being beaten by his dad, and called 'a useless piece of ****' by his mum. However, as other group members shared their experiences of childhood sexual abuse, bullying at school and other traumas, Scott felt he was not alone. When he talked about his childhood the group were extremely supportive. The group shared childhood memories of being bullied by other children because of their ID. Scott remembered being called 'spastic' by the children on his road. As the months went by, Scott's night terrors and panic attacks stopped. He was no longer having to work hard to suppress his memories of abuse. He had processed these, and while he still felt sad when he thought about his family, he was no longer overwhelmed by distress. He was able to go back to his supported employment working three days a week at a community café, and felt much more positive about his life.

Family work

Case study: Joseph

Joseph is a 21-year-old man who has diagnoses of ID and autism and lives at home with his parents. His verbal ability is fairly good, although he does have a tendency to say what he thinks professionals want him to say. Over the past few months his self-harming behaviour of biting his hands and banging his head has increased, and he has also been more aggressive towards his mum, pushing her over. These difficulties are only apparent at home and don't occur at college, which he attends five days a week. His parents say that he becomes upset by something at college and ruminates on this at home. They hear him talking to himself about the difficulties but when they try to talk to him he will become angry with them. He has one older brother (25 years old) who is training to be a doctor and one younger sister (18 years old), who has just left home and gone to university. His mum is a nurse and his dad manages a construction business.

Upon discussion with the family, it emerged that Joseph's ID resulted from him being starved of oxygen during his birth, and both parents felt the difficulties during birth were not responded to quickly enough by professionals. They spoke about their experience of not being supported throughout his childhood and of coping by themselves. They felt that the advice from professionals would not work, and the complexities they saw in Joseph made him different to anyone else supported by the team. They were struggling with the idea of him leaving home – they felt that he would not be able to cope, would end up hurting people, and would be very vulnerable in the community, even if he had support.

In family therapy the family had the opportunity to talk through their struggles and how they had overcome difficulties in the past. In the sessions, the therapists highlighted their strengths as a family and explored how they could use these when facing current issues. Over time the family reported fewer arguments and incidents of aggression. As the family felt they were being listened to and understood by professionals, they were better able to accept support, and, with the support of his care manager, Joseph was able to move out into supported living.

Family therapy can help families explore and exploit the resources within themselves to overcome difficulties (Baum & Lynggaard, 2006). Working with families can be particularly helpful if the difficulties are clearly relational in nature, either conflict between parents and child, or between professionals and the family. In the case study above, the attempted interventions so far had been experienced by the family as intrusive and blaming.

When families have a child with ID, there may be a sense of losing the 'healthy child' that is hoped for before the birth (Sinason, 2010). Each time of transition can act as a reminder of this loss and the grief associated with it. For the family above, the youngest child leaving home serves as a stark reminder of how things are different for her older brother. A family intervention may help to explore that pain and loss, and normalise some of the unspoken thoughts that may be especially painful or guilt-inducing for the parents.

Family work, like other psychological interventions, can also enrich the narrative about someone. Joseph's story can develop from just being someone with ID and autism who hurts himself, to someone who misses his siblings, wants more independence and is doing well at college. Although family work can't solve the intractable issue of Joseph being a person with a disability, hopefully, by allowing the family to explore their difficulties, they may rediscover ways of being that are mutually beneficial.

Systemic work with staff

If someone is referred because of concerns about their challenging behaviour, it may be decided that work can be done to try to change the environment in order to help reduce the frequency or severity of the behaviour. However, sometimes it might be decided that no more can be done to address the behaviour directly and it may be helpful to do some work with the staff team who support the person in their home and/or day centre, to help address their views about the person and their behaviour instead. Working with someone who expresses their distress by hitting themselves or others, spitting, screaming or throwing things can be exhausting, shift after shift. Sometimes this can result in the staff team developing a negative view of the person. A clinical psychologist, or a systemic therapist, might facilitate conversations with the team encouraging them to focus on the times when the person is not engaging in challenging behaviour (Baum & Lynggaard, 2006). As the staff focus on more enjoyable interactions with the person they hopefully start to develop a more positive view of them. This may help the staff to look forward to spending time with the person, rather than dreading each shift. Meanwhile, the person who exhibits behaviour that challenges feels more cared for and content, improving everyone's quality of life.

Key learning points

- A psychological formulation is central to all psychological interventions. It is a description of the difficulties, which includes an explanation of the possible causes in the context of the person's life and history.

- The psychological practitioner should agree with the person with ID, and/or their carers, as to which psychological intervention would be most appropriate, based on the formulation.

- It is important to adapt the intervention to take account of the person's abilities and communication difficulties.

- In all psychological interventions with adults with ID, it is important to consider whether the involvement of carers would enhance the effectiveness.

References

Baum S & Lynggaard H (2006) *Intellectual Disabilities: A systemic approach*. London: Karnac Books.

Department of Health (2001) *Valuing People: A new strategy for learning disability for the 21st century: a white paper*. London: DoH.

Department of Health (2009) *Valuing People Now: A new three year strategy for people with learning disabilities*. London: DoH.

Finlay WM & Lyons E (2002) Acquiescence in interviews with people who have mental retardation. *Mental retardation* **40** (1) 14–29.

Mattison V & Pistrang N (2000) *Saying Good-bye: Stories of separation between care staff and people with learning disabilities*. London: Free Association Books.

National Institute for Health and Care Excellence (NICE) (2016) *Mental health problems in people with learning disabilities: prevention, assessment and management. NICE Guideline* [NG54] [online]. Available at: https://www.nice.org.uk/Guidance/NG54 (accessed January 2018).

Sinason V (2010) *Mental Handicap and the Human Condition: An analytic approach to intellectual disability* (2nd Ed). London: Free Association Books.

Stenfert Kroese B, Dagnan D & Loumidis K (1997) *Cognitive-Behaviour Therapy for People with Learning Disabilities*. East Sussex: Routledge.

Chapter 18: The Mental Health Act

By Jane Barnes

Summary

Historically, many people with intellectual disabilities (ID) were incarcerated for long periods of time in institutions without rights of appeal or independent review. The Mental Health Act (1983) (MHA) was heavily influenced by the civil liberties movement and covers people with ID where certain criteria are met. The 2007 amendments to the MHA resulted in the inclusion of autism. However, there is still a reluctance to use the act with these groups and the revised MHA Code of Practice impresses upon professionals the need to be absolutely sure of the evidence before they use the MHA in these cases. This chapter looks at what the MHA and the Code say, and considers when and how they might be used.

Terminology

The terms 'intellectual disabilities' (ID) and 'autism' are used throughout this chapter. However, the MHA Code of Practice uses the terms 'learning disability' and 'autistic spectrum disorder', so, where directly related to text from the MHA and the Code of practice, these terms are also used. The chapter refers only to current law in England and Wales.

Guiding principles of the MHA

Least restrictive option and maximising independence. Where it is possible to treat a patient safely and lawfully without detaining them under the MHA, the patient should not be detained. A patient's independence should be encouraged and supported with a focus on promoting recovery wherever possible. Any restrictions should be the minimum necessary to safely provide the care or treatment required, having regard to whether the purpose of the restriction can be achieved in a way that is less restrictive of the person's rights and freedom of action.

Empowerment and involvement. Patients should be fully involved in decisions about their care, support and treatment, as far as they are capable of being so, and consideration should be given to what assistance or support a patient may need in order to participate. This includes being given sufficient information about their care and treatment in a format that is easily understandable to them. The views of families, carers and others, if appropriate, should be fully considered when taking decisions. Where decisions are taken that are contrary to views expressed, professionals should explain the reasons for this.

Respect and dignity. Practitioners performing functions under the MHA should respect the rights and dignity of patients and their carers, while also ensuring their safety and that of others. They must recognise and respect the diverse needs, values and circumstances of each patient.

Purpose and effectiveness. Decisions about care and treatment should be appropriate to the patient, with clear therapeutic aims, and treatment should be performed to current national and best-practice guidelines. Patients should be offered care and treatment in environments that are safe for them, for staff and for any visitors, and which are supportive and therapeutic.

Efficiency and equity. Providers, commissioners and other relevant organisations should work together to ensure that the provision of mental healthcare services are of high quality and are given equal priority to physical health and social care services. All services should work together to facilitate timely, safe and supportive discharge from detention. There should be clear mechanisms for accessing specialist support for those with additional needs.

The use of the MHA

The MHA is rarely considered when the needs of people with ID or autism are assessed. There may be a number of reasons for this:

- It is not felt appropriate to use the MHA for people with ID or autism.
- Generic consultant psychiatrists and approved mental health professionals may have little experience of people with ID or autism.
- Practitioners in ID teams may not have a good knowledge of the MHA.
- There is little joint working.
- There is a shortage of specialist units.
- Consultant ID psychiatrists often do not have access to beds.

- 'Acute' units are felt to be inappropriate for people with ID or autism.
- ID and autism are viewed as untreatable.

We must, however, consider the implications of this situation:

- People can be left in unsafe situations at home or in placements that may pose a risk to themselves or others.
- Parents or carers can be left to manage unsafe situations.
- Mental illness may be present but does not get identified or treated.
- Autism is frequently missed or misdiagnosed.
- People are admitted to hospital informally without any understanding of their rights and without an independent review of their treatment.

How should we be using the MHA?

- The MHA is not just about mental illness. It is concerned with the reception, care and treatment of mentally disordered patients. In the MHA, mental disorder means any disorder or disability of the mind.
- Section 2 of the MHA states that a person can be detained in hospital for up to 28 days for assessment if it can be shown that:
  - he is suffering from mental disorder of a nature or degree which warrants his detention in hospital for assessment (or for assessment followed by treatment) for at least a limited period; and
  - he ought to be so detained in the interests of his own health or safety or with a view to the protection of other persons.
- Section 3 of the MHA states that a person can be detained in hospital for up to six months for treatment if it can be shown that:
  - he is suffering from mental disorder of a nature or degree which makes it appropriate for him to receive medical treatment in hospital; and
  - it is necessary for the health or safety of the patient or for the protection of other persons that he should receive such treatment and it cannot be provided unless he is detained under this section; and
  - appropriate treatment is available.

For the purposes of the MHA, 'learning disability' is defined as, '*a state of arrested or incomplete development of the mind which includes significant impairment of intelligence and social functioning*'. The presence of learning disability alone would not be sufficient to fulfil the criteria for detention for treatment under section 3, or to make an application for Guardianship, or allow the making of a hospital order (made by the court) or community treatment order, unless it can be shown that it is associated with abnormally aggressive behaviour or seriously irresponsible conduct. This additional criterion is not required for detention under section 2 or any of the sections of the MHA that cover emergency situations. It would also not be required if the person with ID was suffering from an additional mental disorder such as mental illness, personality disorder or autism.

Autistic spectrum disorders are considered to be mental disorders within the meaning of the MHA in their own right and without any additional criteria. This includes Asperger's syndrome.

'The Act's definition of mental disorder includes the full range of autistic spectrum conditions, including those existing alongside a learning disability or any other kind of mental condition.' (DH, 2015)

Case study: Helen

Helen is a 38-year-old woman who has autism, ID and challenging behaviour. She has been in residential care since leaving school and was in her last placement for seven years before her behaviour became unmanageable. She was verbally and physically abusive to other people, self-harming and behaving in a very disinhibited way by taking her clothes off and laying on the floor with her legs open. Eighteen months ago, she was admitted to the local learning disability ward as an informal patient. She is under constant supervision, often refuses medication and requires frequent restraint for the protection of others. Her parents are elderly and her father is disabled. They are Italian and do not speak very good English. It is the view of professionals from the community ID team that Helen's parents would not like their daughter to be under the MHA, but nobody has spoken to them.

Issues for consideration
1. Is it legal and appropriate for Helen to be treated as an informal patient?
2. What rights would detention under the MHA give Helen?
3. What rights would it give her parents?

Answers
1. No, it is not. There must be lawful authority for her deprivation of liberty and regular restraint. There is evidence that she is objecting to her treatment so it would be necessary for her detention to be authorised by the MHA.
2. Helen would have rights to an advocate, appeals to the Associate Hospital Managers and the Mental Health Tribunal with legal representation in the latter,

oversight of her treatment after three months by a Second Opinion Appointed Doctor and visits from the CQC. If she was detained under section 3, she would be entitled to after-care under section 117.

3. Her parents would have the right to be consulted about the making of a section 2 and the right to object to the making of a section 3, which would require a court order to overrule. They have the right to request her discharge and to give their views to a Managers' or Tribunal hearing, and to have their views considered in any after-care plan.

'Abnormally aggressive' or 'seriously irresponsible' behaviour

Neither of these terms are defined in the MHA and it is not possible to define exactly what kind of behaviour would fall into either category. When considering whether a person's ID is associated with abnormally aggressive behaviour, relevant questions to ask include:

- When such aggressive behaviour has been observed, how persistent and severe has it been?

- Has it occurred without a specific trigger or does it seem out of proportion to circumstances that triggered it?

- Whether and to what degree has it in fact resulted in harm or distress to other people or actual damage to property?

- How likely, if it has not been observed recently, is it to recur?

- How common is similar behaviour in the population generally?

When considering whether a person's ID is associated with seriously irresponsible behaviour, relevant questions to ask include:

- Does the behaviour suggest a disregard or an inadequate regard for its serious or dangerous consequences?

- How recently has such behaviour been observed and how persistent has it been?

- How seriously detrimental to the patient or to other people were the consequences of the behaviour, or how detrimental *might* the consequences have been?

- Whether and to what degree has the behaviour actually resulted in harm to the patient or the patient's interests, or in harm to other people or damage to property?

- If it has not been observed recently, how likely it is to recur?

The MHA Code of Practice states that, '*When assessing whether someone with a learning disability should be detained under the MHA, it is important to establish whether any abnormally aggressive or seriously irresponsible behaviour stems from difficulties in communication, an underlying condition or unmet need.*' (DH, 2015)

Autism

It is possible for someone on the autistic spectrum to meet the criteria for detention under the MHA without having any other form of mental disorder. There is **not** a requirement for it to be associated with abnormally aggressive or seriously irresponsible behaviour as is the case for people with ID alone. However, the MHA Code of Practice takes the view that hospitalisation will usually not be helpful: '*Compulsory treatment in a hospital setting is rarely likely to be helpful for a person with autism who may be very distressed by even minor changes in routine and is likely to find detention in hospital anxiety provoking.*' (DH, 2015)

It is certainly true that going into hospital is very anxiety provoking for people with autism, as is any change to their environment, routine or the people around them. However, once they have got used to their new situation they can do very well in hospital if they are on an appropriate unit, because ward life is based on routine, regular activities and familiar staff. Their anxiety is reduced and they have the opportunity to access psychological therapies and have a proper review of their difficulties including any additional mental or physical health problems. They may have required specialist assessment and treatment to properly understand the nature of their difficulties, treat any additional mental disorder and develop their skills so they can fulfil their potential.

It is discharge planning that proves to be the challenge, because they often do not want to leave the safety of the hospital. After care must be properly suited to their needs and the staff who will support them need to have a good understanding of autism.

Case study: Colin

Colin is a 21-year-old white British man living in the community with a diagnosis of Asperger's syndrome. After his parents separated he was given the tenancy of a flat with support from the National Autism Society. He was so anxious when anybody came to the door that, on one occasion, he jumped out of a window on the first floor. He has now taken himself back to the old family home, which has been locked up because his father is working away. He has a fascination with trains and will often get on one without a ticket. When he gets thrown off, he has been seen walking down the railway tracks. He is being exploited by local youths who take his money and phone and use him to buy cigarettes and alcohol. He is neglecting himself and smearing faeces on the walls. His mother, who now lives elsewhere, is very worried about him and has written several letters to local services asking for help. However, there is a disagreement between mental health services and learning disability services about the nature of his mental disorder and who should take responsibility.

Issues for consideration

1. What are the risks of leaving the situation as it is?
2. How might services have responded to his mother's requests for help?
3. How would you gain entry if Colin wouldn't let you in?
4. Could the police assist in any way?
5. Does Colin meet the criteria for detention under the MHA?
6. Would it be possible to treat him in hospital without the use of the MHA?

Answers

1. Colin could be seriously injured. His self-care and mental state may deteriorate further. He could suffer further and more serious exploitation.
2. They could have referred Colin to the local approved mental health person (AMHP) service, who would have had a responsibility to take Colin's case into consideration and, if appropriate, organise an assessment under the MHA.
3. If the AMHP service had not been able to gain entry, they could have applied to the court for a warrant under section 135(1) to remove him to a place of safety for assessment.
4. When Colin was seen walking down the railway tracks, the police could have been called and they could have removed him to a place of safety for assessment under section 136.
5. Colin has a diagnosis of Asperger's syndrome, which is a mental disorder within the meaning of the MHA. He may also have an additional mental illness that requires assessment and treatment. Colin fulfils the criteria for detention under section 2 or section 3. As he has not been in hospital before, it would be appropriate to use section 2 in the first instance.
6. If Colin lacks capacity and is not objecting to admission, it would be possible to treat him under the MCA. However, he is likely to be under constant supervision on the ward and not free to leave, so an application under DoLS would also need to be made. Given the level of risk involved in Colin's presentation, it is likely that the AMHP would consider the MHA to be more appropriate.

Guardianship

Guardianship under section 7 of the MHA was intended to support people with mental disorders in the community, the criteria being that it is, '*necessary in the interests of the welfare of the patient or for the protection of other persons*'. Guardianship lasts for six months in the first instance, but can be renewed after review if it is felt appropriate. A comprehensive care plan is required, which includes arrangements for suitable accommodation, access to activities, education, treatment and personal support. The guardian can be a named person but the application must be accepted by the local authority in any event.

Guardianship places certain requirements on the service user:

■ to reside at a place specified by the authority or person named as guardian.

■ to attend at places and times so specified for the purpose of medical treatment, occupation, education and training.

■ to see a doctor, approved mental health professional, or another person so specified at the place where they live.

Guardianship does not permit someone to be treated against their will if they have the capacity to refuse, but if the person lacks capacity it would be possible to give them treatment under the MCA if it is deemed to be in their best interests.

The MHA confers on the guardian the power to convey the person to the required residence and to return them there if they leave without permission, but it does not authorise deprivation of liberty. Therefore, if the person was under constant supervision, then an additional application under the Deprivation of Liberty Safeguards would be required.

People with ID or autism often do very well under Guardianship because they are clear about the rules and have support. Carers also feel the benefit as they have professionals they can call on for advice or support. Unfortunately, however, the use of Guardianship has decreased dramatically since 1983. One of the reasons for this is probably because the criteria of abnormally aggressive or seriously irresponsible behaviour have to be met for those with ID to be placed on a Guardianship order.

Supervised community treatment using a Community Treatment Order

Supervised community treatment has been introduced as part of the amendments to the MHA and is designed to support people who have been detained in hospital for the treatment of mental disorder, and to prevent their relapse in the community. It is only available to those who are currently detained under section 3 or section 37 of the MHA (hospital order made by the court). It enables the responsible clinician (RC) to make the person subject to certain conditions following discharge from hospital. These conditions are intended to:

- ensure the person receives medical treatment for mental disorder

- prevent harm to the person's health or safety

- protect other people.

If a person fails to follow these conditions following discharge, the clinician can recall them to hospital. This may just be for a short time, in which case the community treatment order (CTO) will remain in place. However, if the RC subsequently revokes the CTO, the person will then be back on their original detaining order. Supervised community treatment was subject to a lot of controversy during the period when the changes to the MHA were being discussed. However, it is being used much more than was originally expected. It is also worth noting that the person does not have to have the capacity to understand the conditions in order to be made subject to a CTO.

How is an assessment under the MHA organised?

In order for someone to be detained in hospital under section 2 or 3, or made subject to Guardianship, there must be two medical recommendations and an application by an AMHP or the nearest relative. One of the medical recommendations must be from a doctor who is registered under section 12 of the MHA – usually a consultant psychiatrist. Ideally, one of the doctors should have previous knowledge of the person being assessed (often their GP). The two doctors must have seen the person with no more than five days between the two assessments. The AMHP must be warranted by the local social services authority and is required to look at all the circumstances of the case, not just the medical issues, and to consult with the nearest relative as well as interview the person concerned. The AMHP application must be made within 14 days. If it is not possible to locate the nearest relative, the

AMHP can go ahead if it is felt that consultation is not reasonably practicable or would involve unreasonable delay. If there is consultation and the nearest relative objects to the making of a section 3 order or guardianship, the application cannot go ahead without taking the case to court. A section 2 order can, however, go ahead even if the nearest relative is objecting.

If carers or members of the family feel that there should be an assessment under the MHA they can contact the GP in the first instance, who would then liaise with social services. An AMHP has a responsibility to look at the least restrictive alternative to detention in hospital, so the outcome may be support or treatment in a different setting, or provided in the home or on an outpatient basis. In cases of urgent necessity, it is possible for a person to be admitted to hospital for assessment under section 4 of the MHA on the basis of only one medical recommendation and an application by an AMHP or nearest relative. Once the order is made it will only last for 72 hours during which time a second doctor must see the person and decide if the order should be converted to detention under section 2 of the MHA, which lasts for 28 days.

If after the assessment the AMHP concludes that the person does need to be in hospital **and the person has the capacity to consent** to such an admission, they can be admitted as an informal patient. The person has the right to refuse treatment or to leave at any time. If the AMHP is concerned that this would be unsafe for the person or others, they would make an application under the MHA.

If after the assessment the AMHP concludes that the person needs to be in hospital and is not objecting to such an admission **but lacks the capacity to give consent**, the AMHP must decide on the appropriate legal framework. It would be possible to admit the person under the MCA, but, if the person's care and treatment on the ward is likely to amount to a deprivation of liberty, the MCA alone does not provide sufficient authority. There would therefore need to be an application under the Deprivation of Liberty Safeguards (DoLS; see Chapter 20). Any deprivation of liberty must be authorised. In a care or health setting this must be done in one of three ways:

- Detention under the MHA.
- Authorisation under DoLS.
- An order from the Court of Protection.

Anyone who is detained under the MHA is entitled to ask to see an independent mental health advocate (IMHA). The advocate can represent the patient's views to the treating team and be involved in meetings to review their progress.

People who come into contact with the police and courts

Part III of the MHA covers situations where the police are involved or where people with mental disorder have come before a court.

Section 135: This authorises a warrant to search for and remove a person to a place of safety for assessment on evidence, provided by an AMHP, that a person believed to be suffering from mental disorder is being ill-treated or neglected, or is unable to care for himself or is not under proper control.

Section 136: If a person appears to be suffering from mental disorder and to be in immediate need of care or control, the police may remove that person to a place of safety in order that they can see a registered medical practitioner and an AMHP within the defined time scales. Under section 136, a person cannot be removed from their own home. Both sections 135 and 136 have recently been amended so that a person can only be kept for up to 24 hours while an assessment is carried out. In exceptional circumstances this can be extended by a further 12 hours in order for a decision to be made about whether the person requires detention in hospital.

Appropriate adult

If someone with ID or autism is arrested by the police they must have an 'appropriate adult' present at their interview (Police and Criminal Evidence Act (1984)). This could be a relative or a carer or someone from the local authority's Appropriate Adult scheme. The appropriate adult is there to ensure that the interview is conducted fairly and sensitively, taking into account the person's vulnerabilities.

The MHA after charges or convictions

If a person with mental disorder appears in court having been charged or convicted of an offence, the courts have the option of using the MHA if they feel the person requires assessment or treatment. These include:

Section 35: Remand to hospital for a report on the accused's mental condition.

Section 36: Remand of accused person to hospital for treatment.

Section 37: This empowers a court to order hospital admission or Guardianship where a person is convicted of an offence punishable with imprisonment. Hospital orders under section 37 are very like treatment orders under section 3 and last for the same length of time.

Section 38: Interim hospital order. This is used when a person has been convicted of an offence punishable with imprisonment and it is unclear whether he will respond to treatment in hospital.

Section 41: If the Crown Court has made a hospital order and the offence is particularly serious it can add a restriction order, which means that the person can only be given leave from hospital or transferred with the permission of the Ministry of Justice, and can only be discharged by the Ministry of Justice or a mental health tribunal.

What does the MHA mean by 'treatment'?

For the purposes of the MHA, 'medical treatment' includes nursing, psychological intervention and specialist mental health habilitation, rehabilitation and care, as well as medication. The purpose of treatment is to alleviate or prevent a worsening of a mental disorder or one or more of its symptoms or manifestations. It can be seen from this that the definition of 'treatment' in the MHA is very wide.

People detained on emergency orders such as sections 4, 135 or 136 cannot be treated for their mental disorder without their consent. If the person lacks the capacity to give or withhold consent, a decision could be taken to treat them in their best interests following a capacity assessment. In the event of urgent necessity, the person may be treated under the 'common law'. People detained under assessment or treatment orders such as sections 2, 3 and 37 can be compulsorily treated for their mental disorder without their consent whether they have capacity or not. Any treatment that goes on for longer than three months must be authorised by a second opinion appointed doctor (SAOD) provided by the Care Quality Commission (CQC). There are also additional safeguards before certain treatments can be authorised, such as electroconvulsive therapy (ECT).

Reviews, appeals and discharge

People who are detained under the MHA should have regular reviews as well as rights of appeal if they do not agree with their detention in hospital. The RC in charge of their treatment can discharge patients under sections 2, 3 and 37 at any time. Patients can also appeal to the Associate Hospital Managers or to the Mental Health Tribunal for an independent review of their detention and a decision about whether they need to stay in hospital, or if their discharge should be ordered. Other patients who are on court orders with restrictions may only be discharged by a tribunal and may have conditions imposed upon them. At the tribunal hearing, patients are entitled to free legal representation. People on CTOs and Guardianship orders can be discharged by the community RC and have rights of appeal to the Mental Health Tribunal. Guardianship orders can also be discharged by the local authority or the nearest relative.

After-care

Under section 117 of the MHA there is an entitlement to after care for people who are, or have been in the past, detained under sections 3, 37, 45A, 47 or 48 of the MHA. It requires clinical commissioning groups (CCGs) and local authorities, in co-operation with voluntary agencies, to provide or arrange for the provision of after care services until such time as they are satisfied that the person concerned is no longer in need of such services. This is an important entitlement for people who have been detained in hospital for the treatment of their mental disorder. It is also important to know that patients cannot be charged for any services provided for them under section 117.

Conclusion

When assessing the needs of people with ID or autism, it is the responsibility of us all to be aware of the options available and to use the tools we have effectively. The care and treatment of people with ID and autism is still organised in a very paternalistic way, with little emphasis on the protection of their rights. It is important that staff involved in their care are aware of these protections and use them appropriately. We should not dismiss the MHA as being inappropriate for people with ID or autism without proper consideration. It might actually be very helpful in ensuring that someone obtains the assessment, treatment and protection they require, as well as supporting the carers who may be so overwhelmed that they cannot make those decisions.

Key learning points

■ The use of the MHA with people who have ID or autism should be considered in mental health services.

■ A culture of paternalism among carers and professionals does not take into account the protection of rights.

■ The MHA ensures access to assessment and treatment.

■ The MHA provides a risk management framework.

References

Department of Health (2015) *Code of Practice: Mental Health Act 1983* [online]. Available at: https://www.gov.uk/government/publications/code-of-practice-mental-health-act-1983 (accessed January 2018).

Department of Health (2008) Refocusing the Care Programme Approach: Policy and positive practice guidance.

NHS England (2014) Winterbourne View, Time for Change. Transforming the commissioning of services for people with learning disabilities and/or autism.

Chapter 19: Consent to treatment, the Mental Capacity Act and the Deprivation of Liberty Safeguards

By Jane Barnes and Steve Hardy

Summary

Making your own decisions is a fundamental right for all adults. This chapter explores how capacity to make decisions is assessed and how decisions are made on behalf of people who lack capacity on any particular issue. The chapter focuses on capacity law in England and Wales (The Mental Capacity Act (2005)). Scotland has the Adults with Incapacity (Scotland) Act (2000) and Northern Ireland has the Mental Capacity Act (Northern Ireland) (2016). Despite these different acts, the general principles of capacity and consent are similar throughout the UK. The chapter also looks at the Deprivation of Liberty Safeguards.

Introduction

Mental capacity is an individual's ability to make decisions. It can be about small day-to-day decisions, such as deciding what to wear or what to eat, through to more significant decisions such as where to live or whether to have medical treatment. The Mental Capacity Act (MCA) is applicable to anyone who cares for a person who may lack capacity. This includes family, paid carers and professionals. The MCA is underpinned by five guiding principles:

1. We must assume a person has the capacity to make a decision unless proved otherwise.

2. All practical steps must be made to support an individual to make a decision.

3. A person is not to be treated as unable to make a decision merely because he or she makes a decision that is deemed unwise by others.

4. Anything done for or on behalf of a person who lacks capacity must be done so in their best interests.

5. Any decision made in the best interests of an individual should be the least restrictive of their basic rights and freedoms.

According to the MCA: *'a person lacks capacity in relation to a matter if, at the material time, he is unable to make a decision for himself in relation to the matter because of an impairment of or disturbance in the functioning of the mind or brain.'*

The person should be able to understand the reasonably foreseeable consequences of deciding one way or the other or of failing to make the decision. Often these assessments are not clear cut so a conclusion about someone's capacity in any particular situation must be decided on the balance of probabilities dependent on the evidence available at the time. Consent is invalid without capacity. For consent to be valid, it must be freely given and informed, so the person must be able to understand the effects, risks and alternatives. If the person can do this then they are entitled to make any decision they wish. Consent given under undue pressure cannot be deemed to be valid consent and nobody else can consent for you without legal authority. This sometimes comes as a surprise to families and care staff who assume that they can make decisions on behalf of adult service users without reference to the MCA.

Assessing capacity to give consent

The vast majority of people are able to make the complete range of decisions that affect their life and their capacity is unlikely to be questioned. The MCA indicates that when a person has a 'mental disorder' (a definition that includes ID), capacity may be assessed. This does not mean that the person lacks capacity – the assessment will establish this.

The judgment as to whether or not an individual has capacity is based on their ability to understand the nature and effects of the decision to be taken at the time it needs to be taken. Each decision is assessed independently, as the information pertaining to each decision will be unique, and some individuals may be able to make some decisions but not other, more complicated ones, for example. A person's capacity to give consent is not static – it can change.

The functional approach

The MCA has adopted a 'functional approach' to assessing capacity and this has been developed through several key court cases (British Medical Association & The Law Society, 2009). The functional approach to assessing capacity is a four-stage test and all stages should be passed.

1. **Understand the information relating to the decision**
   The person should be given all relevant information relating to the decision that needs to be made. They need to understand the information and believe it to be true.

2. **Retain the information**
   The person should be able to remember the information long enough to reach a decision. The MCA sets out no time frame for information to be retained; this would be a matter of professional judgement.

3. **Weigh, balance and use the information**
   The person should be able to weigh the information, looking at both the possible positive and negative outcomes of making the decision, and the same for any alternative options. They should be able to balance these and use this information to come to a decision.

4. **Be able to communicate the choice**
   The person needs to be able to communicate their decisions. Communication does not just mean verbally; it could be any form of communication that the person uses (sign language, pictorial symbols etc.).

In regards to capacity to consent to treatment, the individual responsible for completing the assessment is the professional who would implement the treatment (e.g. for dental treatment, the dentist). But the responsible professional might not have met the person before or know how they communicate, so it is good practice for them to seek the help of those who know the person well (e.g. family or support workers) or have expertise in working with people with ID. Once an individual has been given sufficient information about the decision and enough time and support to absorb the information, the assessor will interview the person to ascertain if they pass the functional test.

Etchells *et al* (1999) developed a tool called *The Aid to Capacity Evaluation*, which offers guidance on the type of questions that should be asked in an assessment (see Box 1).

Box 1: Assessment questions

- Ability to understand the medical problem
  - What problem are you having right now?
  - Why are you in hospital?

- Ability to understand the proposed treatment
  - What is the treatment for?
  - What can we do to help you?

- Ability to understand the alternatives to the proposed treatment (if any)
  - Are there any other treatments?
  - What other options do you have?

- Ability to understand the option of refusing treatment (including withdrawing treatment)
  - Can you refuse?
  - Could we stop the treatment?

- Ability to appreciate the reasonably foreseeable consequences of accepting the treatment
  - What could happen if you have the treatment?
  - How could the treatment help you?
  - Could the treatment cause problems or side effects?

- Ability to appreciate the reasonably foreseeable consequences of refusing the treatment
  - What could happen to you if you don't have the treatment?
  - Could you get sicker/die without the treatment?

- The decision is not substantially based because of hallucinations, delusions or cognitive signs of depression
  - Why have you decided to accept/refuse the treatment?
  - Do you think we are trying to harm you?
  - Do you deserve to be treated?
  - Do you feel you are being punished?
  - Do you feel that you are a bad person?

(NB. These questions may need to be simplified when interviewing people with ID).

Before the assessment, the assessor should have a clear understanding of where to set the bar as to passing or failing the functional test. This would include what pertinent information the person should know and understand about the decision. The 'bar' for people with ID would be the same as any other person. It is the way in which we deliver the information and ask the questions that might differ. Whatever the outcome of the assessment, it should be clearly recorded in the person's records and have clear reasoning supporting the conclusion. This should also be communicated to the person.

Acting in a person's best interests

If, after assessment, the person is deemed to lack the capacity to make a decision about the matter in question, any decision made or act done on their behalf must be done in their best interests. Decisions may be made by attorneys, deputies and the Court of Protection. Decisions will often be made by staff involved in care and treatment. The decision maker will generally be the professional that will implement the decision (e.g. a medical procedure). The MCA provides a best interests checklist that decision makers should follow.

Best interests' checklist

- **Consider all relevant circumstances.**
  This might include diagnosis and prognosis, physical and emotional needs, the care the person needs and risk assessment. Is there an applicable Advance Decision, Lasting Power of Attorney or order from the Court of Protection?

- **Consider the person's reasonably ascertainable past and present wishes, beliefs and values.**

- **Consult others who have an interest in the person's welfare.**
  This would include family, friends and professionals. If none of these people is available and it is a serious medical decision or a proposed change in accommodation (provided/commissioned by the NHS or social services), an independent mental capacity advocate (IMCA) should be sought. The IMCA's role is to represent the person, not to make the decision.

- **Consider less restrictive options – can the same result be achieved in a less restrictive way?**

- **Is the person likely to regain capacity in the future and can the decision wait?**

- **Encourage and permit the person to participate.**

- **Do not base the best interests' decision solely on age, appearance, behaviour or condition.**

- **If the decision is about life-sustaining treatment, do not be motivated by a desire to bring about the person's death.**

Table 1: Examples of issues for consideration

	Possible areas for consideration
Emotional	Short and long-term reaction to event/procedure
Medical	Risks and benefits and likelihood of each option occurring Pain Aftercare
Social welfare	Where the person lives Independence Relationships Occupation/daytime activity

In relation to any proposed treatment, the decision maker also needs to consider any alternatives that are available and their associated benefits/risks and the impact on the person's life. The decision maker may not have met the person before and only know them in the context of the treatment decision. It is good practice in these situations for a best interests meeting to be held. This offers all parties who care for or work with the person the opportunity to discuss the decision, ensure the MCA best interests' checklist is followed, and weigh up the pros and cons. Once the best interests decision has been made, the details should be clearly recorded and, if a best interests meeting was held, minutes should be produced. Both records should detail the outcome of the best interests checklist, the decision, how it was reached and how it will be implemented.

In the event that agreement cannot be reached about what is in the person's best interests or if the decision is a very serious one, an application should be made to the Court of Protection. If staff are in doubt about whether a decision should be referred to the Court, they should seek legal advice from the relevant trust/local authority/ provider agency. There are some decisions which are deemed to be so personal that only a person with capacity can make them. These include sexual relationships, marriage, voting and adoption. Other decisions can only be made by the Court of Protection. These include organ donation and non-therapeutic sterilisation.

Restraint

Care staff will often say that their organisation's policies do not allow them to use restraint. However, this is not what the MCA says and law will always have greater authority than policy. Under the MCA, staff are empowered to use restraint if they reasonably believe:

- the person lacks the capacity to consent to the act in question

- it needs to be done in their best interests

- restraint is necessary to protect the person from harm

- it is a proportionate response to the risk posed.

Examples of when this may happen could include holding someone who requires an injection or eye drops because they lack the capacity to consent to it and it needs to be given in their best interests. It could also include preventing someone who does not understand the danger of cars from running into the road. Restraint cannot amount to deprivation of liberty, which requires separate authorisation under DoLS (see below). Also, restraint under the MCA does not cover harm to others. Clearly, however, staff have a duty of care to all their service users and they may, under common law, take appropriate and necessary actions to restrain the person to prevent harm to others or themselves.

When carrying out acts of care or treatment for a person who lacks capacity, staff will be legally protected under section 5 of the MCA provided that:

- they have taken reasonable steps to assess capacity

- they reasonably believe the person lacks capacity to consent to the act in question

- they reasonably believe the act is in the person's best interests.

Advanced Decisions

An adult over the age of 18 who has the capacity to make decisions about their treatment may decide that there are certain treatments they would not wish to have in the future if they lost the capacity to make those decisions. This is called an Advance Decision. It has also been called an Advance Directive or a Living Will. Decisions can be verbal, unless it involves life-sustaining treatment in which case it must be put in writing, signed and witnessed. It can only be used to refuse treatment; it cannot be used to dictate what treatment the person would like as that is a clinical decision that only a doctor can make. Medical staff must take notice of an Advance Decision if it is valid and applicable.

Lasting Power of Attorney (LPA)

Under an LPA, a person over the age of 18 can, while they still have the capacity to make decisions, appoint another person over the age of 18 years to make decisions on their behalf should they lose capacity in the future. There are two types of LPA:

1. Personal welfare including healthcare.

2. Property and affairs (financial matters).

People can choose to have one or both, but the person being appointed must agree to take on the role and it must be written down and registered with the Office of the Public Guardian before it can be used.

Mental disorder

The MCA can cover treatment for mental disorder as well as physical conditions but it does not authorise deprivation of liberty without DoLS. If a person needs to be admitted to hospital for the treatment of mental disorder, lacks capacity, and is not objecting, then either the MHA or DoLS could be used and it would be up to the AMHP to decide which would be the most appropriate in that particular case. If a person is detained under the MHA they can be treated without their consent for their mental disorder. However, if they require treatment for a physical disorder this would still be covered by the MCA and would be subject to a capacity assessment.

Case study: D

D is a 48-year-old man (white British) with a diagnosis of autism and mild ID. He has a history of placement breakdown due to verbal abuse of staff and other residents and aggression to property. He is currently in a specialist unit detained under the Mental Health Act. He does not engage in many activities although he does like to go out and he attends sessions with the psychologist. He is monosyllabic when spoken to and sometimes abusive. He has a history of stealing ladies' underwear from washing lines. He still likes to wear ladies' underwear and has asked staff to help him buy it.

D has significant health problems exacerbated by obesity and smoking. He does not want to address either of these problems. He has started to go blue when resting and, on one occasion, was rushed to the general hospital by ambulance. He has been diagnosed with COAD (chronic obstructive airways disease) and has been provided with a breathing mask at night. He is refusing to wear the mask and fights the staff if they try to put it on him. D has a supportive family who visit him and attend his reviews.

Issues for discussion

1. Does the MHA have a part to play in a consideration of the issues concerning the ladies' underwear or COAD?

2. Is the issue of the ladies' underwear a capacity issue?

3. How should D's capacity to consent to the use of the mask be assessed?

4. If he is deemed to have capacity in relation to the treatment of his COAD, is he entitled to refuse the use of the mask?

5. If he is deemed to lack capacity in relation to the treatment of his COAD, how should the team go about deciding what would be in his best interests?

6. If it is decided that he lacks capacity in relation to the treatment of his COAD and it would be in his best interests to use the mask, could restraint be used to ensure he uses it?

Answers

1. No. The MHA is only concerned with the treatment of mental disorder.

2. No. This is a sexual preference and should be accommodated if it can be in a way that does not cause offence or distress to other people. The staff managed this by taking him to buy the underwear and getting an agreement from him that he would only wear it on show when he was in his own room.

3. His condition and the need for the mask should be carefully explained to him by a doctor in a way that gives him the best chance of understanding. It would be helpful to have someone there that D knows well and trusts – perhaps a member of his family or the psychologist that he gets on well with.

4. Yes, he is, even though this may mean that his condition deteriorates and leads to his death. Staff often find this difficult to tolerate but that is his right if he understands the issues and the risks. Alternative treatments should be explored if they are available as they might be more acceptable to him.

5. Follow the best interests' checklist, get his views and consult all those with an interest in his welfare. This could be through a best interests meeting.

6. Yes, it could. Again, staff often find this very difficult and do not want to do it, but to decide that it would be in his best interests because without it he may die and then not do it would be negligent. (In fact, it did not take too long for D to get used to the mask and it led to a significant benefit.)

Deprivation of Liberty Safeguards

At the same time that the MHA was amended, the Mental Capacity Act was amended to include the Deprivation of Liberty Safeguards (DoLS). These came into force in 2009 and apply to adults:

- over the age of 18 years in care homes or hospitals
- who suffer from a disorder or disability of the mind
- who lack the capacity to consent to their care and treatment
- whose care and treatment amounts to a deprivation of liberty
- whose care arrangements are attributable to the state.

These safeguards were introduced in response to a famous case called the Bournewood case (R v Bournewood Community and Mental Health NHS Trust, *ex parte L*). This case involved a 48-year-old man with ID, autism, very little speech and challenging behaviour. In 1997 he was admitted to the Bournewood Trust and kept there for several months without being detained under the MHA and without his carers, Mr and Mrs E, being allowed to visit him. They were very unhappy about this as they did not feel he needed to be in hospital and did not feel it was right that he could be kept there and that they should be prevented from seeing him on the opinion of one psychiatrist. They took out a legal case against the Trust which went through the High Court, the Court of Appeal and the House of Lords. Although the Trust was not found to have acted unlawfully, the case highlighted that apparently compliant, incapacitated patients would not have the specific protections provided by the MHA. This came to be known as the 'Bournewood gap'. The case was eventually heard in the European Court of Human Rights, which ruled that the man's detention in hospital was contrary to the Human Rights Act, article 5, because someone should only be deprived of their liberty through a process of law and such detention must be subject to independent legal review. It said that the MHA should be used where it applies and the UK government should develop other procedures for people who lack capacity where the MHA does not apply and where their care and treatment amounts to a deprivation of liberty. In 2009 the UK government therefore brought in DoLS.

Between 2009 and 2014 the number of referrals for DoLS assessments was low throughout the country. The safeguards were not well understood by organisations providing care and treatment, and there was a lack of agreement among professionals about what constituted deprivation of liberty. A number of cases were eventually heard in the Supreme Court, which ruled that there are two key questions which provide the 'acid test' for whether someone is objectively deprived of liberty:

- Is the person subject to continuous supervision and control?
- Is the person free to leave?

Being free to leave does not mean just being able to go out, but whether the person is free to live somewhere else if they wished to. Factors that are no longer relevant when considering whether someone is being deprived of their liberty include their compliance or lack of objection, how they compare to other people with disabilities or the reason/purpose behind a particular placement.

This ruling has had a significant impact on both local authorities and care providers. Because the threshold has been lowered it means that there are far more people who should now be covered by the safeguards. There are also a significant number of service users in supported living whose care amounts to a deprivation of liberty. It may even apply to people cared for in their own homes. They cannot be made subject to DoLS because those procedures only apply to care homes and hospitals. Their cases therefore need to be referred to the Court of Protection. Local authorities fulfil the role of supervisory body for all care providers and hospitals in their area. This means that they must arrange DoLS assessments, scrutinise those assessments and issue authorisations as appropriate for people in care homes and hospitals, and make applications to the Court of Protection as appropriate for those in other types of situations.

Care providers have specific responsibilities:

- to assess the capacity of their residents to consent to their care and treatment
- to identify those who lack capacity in this regard and whose care amounts to a deprivation of liberty, or may amount to a deprivation of liberty
- to ensure that the resident cannot be cared for in a less restrictive way
- to make referrals to the supervisory body for a DoLS assessment, where appropriate
- to facilitate that assessment
- to comply with any authorisation and conditions
- to inform the supervisory body of any changes or moves.

The DoLS assessment

If the service user is in a hospital or care home, the manager should complete an urgent authorisation to cover the immediate situation while a full DoLS assessment is organised. An urgent authorisation lasts for seven days and can be renewed for a further seven days if necessary. A DoLS assessment is carried out by two professionals: a mental health assessor and a best interests assessor (BIA). Between them they have to carry out six assessments:

- Age – the person must be over 18 years.

- Mental Health – the person must have a mental disorder within the meaning of the MHA (note, the criteria for ID does not need to include seriously irresponsible or abnormally aggressive conduct).

- Mental capacity – in relation to care and treatment.

- Best interests – is being cared for in a way that amounts to a deprivation of liberty in their best interests?

- Eligibility – the person is not already detained under MHA or should be.

- No refusals – a DoLS authorisation must not conflict with a valid advance decision, lasting power of attorney or an appointed deputy.

If all of these assessments are satisfied, the BIA will recommend that an authorisation under DoLS is made and how long the authorisation should last for, up to a maximum of 12 months. The BIA will also appoint a representative for the person who should be someone who will keep in contact with them and represent their interests. If there is nobody suitable to fulfil this role, the BIA will appoint an Independent Mental Capacity Advocate (IMCA). The BIA may also recommend that certain conditions are put in place to lessen the effect of the deprivation of liberty. Both the person and their representative can appeal to the Court of Protection to vary the conditions or terminate the authorisation. The BIA will write a report that will be made available to the care providers detailing the evidence and how they have arrived at their conclusions. The supervisory body will issue the authorisation. In the case of service users in supported living or at home whose care amounts to deprivation of liberty, the local authority will arrange for an assessment and care plan to be presented to the Court of Protection for authorisation.

Case study: S

S is a 23-year-old man (black British) with autism and ID. He has very little speech and uses some Makaton. He has lived in the same residential placement for several years. He can become agitated and distressed, at which times he is encouraged to go to his room until he feels calmer, but generally he has been settled and appears happy at the placement. He has quite a busy timetable, which includes a paper round and a job cleaning cars. He is always escorted by a member of staff whenever he goes out, including visits to his family. They like the placement and feel he is doing well there.

Issues for discussion

1. What are the two questions that staff need to ask to decide if S is deprived of his liberty?

2. Based on the answers to those questions, is S deprived of his liberty?

3. If he is deprived of his liberty, is he eligible for DoLS?

4. If he is eligible for DoLS, what should happen next?

Answers:

1. Is he under continuous supervision and control? Is he free to leave?

2. Yes, he is, because that is his concrete situation even though he is happy and settled and his family like the placement.

3. Yes, because he is in residential care which is covered by the legislation.

4. The managers of the placement should make him subject to an urgent authorisation under DoLS then refer his case to the local authority for a full DoLS assessment. They should facilitate that assessment and support S through it. They will need to talk to the assessors and make all S's records and care plans available to them. If DoLS is authorised then they need to take account of any conditions or recommendations the BIA has made and be aware when the order will expire, or inform the local authority if S moves or his condition changes so he no longer needs those restrictions.

Conclusion

Historically, people with ID have had very little choice in their lives. The Mental Capacity Act is designed to ensure that everyone has a responsibility to support choice and decision making whenever individuals have capacity, and provides a structured approach to making decisions on behalf of those who lack capacity. Care staff need to understand it and be confident in using it. They also need to be aware when their service users are being cared for in a way that amounts to a deprivation of liberty and how that should be authorised.

Key learning points

■ Health professionals are required to make a capacity assessment before carrying out any care or treatment. The more serious the decision, the more formal the assessment should be.

■ Generally, the person who will implement the decision is responsible for assessing capacity, but it is good practice for them to consult those who know the individual.

- If the person is deemed to have capacity, they can make whatever decision they choose even if others think it is unwise. If the person is deemed to lack capacity, the decision should be made in their best interests following the best interests checklist.

- If a person who lacks capacity to consent to their care and treatment is being cared for in a way that amounts to deprivation of liberty, this must be authorised through the DoLS procedure or by the Court of Protection.

References

British Medical Association and The Law Society (2009) *Assessment of Mental Capacity*. London: The Law Society.

Department of Constitutional Affairs (2005) *Mental Capacity Act 2005: Code of Practice*. London: TSO.

Etchells E, Darzins P, Silberfeld M, Singer PA, McKenny J, Naglie G, Katz M, Guyatt GH, Molloy DW & Strang D (1999) Assessment of patient capacity to consent to treatment. *Journal of General Internal Medicine* **14** 27–34.

Ministry of Justice (2008) Deprivation of Liberty Safeguards: Code of Practice to supplement the main Mental Capacity Act 2005 Code of Practice. London: TSO

Re C *(adult: refusal of medical treatment) (1994)* 1 All ER 819.

Chapter 20: Key facts, concepts and principles in the mental health of people with intellectual disabilities

By Colin Hemmings, Deepa Jain and Sidney Htut

Summary

This chapter highlights some of the key facts, concepts and principles in the field of the mental health of people with intellectual disabilities. It considers epidemiology, diagnostic overshadowing, the complexities of assessment and treatment and the need for biopsychosocial and integrated approaches, as well as the need for ongoing research and for training for everyone who works in this area.

Introduction

Over the last few decades, the mental health of people with intellectual disabilities (ID) has developed into a well-recognised area of clinical practice and research. It is widely (although not universally) agreed that it includes the assessment and management of challenging behaviours, when these are accompanied by major risk to themselves or others, as well as diagnosable mental disorders. The field therefore differs in focus from the general medical health care of people with ID, and the practice and delivery of their social care and education.

Epidemiology

The mental health of people with ID, as an area of clinical practice, is based on two key facts:

1. People with ID experience mental health problems like the rest of the population, although sometimes with atypical presentations.

2. People with ID actually experience higher rates of mental health problems than the rest of the population.

(Hemmings, 2016)

Epidemiological studies have found that some mental disorders appear significantly increased in people with ID (for example, schizophrenia), while the prevalence of others is often similar to, or at least not substantially greater than, people with more typical IQ (Buckles, 2016). What has always been very clear is the significantly increased prevalence of challenging behaviours in people with ID. When challenging behaviours are not included with diagnosable mental disorders, the prevalence of mental disorders overall in people with ID is still increased over that of the general population, but is much less marked.

Another key fact is that assessing the mental health of people with ID is usually more difficult than for people with more typical IQ. Mental disorders are diagnosed using standardised language-based criteria (such as the WHO's International Classification of Diseases – ICD-10). A key principle here is that these standardised diagnostic criteria become less and less useful in people with increasingly severe ID, as people are less and less able to express their internal mental states verbally. There can therefore be problems of both over- and under-estimating the prevalence of mental disorders in people with ID.

Diagnostic overshadowing

Another important factor in the under-diagnosis of mental health problems in people with ID is known as 'diagnostic overshadowing', which is a critical issue in the mental health of people with ID. Diagnostic overshadowing was originally described (and usually still is) as a medical professional ascribing a person's mental health symptoms to their ID, rather than looking further for the cause. It can also happen because symptoms are ascribed to other diagnoses present, such as autism or epilepsy.

The presence of autistic traits are of huge importance when assessing other mental disorders and challenging behaviours in people with ID. Staff who have had no training in ID services are gradually becoming more aware of autism, and better able to recognise it. It is therefore becoming more common for autism to be diagnosed in generic mental health services. It is also essential that comorbid mental health problems are not missed in people with ID and autism owing to another type of diagnostic overshadowing, in which some staff trained in ID are more inclined to see autism than mental illness (Hemmings, 2016).

Tom's cases study below illustrates a case of diagnostic overshadowing.

Case study: Tom

Tom is a white British male who lives in residential accommodation. He has moderate ID, autism and challenging behaviour, and has been prescribed an antipsychotic medication (zuclopenthixol). He speaks with a loud voice and has echolalia, repeating words and phrases uttered by others. He often gets anxious and agitated, pacing up and down, is verbally aggressive, and he throws things when he is upset. He is obsessed with watches, often insists on going to the toilet when he has no need to use it, takes a bath many times during a day, changes his clothes often and likes wearing female clothes. However, until six years ago he had never hit anyone or shown self-injurious behaviour. Then, aged 50, he started slapping his face and banging his head in addition to his previously known challenging behaviours. No obvious trigger for this behavioural change could be identified. His zuclopenthixol dose was increased, which was associated with an improvement in his challenging behaviours.

He developed deep vein thrombosis aged 54 and his behaviour then deteriorated further, including increased self-harming. His zuclopenthixol dose was increased again and his challenging behaviours improved again for over two years.

Now aged 56, Tom had a medication review when he had urinary incontinence and weight gain, which were thought to be side effects of the medication. His zuclopenthixol dose was slowly reduced to replace it with risperidone – a newer 'second generation' antipsychotic. Tom then became more irritable and elevated in mood with increased physical and verbal aggression. He was pacing up and down all the time, much more talkative, and all his other behaviours were amplified. His sleep reduced to less than four hours per day and he started going into other resident's rooms at night and was causing distress.

He began to place himself in danger (for example, by running into traffic) and also lost many of his social inhibitions and began to display hyper-sexualised behaviours, such as masturbating in public and touching others in a sexual way.

Questions:

- Is there any chance of diagnostic overshadowing?

- Might this be an episode of mania?

Answers:

- Tom has a diagnosis of moderate ID with impairment of behaviour ('challenging behaviours') and autistic spectrum disorder (ASD). Tom was on zuclopenthixol, which is usually prescribed for someone who has either schizophrenia or psychosis and it is not an evidence-based or licensed treatment for challenging behaviour. There is a chance of diagnostic overshadowing here, since Tom's ID and ASD may not explain his improvement with zuclopenthixol, nor his deterioration when it was reduced. It is therefore important that a comorbid mental health problem should be considered. He is showing common symptoms of mania, and so it is important not to assume the challenging behaviours are only due to his moderate ID and ASD.

- Staff therefore need to probe further into his history to look for a change from his premorbid state and for other symptoms of physical and mental health problems, including mania. Increased talkativeness could be an indication for pressure of speech. Reduced sleep is another possible symptom of mania. Moreover, other symptoms like distractibility, reckless behaviour (placing himself in danger like running into traffic), new and hyper-sexualised behaviours that are out of character for Tom like masturbating in public, touching others in a sexual way and loss of usual social inhibitions must also be explored. The presence of any three symptoms as described above might fulfil the diagnostic criteria for a manic episode.

The high prevalence of challenging behaviours

There is no universal definition of 'challenging behaviour', but it is commonly cited as:

'...culturally abnormal behaviour of such an intensity, frequency or duration that the physical safety of the person or others is likely to be placed in serious jeopardy, or behaviour which is likely to seriously limit use of, or result in the person being denied access to, ordinary community facilities.' (Emerson, 1995)

Challenging behaviours, such as aggressive, self-injurious and destructive behaviours are often the primary reason that people are referred to specialist ID services, and they can often fluctuate over years and so be chronic in duration. Referrals to specialist ID services are often made for people with more severe levels of ID, who tend to have more frequent and more severe challenging behaviour compared to those with milder ID.

The mainstay of interventions for challenging behaviour should always include psychological (including behavioural) interventions, possibly coupled with changes to the person's social and physical environment. However, challenging behaviours are widely considered to be caused by a range of factors (see box 1 below). Before moving towards the implementation of psychological interventions, it is important that a person with ID and challenging behaviour is screened to check for all other factors that may be causing or exacerbating the challenging behaviours (see also Chapter 13).

Box 1: Some factors associated with challenging behaviours

- Learned behaviour
- Responses to life events, e.g. change of key worker, bereavement
- Attachment problems
- Social environment
- Physical environment
- Communication difficulties
- Sensory difficulties
- Genetic syndromes/behavioural phenotypes
- Physical health problems, including pain, infections, constipation,
- Dementia
- Epilepsy
- Drugs and alcohol and withdrawal states
- Mental illness
- Personality disorder
- Autism
- ADHD

It is important to remember that some challenging behaviours may also be developmentally appropriate behaviours in a person with ID.

Case study: David

David is 73-year-old white British man living in a residential home. He has mild ID, a history of psychotic illness and challenging behaviour. His medical history includes obesity, hypertension, recurrent urinary tract infections, a long history of urinary incontinence and dermatitis. He worked for 20 years at the local docks as a labourer. He is now dependent on the care staff for his all personal care needs.

He has a long-standing history of contact with mental health services from early adulthood and had several short admissions, possibly for more florid psychotic features, but reportedly also for behavioural and physical health problems. There were a few references in his history to sleeplessness, confusion, delusions or hallucinations during these admissions. During one hospitalisation he was reported to have had the delusional belief that he was pregnant and that his baby had died, while on another occasion in A&E he believed that his carer was a prison officer who had come to take him to prison. His urinary incontinence was often thought to be 'behavioural'.

David was discharged from a general hospital to a care home for people with ID. During hospitalisation it seemed he had become dependent on a wheelchair. He subsequently developed some wasting of his thigh and leg muscles through disuse, and later degenerative changes in his hip were noted on a scan. David started showing deterioration in his mental health and challenging behaviour soon after the move to the care home. He was verbally abusive and occasionally physically aggressive to the care staff. On occasion he seemed to be experiencing visual hallucinations, stating that his girlfriend was in the room and he was often seen talking to himself or to the television. He stayed in his room, appearing confused, sometimes sobbing and picking at his skin. During these relapses in his mental health he refused to eat or drink, and he spoke incoherently in a high-pitched, child-like voice. He often slept in his chair, threw urine and faeces at the care staff and urinated on himself. He was intermittently compliant with oral medication.

On continued assessments over the year, three main factors for his challenging behaviour were identified – mental, physical and social/environmental.

Mental health: David was started on antipsychotic injections and a positive change in his mental health was soon noted. He became calm, co-operative, friendly and chatty, and had no evident side effects.

Physical health: He received input from a urologist, a physiotherapist, a community ID nurse, district nurses and from his GP. He was prescribed antibiotics in case of possible urinary infection, as well as for dermatitis and for skin infections between his toes. An ultrasound scan then showed 20 bladder stones, and their subsequent surgical removal led to a reduced frequency of his recurrent urinary infections.

Social/environmental: David was under-stimulated in his environment as he appeared to be of a much higher intellectual ability than most of the other residents. Following continued liaison with his social worker, he was given increased individual care support with more opportunities to socialise, including outside of the care home.

His quality of life has now improved and he enjoys going on days out to the zoo or to the beach to watch the ships, as well as visiting cafes.

Discussion: This case illustrates the importance of a comprehensive (biopsychosocial) assessment. David's history indicated a decline in his functioning and a loss in his independence over the years, with chronic psychosis in the presence of long-standing physical health problems. The case demonstrates how, for people with ID, underlying physical health issues can be neglected or missed and often misinterpreted as challenging behaviour/mental illness.

The relationships between mental and physical health problems and challenging behaviours

It is vital that specialist ID staff and services are aware of the link between challenging behaviours and physical and mental health problems. It is widely accepted that mental health problems are often associated with challenging behaviours in people with ID, and there are several reasons why this should be the case (Hemmings, 2007). Moss *et al* (1999) argued that the relationship between psychiatric symptoms and challenging behaviours could work in three main ways:

- First, some challenging behaviours might actually be atypical symptoms of a mental illness. For example, aggression and self-injurious behaviours might sometimes be manifestations of depression in people with severe ID, and someone unable to express feelings may manifest them as behaviours.

- Second, mental illnesses may produce the conditions for the expression of challenging behaviours that are maintained by behavioural processes. For example, depression may be associated with a resistance to socialising, thus turning social activities into negative reinforcers. Events might only become aversive when a person with ID is also experiencing a particular psychiatric symptom.

- Third, it is also possible that challenging behaviours may contribute to the development of psychiatric symptoms, such as low mood, rather than indicate them.

The relationships between ID, physical health problems, mental health problems and challenging behaviours are therefore very complex. Physical and mental health problems may be an important or even primary contributory factor to some challenging behaviours. However, the bulk of challenging behaviours are not likely to be associated with physical or mental health problems. Even when they co-exist, they are not necessarily related. It is important to neither overplay nor underplay the importance of mental health problems when considering challenging behaviours in people with ID. In complex cases, single answers or diagnoses can be superficially attractive but in practice they are unlikely to explain all of the presentation or lead to a simple solution. Perhaps it is most important to hold the principle that complexity and multifactorial causation in cases of challenging behaviours are more the norm than the exception. The case study below illustrates this complexity.

Case study: Debbie

Debbie is a 28-year-old white British female who lives with her mother. She has diagnoses of moderate ID, Down's syndrome, gait difficulties, astigmatism and eye squint. Her communication abilities are significantly limited and she is dependent on others for all her personal care needs. She was assessed following a four-month period of experiencing difficulties, including a deterioration in mood and behaviour with agitation, sleep disturbances, appearing distracted and apparently responding to unknown stimuli. She was prescribed risperidone (an antipsychotic) and zopiclone (a sleeping tablet) for possible psychosis and sleep disturbances. She initially showed some improvement in her symptoms, however her urinary incontinence worsened (probably due to risperidone) for which she was treated with oxybutynin (an anticholinergic medication for overactive bladder). After a six-month period of some improvement, she started deteriorating again and worsened quickly. She exhibited episodes of sudden onset 'trembling', shouting, agitation, appearing frightened and withdrawn, curling into a foetal position on the floor, keeping her neck stiff, constantly moving her eyes and covering them and refusing to eat or drink. She was not sleeping or engaging, and she posed a risk of self-harm and self-neglect.

Her mother revealed that Debbie had appeared unhappy about six months ago, apparently when a particular taxi driver drove her to day care centre for about a month. Subsequent physical examination and urine test by GP were normal, although she remained anxious. The possible differential diagnoses were numerous, and included seizure/pseudo seizure activity, psychosis, mixed anxiety and depression, panic attacks, post-traumatic stress disorder, dissociation reaction and migraine. Debbie was also prescribed clobazam (antiepileptic medication) by a neurologist for the suspected seizures. She was taken to A&E several times. Blood investigations, MRI, EEG did not reveal any evident physical health problem or epileptic activity. Clobazam was stopped after a brief period in the absence of a response.

A change in antipsychotic medication to aripiprazole led to some improvement in Debbie's psychotic symptoms without side effects. She was also provided with psychological and individual care support at her home, which helped her mother to cope. With the different interventions provided, Debbie is now once again leading a happy life.

Discussion: This case illustrates how complex an assessment can be when someone presents with psychotic symptoms in the presence of ID, and where the person has limited communication abilities. With Debbie's presentation, it was difficult to establish whether her difficulties were primarily mental, physical, psychological or psychosocial in nature, or whether they were multifactorial. It also signifies the difficulties when managing someone who has experienced mental health issues following a suspected abuse. In such cases, the clinicians often have to rely on family/carers for a history, and if that history is not detailed or not disclosed, it is easily possible to miss relevant issues. Thus, this case also highlights the importance of taking a careful history that covers all aspects of the person's life including their vulnerability, and making objective observations of the person. People with ID can also show increased sensitivity to psychiatric medications and are often unable to report the side effects.

Guidelines to aid practice

Reiss (1994) gave some useful guidance for practising clinicians when considering challenging behaviours:

■ They must assess whether or not there has been a clear change in behaviour from baseline levels of fluctuation.

■ They must then consider whether any behavioural disturbance may be part of a symptom pattern that corresponds to a mental disorder.

■ They should remember that there is always the possibility that challenging behaviours may be exacerbating a coexisting mental disorder, as well the fact that mental disorders can manifest as new or increased challenging behaviours.

■ Allowances should be made for the impact that differing levels of intellectual functioning have on the expression of the symptoms.

■ Accept that the cause of the behaviours may ultimately be ambiguous – in more severe ID, diagnoses of mental disorders are generally tentative, often to be treated more like hypotheses.

More recently, Deb *et al* (2006) published guidance about the use of medications for challenging behaviours in people with ID. The National Institute for Health and Care Excellence has also published important guidance for the assessment and treatment of challenging behaviours (NICE, 2015) and mental health problems (NICE, 2016) in people with ID.

Biopsychosocial approaches and the need for multidisciplinary working

The assessment and management of challenging behaviours is a perfect illustration of how approaches to the mental health of people with ID need to be multidisciplinary. People with ID are more likely to have complex needs than people without it. It is not uncommon to find people with ID who also have mental illness, multiple physical health problems, sensory needs and communication difficulties, as well as a range of unmet social needs. This makes assessment much more complicated.

As challenging behaviours are invariably multi-factorial in causation, it is important not to reduce them to simply being 'biological' or 'psychiatric', or alternatively as simply 'behavioural'. The term 'behavioural overshadowing' refers to psychiatric symptoms being ascribed to learned behaviour and there is no consideration given as to whether they are perhaps symptoms of a mental illness. If behaviour is thought to be 'behavioural' then it is often considered to serve a function or purpose for the person. Conversely, if behaviour is considered to be 'psychiatric' in origin, then very often any other reasons for it are disregarded. Even when some behaviours have a strong biological drive, the environment can still reinforce them or they can provide some function or purpose for the person that may make them suitable for behavioural approaches.

Given the complex causes of challenging behaviours, it does not make sense to artificially and neatly separate them from mental health problems (nor indeed the care of the more severely intellectually disabled from those with milder ID). Any service that manages severe challenging behaviours in people with ID will always need access to physical health assessments and medication, and sometimes even in-patient care, no matter how good the behavioural management or how well the environment can be improved.

There is perhaps no other field in health and social care that has greater need of a holistic (biopsychosocial) and integrated approach than the mental health of people with ID, with partnership working between agencies and with relatives and paid care staff. Various ways of understanding – such as the 'medical', 'biological', 'behavioural' or other 'models' – are ultimately only different aids that should be considered simultaneously. The case study below is an example of the need for multidisciplinary approaches, using the co-ordination of the Care Programme Approach (Department of Health, 1990).

Case study : Harry

Harry is a 23-year-old white British male with mild ID, autistic traits and Landau-Kleffner syndrome. He developed normally but had seizures since he was an infant and became aphasic at the age of three. He could not understand or express language and did not attend school until he was 11, when he went to a residential school for children with autism.

After leaving the boarding school at 16, Harry lived in residential homes, however he had a number of placement breakdowns. Harry has severe challenging behaviour that consists of self-harming, punching himself in the chest, induced vomiting, scratching, and later on, cutting himself superficially with sharp objects. He is also very aggressive towards others, pushing, kicking and punching, and holding people by their throats while pinning them to walls. He has absconded from his residential homes many times, hitch-hiking or taking trains and buses and often getting lost. On these occasions the police have had to return him his home.

He was treated with sodium valproate for his epilepsy and with two antipsychotics, risperidone and aripiprazole, for his agitation. Harry was subject to DoLS as he did not have anywhere to stay apart from his current residential home, which he shared with seven other residents. He was very impulsive and became aggressive when his needs were not met immediately. He was referred to psychology for a functional analysis of his behaviour. The function of his challenging behaviour was not fully understood, although it appeared that many episodes have stemmed out of his impulsivity and anger.

After a few weeks, Harry received behaviour guidelines and his aripiprazole was gradually stopped. Harry got on very well with his key worker, to whom he became very attached. His aggression ceased, he started going out to places and there was no further absconding from his home.

However, after some time the home manager left along with a few other staff – one of whom was Harry's key worker – which destabilised Harry again. He began to abscond from his home again, and this time he was brought back from the home of his previous key worker by the police. There were a few incidents of physical aggression in which Harry hit staff members, threatened them with knives and strangled one of them by her throat. Police were called and a safeguarding alert was raised. Harry also tried to take an overdose of some medication, which he got from the medicine cabinet by stealing the key from the staff, and there was also an incident of fire setting.

Care Programme Approach meetings were arranged and attended by psychiatrists, psychologists, occupational therapists, speech therapists, his care manager, the manager of his home and a community ID nurse. Issues with managing current risks were discussed. To prevent him leaving the care home, Harry was given 1:1 carer support, day and night, and a new lock to prevent him from leaving the house unaccompanied was arranged by the occupational therapist since he was on DoLS. To reduce the risk of fire setting, Harry was not allowed to carry cash in order to prevent him from buying lighters. All sharp objects, including broken CDs, were taken away, and kitchen knives were to be kept in a locked room. The medication cabinet was also placed in a locked room. Agency staff were also not allowed to provide 1:1 support for Harry for both day and night, and his medication was reviewed – he was started on fluoxetine to help allay his anxiety.

The clinical psychologist identified Harry's historical attachment issues, his difficulty with transitions, his inability to differentiate between reality and dreams – which blurred boundaries – and made a new behaviour plan to support him to manage situations and his feelings. The home manager arranged for staff to have breakaway and challenging behaviour training. The speech therapist identified that Harry's main problem was his inability to understand others and to express himself effectively, and to process information. With all of this concerted effort from the multidisciplinary professionals and care staff, co-ordinated through regular CPA meetings, Harry's distress was reduced and he was able to function much better again.

The need for further research and training

Interventions for people with ID have always tended to lag behind those that have long been standard in generic mental health services, not only in terms of medications but also for psychological treatments. While the preceding chapters in this book have shown how various practices and interventions to support the mental health of people with ID are now firmly established, many medications and psycho-social treatments cannot yet be said to be evidence-based for this specific population, and we still need a more substantial body of research to support the further development of new and existing interventions and services for people with ID.

There are many well-documented difficulties in conducting research in people with ID, including funding and recruitment (Lennox *et al*, 2005), and mental health research has therefore frequently excluded this group. The increasingly stringent ethical clearance for research with people with ID may unfortunately lead to less research in people with ID being carried out in future. This unintended outcome is not in their best interests, and it is therefore important that professionals, paid care staff and relatives support and participate in research into the mental health of people with ID.

Many of the key facts, concepts and principles described in this chapter are still not widely known or universally understood, especially by those not trained in the mental health aspects of ID. While publications such as this book can help to inform professional staff, carers and relatives, the training of non-ID staff and care staff and relatives in the mental health of people with ID is more important that ever, and also needs to be researched to see how effective it is at changing knowledge, practice and outcomes.

Key learning points

- Mental health problems, including challenging behaviours, are more common in people with ID.

- The prevalence of some mental illnesses, such as schizophrenia, are greatly increased in people with ID. The prevalence of many others, such as depression, are also increased, but less so.

- The prevalence of challenging behaviours account for much of the difference in the prevalence of mental health problems between people with ID and those without ID.

- Difficulties in diagnosis mean that mental health problems can be both under- and over-diagnosed.

- Wrongly describing problems as being due to a person's ID and not their mental health problems is known as diagnostic overshadowing.

- Mental health problems, including challenging behaviours, are usually multifactorial phenomena that require an integrated, multimodal approach to assessment and treatment.

References

Buckles (2016) The epidemiology of psychiatric disorder in adults with intellectual disabilities. In: C Hemmings and N Bouras (Eds) *Psychiatric and Behavioural Disorders in Developmental Disabilities and Developmental Disabilities* (4th Edition) pp34–44. Cambridge: Cambridge University Press.

Deb S, Clarke D & Unwin G (2006) *Using medication to manage behaviour problems among adults with a learning disability: Quick reference guide*. University of Birmingham, MENCAP, The Royal College of Psychiatrists.

Department of Health (1990) Care Programme Approach: Circular HC(90)23/LASSL(90)11. London: Department of Health.

Hemmings C (2016) Reflections. In: C Hemmings and N Bouras (Eds) *Psychiatric and Behavioural Disorders in Developmental Disabilities and Developmental Disabilities (4th Edition)* (pp279–288). Cambridge: Cambridge University Press.

Hemmings (2007) The relationship between challenging behaviours and psychiatric disorders in people with severe intellectual disabilities. In: N Bouras and G Holt (Eds) *Psychiatric and Behavioural Disorders in Developmental Disabilities and Mental Retardation (3rd Edition)* pp62–75. Cambridge: Cambridge University Press.

Lennox N, Taylor M, Rey-Conde T, Bain C, Purdie DM & Boyle F (2005) Beating the barriers: recruitment of people with intellectual disability to participate in research. *Journal of Intellectual Disability Research* **49** 296–305.

Moss S, Kiernan C & Emerson E (1999) The relationship between challenging behaviours and psychiatric disorders in people with severe developmental disabilities. In: N Bouras (Ed) *Psychiatric and Behavioural Disorders in Developmental Disabilities and Mental Retardation (2nd edition)* pp40–44. Cambridge: Cambridge University Press.

NICE (2015) *Learning Disabilities: Challenging behaviour* [online]. Available at: https://www.nice.org.uk/guidance/qs101 (accessed February 2018).

NICE (2016) *Mental Health Problems in People with Learning Disabilities: Prevention, assessment and management* [online]. Available at: https://www.nice.org.uk/Guidance/NG54 (accessed February 2018).

Reiss S (1994) Psychopathology in mental retardation. In: N Bouras (Ed) *Mental Health in Mental Retardation: Recent advances in practice*. Cambridge: Cambridge University Press.

Other titles from Pavilion Publishing

PAS-ADD Clinical Interview Handbook

Steve Moss

The PAS-ADD Clinical Interview handbook is for the assessment of mental health problems in people with or without intellectual disability.

Mini PAS-ADD Interview Handbook, 3rd Edition

Steve Moss

The Mini PAS-ADD is an assessment tool for undertaking mental health assessments with people with learning disabilities.

PAS-ADD Checklist

Steve Moss

PAS-ADD Checklists written in everyday language for use by carers and family.

ChA-PAS Interview Handbook and Clinical Interview

Steve Moss

The Child and Adolescent Psychiatric Assessment Schedule contains instructions for using the assessment, a semi-structured interview and clinical glossary.

Mental Health Needs of Children and Young People with Learning Disabilities

Raghu Raghavan, Sarah H Bernard and Jane McCarthy

This handbook will provide health and social care professionals with a sound knowledge base for shaping and enhancing their practice.

Anxiety and Depression in People with Intellectual Disabilities: Advances in interventions

Raghu Raghavan

Anxiety and Depression in People with Intellectual Disabilities focuses on the full range of anxiety and depressive illnesses and interventions, support strategies and approaches to working with this population. It includes case formulations, psychopharmacological interventions, cognitive therapy, psychodynamic approaches and solution focused therapy.

An Introduction to Supporting the Mental Health of People with Intellectual Disabilities: A guide for professionals, support staff and families

Eddie Chaplin, Karina Marshall-Tate and Steve Hardy

A mental health guide to those supporting people with intellectual disabilities.

Guided Self-help for People with Intellectual Disabilities and Anxiety and Depression

Eddie Chaplin

This multimedia training resource guides facilitators on how to support people with intellectual disabilities.

I Can Feel Good: Skills training for people with intellectual disabilities problems managing emotions

Bridget Ingamells and Catrin Morrissey

This resource helps people with intellectual disabilities to develop the skills they need to self-soothe and manage emotional distress.

Intellectual Disabilities and Personality Disorder: A integrated approach to support

Dr Zillah Webb

This book gives professionals a framework for approaching issues that arise when an individual has intellectual disabilities and a personality disorder.

Reflections on the Challenges of Psychiatry in the UK and Beyond: A psychiatrist's chronicle from deinstitutionalisation to community care

Professor Nick Bouras

A personal journey through British psychiatry, the NHS and academic life, over a career spanning 40 years.